# of Huck and Alice

Humorous Writing in American Literature

*Financial assistance for this book
was provided by the
Andrew W. Mellon Foundation.*

# of Huck and Alice

Humorous Writing
in American Literature

Neil Schmitz

University of Minnesota Press • Minneapolis

Library of Congress Cataloging in Publication Data

Schmitz, Neil.
Of Huck and Alice.

Includes index.
1. American wit and humor—History and criticism.
2. American fiction—History and criticism. I. Title.
PS430.S35 1983   817'.009   82-23895
ISBN 0-8166-1155-6
ISBN 0-8166-1156-4 (pbk.)

Acknowledgments

I have always admired my mother's amiable sensibility, her resilience, her laughter, so this book is principally for her, Martha Wendland Schmitz. I also owe a great deal to Margaret Wooster who helped me with questions, listened to my complaints, and threw the occasional salutary brick. My children, Nelly, Andrew, Taylor, gave me merriment in the midst of writing. There are significant prompters who urged me through hesitations—John Mastrogiovanni, Ellen Vineski, Edward Griffin. I have closely studied the several routines of three antic scholars, Carl Dennis, Roy Roussel, Martin Pops, and discussed the Venus of Willendorf with H. D. Strachan, Christopher Maier, Roger Levin, Richard Mason, and Harvey Kornspan. I teased a number of students into taking *Tender Buttons* seriously, and some, notably Karen Whitney, became luminous interpreters of that text. I remember the hospitality of the late Frederick Anderson, curator of the Mark Twain Papers in Berkeley. Everyone who studies Gertrude Stein's writing knows the usefulness of Richard Bridgman's *Gertrude Stein in Pieces*, what a provision it is. I want also to thank the editors of *Partisan Review* and *Salmagundi* for permission to reprint material that previously appeared in their journals. The Julian Park Fund at the State University of New York at Buffalo made it possible to illustrate this book.

Contents

of Huck and Alice

Humorous Writing in American Literature

I

The Project of Humor

There is only one world, and that world is false, cruel, contradictory, misleading, senseless. . . . We need lies to vanquish this reality, this 'truth,' we need lies *in order to live*. . . . That lying is a necessity of life is itself a part of the terrifying and problematic character of existence.

Nietzsche

These last two features—the rejection of the claims of reality and the putting through of the pleasure principle—bring humour near to the regressive or reactionary processes which engage our attention so extensively in psychopathology. Its fending off of the possibility of suffering places it among the great series of methods which the human mind has constructed in order to evade the compulsion to suffer—a series which begins with neurosis and culminates in madness and which includes intoxication, self-absorption and ecstasy.

Freud

You don't know about me, without you have read a book by the name of 'The Adventures of Tom Sawyer,' but that ain't no matter. That book was made by Mr. Mark Twain, and he told the truth, mainly. There was things which he stretched, but mainly he told the truth. That is nothing. I never seen anybody but lied, one time or another, without it was Aunt Polly, or the widow, or maybe Mary. Aunt Polly—Tom's Aunt Polly, she is—and Mary, and the Widow Douglas, is all told about in that book—which is mostly a true book; with some stretchers, as I said before.

Mark Twain

Pain soup, suppose it is question, suppose it is butter, real is, real is only, only excreate, only excreate a no since.

Gertrude Stein

1

The first humorous writer in American literature truthfully admits the force of reality in his text, shows us misery and wreckage. He is not a fool. Reality is severe, a big order, bad news. It moves, like the Mississippi, murkily southward, to the Gulf, always testing, trying the alertness of human cunning. This writer, who prepares the way for others, gently, absolutely, displaces the genial humorist whose daft discourse hitherto ruled the humorous text. He describes the recuperative work of humor, begins with an offering of little things—poignant misspelling, a rude raft, and then slips easily into the supposing of humorous questions. Awful frames of reference, the din of a certain harsh defining, this rough reality sorely tries the writer, who must find the portion of pleasure in it, excreate "a no since," whose task is to tolerate existence. The guidance in humorous feeling is therefore always forgiving. It is the first thing Huck Finn does in his book, humor Mark Twain, forgive his lies, and the wherefore is plainly spoken. Everybody lies, Huck tells us, except Aunt Polly, or the widow, or maybe Mary. The world is false, cruel, senseless, everything Nietzsche says it is, particularly in the region roundabout Cairo, and we need lies to endure it, to survive in it. That is Huck's 'truth,' the hard story he will tell. Such a report of reality, of the old hugger-mugger, that it shoots children, should disclose on the spot the "terrifying and problematic character of existence," lead us to expect the impact of some tragic closure, but this fall from humor does not happen, not in the spell of this book, which begins with a loophole and ends with a trapdoor, which holds the place of suffering, the real world, the one world, first and last squarely in the center of a humorous gaze. That is the project of humor, to confront reality, to think, real is only.

As Mark Twain places himself into the *Adventures of Huckleberry Finn*, shows us the culpable humorist, the one who tells white lies, he directs us to Huck's sense of humor, the serious one that will admit black truths. The problem of humor in literature, that it is a lie, an evasion, an understanding, a transformation, is constantly before us in the text. There sits the benign humorist in Chapter XIV, book open on his lap, puffing on a seegar, Huck Finn playing Mark Twain. He has barely escaped the foolishness of blundering into the wreck of the *Walter Scott*, but that ain't no matter. The raft has been regained, we are safely in the woods, and there is the ongoing river. Amiably tolerating Jim's ignorance, Huck explains the fortune of kings. They have the power and the pleasure of absolute mastery. They own everything. "*Ain'* dat gay?" Jim marvels—and then asks the Hegelian question that transfixes Huck, catches him flush in the sudden uncertainty of his learning. "En what dey got to do, Huck?"[1] Here Huck's labor begins: the lie emerges (we should admire the master), the truth appears (the master is not admirable), question follows question, and Huck at last must draw upon the brickbat, *nigger*, to bring this swerving Dialectic to an end. What indeed does a humorist do? That question is deftly written into *Huckleberry Finn*, and the right answer is ultimately given to Tom Sawyer. Huck will learn at least the painful variance in the meaning of the predicate, to humor. Here, fooled, he yields to the instinct for argument, assumes the stance of the explainer. In the humorous text, which variously repeats this particular exchange, the serious rhetorician who severely announces which reality is real always relies finally on the stick. Frustrated, spiteful, unable to disentangle his Solomon from Jim's Sollermun, Huck miserably records the familiar complaint in humorous writing: "you can't learn a nigger to argue" (*HF*, p. 114). The purest statement in American literature of the humorous question, of the humorous refusal to argue, appears first in Huck's poor, unlovely speech, then in the commingled sensibility of the single text Gertrude Stein and Alice B. Toklas share.

Before humor is that wise, however, it is first mad. There are four humours in the classical text, and we know each one on sight as a categorical fool, as lumplike, furious, giddy, morose. Here is Mr. Head-Melancholy, as Robert Burton sees him in *The Anatomy of Melancholy* (1621): "The common signs, if it be by essence in the head, *are ruddiness of face, high sanguine complexion, most part* with a flushed colour, one calls it bluish, and sometimes full of pimples, with red eyes."[2] When the knowledge of physiology changes, such vivid characters lose, along with their pneuma, the credibility of these "common signs." A sense of craziness remains in the term, inhabits the holy talk of blessed simpletons in European writing, and will significantly reappear in American humor, take on a new life in *Krazy Kat*, respelled as kraziness, but for the most part, refigured in the eighteenth century, rationalized, humor comes simply to mean the odd, the eccentric. This shift in the value of the term, the emergence of diverse humorous styles, the disposition to take humorous texts seriously, all this at once produces a distinctive canon and establishes a thriving criticism. What is humor's relation to the other modes of comedy? What indeed does a humorist do? The question in *Huckleberry Finn*, painfully spelled out, humorously resolved, is the primordial question in humorous literature. How does humor preserve itself from savage irony? How far south down the Mississippi can it go? Humor, in its new guise, takes up a precarious existence in the literary text. It is, almost from the start, complicated by the issue of cultural and linguistic difference, by the effort to distinguish Caledonian humor from Castilian. Stuart Tave's *The Amiable Humorist* (1960), which examines the concept of humor in eighteenth-century and early nineteenth-century English literature, reveals how the theorists of the new congenial interpretation politically justified their notion of "True Humour," shows us, in fact, how these theorists restricted their sense of humor. William Hazlitt believed, for example, that the establishment of the Protestant ascendancy and the succession of the House of Hanover had much to do with the sweetening of the English temperament. Courtiers demand wit, citizens prefer humor. English liberty, the English suggest, encourages the generosity of humorous feeling. It becomes an undertaking in European literature, to describe sentimental English humor, capricious Italian humor, heavy German humor, and in the urgent, often chauvinistic account of the various styles and modes the actual achievement of humorous thought is frequently lost.

Specifically, there is an English version and a German reading of the problem in the humorous text that bears directly on the American project. Humor, Corbyn Morris writes in 1774, is *"any* whimsical Oddity *or* Foible, *appearing in the* Temper *or* Conduct *of a* Person *in* real Life." A humorist is a person *"obstinately attached to sensible peculiar* Oddities *of his own genuine Growth"* who, though he may have his narrow side, nonetheless "stands upon a very enlarged Basis."[3] There is still some craziness here, but the "Humourist" who allows his *"sensible peculiar* Oddities" their full expression, whose own humorous intelligence alters the very basis of self-evaluation, is now given a certain validity. What we see in his strangeness, his queerness, is not merely derangement, but difference. His alogical view of things, so obstinately held, starts from a different a priori, proves to be sufficient, and brings the adequacy of our own assumptions about reality into doubt. Before the definition of humor becomes a nationalistic enterprise, Morris exactly describes the psycholinguistic work that takes place in humorous writing. Shakespeare's ample representation of Falstaff effectively becomes the subject of Morris's treatise. Unlike Wit, Raillery, Satire, and Ridicule, where the verbal strokes are like "sudden Flashes" quickly gone, Humour is "compleat and perfect" in its rounded vision of experience. Shakespeare's portrayal of Falstaffian desire, of Falstaffian suffering—so unstinting, so generous—enables Morris, otherwise a steadfast Whig and prudent economist, to forgive at least this one bawdy and reckless squire his profligacy. In the spell of humor, deftly alienated from his judgment, Morris loves Falstaff. So the meaning of humor is turned.

When Laurence Sterne's *Tristram Shandy* appears in 1760, humorous writing, instantly mature, promptly establishes what it will suppose. Tristram precedes Huck, writes in a different period, in a different discourse, keeps pretty much to dry land, is certainly smarter, yet his overall project in the narrative is very much like Huck's—to confront the sad pull of gravity, the doomsward movement of rushing time, and transform the feeling of it. Sterne's text exhibits the stylistic gamble all subsequent humorists must take. Indeed, not until we come upon Gertrude Stein's experimental writing at the start of the modern period do we find such a skillfully wrong presentation of text and tale. Mounted on their hobby-horses, fixed in their obsessions, Walter and Toby Shandy are continuously sustained in their radiant absurdity by the lift of Tristram's style. The sentence that takes up as its grave subject the moment of death also disperses the force of it. "Nature instantly ebbed again,—the film returned to its place,—the pulse fluttered—stopped—went on—throbbed—stopped again—moved—stopped—shall I go on?—No."[4] As it takes us, dash-dash, toward that decisive instant, *Tristram Shandy* reveals the paradoxical seriousness of humorous writing. No aversion or sublimation here—Le Fever's dying is immediate. Nothing, not death, not even nihilism, is outside the capability of Tristram's style, which turns its ironies so tenderly that the line between nullifying irony and affirming humor is veritably erased. Tristram is the exemplary English humorist, Huck's precursor; he, too, will lecture and be lectured, observe his father, Walter Shandy, batter an impervious Uncle Toby with right opinions.

The German romantics, who read Sterne enthusiastically, devised in their conception of the humorist a quite different figure, one that bears an odd resemblance to the Mark Twain whose principal hero is Tom Sawyer. In Jean Paul Richter's *School for Aesthetics* (1804), the romantic humorist strides scornfully about in the "low *soccus*," a funny shoe. He is armed with a thyrsus staff, for thumping, and loosely carries a tragic mask. Because he sees no ultimate sense in the world, sees the world simply as the field of folly, this humorist is free to discover exceptional meaning in private folly and will empathetically represent the pathos of such doomed assertion. "When man looks down, as ancient theology did, from the supernal world to the earthly world, it seems small and vain in the distance; when he measures out the small world, as humor does, against the infinite world and sees them together, a kind of laughter results which contains pain and greatness."[5] The English Romantics—Coleridge, De Quincey, the young Carlyle—readily took up Richter's "kind of laughter" and adapted it to their own definition of humor, their own reading of *Tristram Shandy*. Richter would become "the German Sterne," enjoy a certain vogue as the perfected humorist whose romances lifted humorous writing to the highest loft in literature, whose critical theory explained its power. Yet there is a problem hidden in the clarity of Richter's formula. It is the act of measuring, and what is recognized, that makes this romantic humorist suspect, for what he perceives in that instant is paradox, disproportion, dread, the abrupt inversion of the sublime (mania). These are irony's things, the entire rack. Just here, as he sees his small against the large, he laughs. It is the rueful mirth of a foiled male narcissism, and laughed inside a privileged discourse. Richter advocates the seriousness of humorous writing, discusses its relation to sensuousness, takes up (long before Gertrude Stein) the curiosity of its relation to grammar, and at the same time yields to the temptation of the mask, looks at his subject through it. Humor is a shade of irony; the humorist, a kind of ironist. Those German Romantics who follow Richter in the interpretation of humor, notably K. W. F. Solger, simply extend this aspect of Richter's analysis. Humor, Solger will argue in 1815, does more than just measure the great and the small; it annihilates the very *Grund* that sustains them.

A proper humorist, a resilient humorist, looks twice at the service of the tragic mask. After all, the practical sense of humor is that it transforms the effect of error, the result of wrong, and reformulates pain as pleasure. In this sense of humor, less romantic, still knowing, an artist (writer or performer) discovers something amiss, something loose, in the solidity of seriousness, in the fit of the mask, and therein creates a release, admits a measure of enabling tolerance. What's wrong is not just out there in the world of experience, the world of objects, but here in the very language that represents the wrong as wrong. Huck and Jim are in a routine as they discourse in the woods about the fortune of kings, a routine recognizably imported from the low comedy of the minstrel show, and this form, which Mark Twain does not contradict, holds the blackfaced intensity of the exchange. "En what dey got to do, Huck?" The uses of the tragic mask are left to the King and the Duke. When these "reglar rapscallions" appear in the text, spouting romantic legend, telling tragic tales, Huck and Jim will repeat the question in the routine (Should we admire the master?), this time in a perfect harmony of opinion. The humorist finds a style, the voice, in which the serious can be wisely entertained, but not appropriately expressed. This grave feeling, this painful situation, he capably shows us, is not all that it seems. Some hard things will bounce, or shatter into different meanings.

So a brick is thrown at Krazy Kat.

The emphasis is on the heart in George Herriman's cartoon. Almost out of the picture, the heart of humor nonetheless decides the flow of the sequence. It turns the hurt of the brick into the bliss of the brick. Ignatz hurls *I hate you*, but Krazy Kat's heart is not broken. It is rather liberated, set free. No hemorrhage of the heart—there it is, tingling with rapture—and no cerebral hemorrhage either. How is it possible that Krazy Kat should adore Ignatz Mouse, suffer repeatedly the ignominy of Ignatz's spiteful rejection, brick after brick after brick, and still love him? Offisa Pupp, who admires Krazy Kat's gentle and confiding sensibility, his sweet craziness, looks on, properly bewildered. Surely Herriman has got the order of things all wrong: the dog loves the cat, the cat loves the mouse, and the mouse scorns both dog and cat. A perfect equanimity rules this reversed world: the soft and yielding presence of Krazy Kat's good nature. Each act of violence, each aggression, is embraced, beautifully misunderstood. The whole history of grief is reduced to the size of a small black brick and construed as a love letter.

We are in the topsy-turvy world of Coconino County, where the sustaining *Grund* continually changes its formation. Sweetness, chattering in its lingo, is constant. Yet for all its charm, Herriman's depiction of the scene plainly draws the reality of malevolence. The most prominent piece of architecture in the cartoon is the Jail. "Sic transit Sin," Offisa Pupp remarks, watching a brick whiz by on its certain trajectory. Here, against a whimsical horizon of funny buttes and odd mesas and flat desert floor (Herriman's tribute to the 'real' Coconino County in northern Arizona, the site of the Grand Canyon), these exemplary creatures, whose ancestors are to be found in *The Parliament of Fowls*, take their places, and we see at a glance their relation, that the humblest is highest. Wit, always nasty, continually looking to score a hit, darts a missile, *zip*. Humor happily suffers it, *pow*. And there, with its badge and club, is Irony. Irony would erase the brick in midair, if it could, and therefore it has, at best, a marginal standing in the humorous text. Like the onlooking Offisa Pupp, whose power to police meaning in *Krazy Kat* is effectively useless, irony can only interfere in the fierce play of a humorous exchange. "Insupportable nonentity," Ignatz says of the flatfooted Pupp, "how I love to hate him."[6] Humorists who manage to humor the critical voice of irony in their texts, to draw this picture, keep themselves alight in good humor.

"True humour," to borrow from Tave, is amiable, of the heart, warm and moist. A heart is the emblem of Krazy Kat's being, and heart is what Huck Finn principally has. Romantic humorists, caught between the finite and the infinite, and black humorists, for whom there is no consolation, write in a different sense of humor, are headwise, witty, usually cold and dry in their style, and always ironic in their outlook. What indeed distinguishes those prodigies of redemptive humor in American literature—*Krazy Kat*, the speechless performance of Harpo Marx, Mark Twain in Huck's voice, Gertrude Stein loose in her "continuous present"—is their different relation to irony, the extent to which each humorist has undertaken that inspection and seen through it. Their refusal of irony, of course, is a criticism of irony, a complaint, not unlike Alex Portnoy's, that irony is too keen in its accounting and therefore not adequate in its negative representation of reality. Too much, for example, is. So humor questions a specific knowledge, does not understand what is proper, requires an explanation, is always being taught (as in a writing lesson), and affords us, as the knower explains himself, the edifying spectacle of the insufficient answer. Or humor itself responds to a question, thinks it over, and provides an answer that is at once beside the point and beyond it. Humor, in brief, is skeptical of any discourse based on authority—misspeaks it, miswrites it, misrepresents it. As Ignatz discovers, you can't learn Krazy Kat to argue. The flung brick in Herriman's picture is the book in *Huckleberry Finn*, the lurid book Tom throws at Huck, the Book of Kings Huck tries to throw at Jim, an aggressive argument, an imperative statement about knowledge as power.

Although this particular routine recurs in humorous literature, not all humorists turn it around upon themselves. The humorist as entertainer, as interlocutor, controlling the compass of his or her text, does not appear in *Huckleberry Finn*, except by ignoble proxy, and in Gertrude Stein's work the appellation 'humorist' simply does not figure, though *Tender Buttons*, *Lifting Belly*, *The Autobiography of Alice B. Toklas*, and *Ida*, are, in their different modes, humorous texts. Each writer submits his or her writing to humorous skepticism, yields, as it were, to the play of another voice, another value, and creates a knowing, supple, perverse style that at once entertains and abjures ironic knowledge. By forgiving the humorist his lie, Huck allows Mark Twain to open the general course of his writing, specifically the writing of *The Adventures of Tom Sawyer*, to humorous scrutiny. It is not just the "style" of Tom's tale that lies exposed in Huck's wistful narration, but as well the ironic distance Mark Twain achieves as the writer of the earlier book. As a voice in the text, as the signifier of a particular feminine intelligence, Alice B. Toklas is the Huckish presence in Gertrude Stein's writing. As soon as she figuratively enters Gertrude Stein's work, appearing near the abbreviated end of *A Long Gay Book* (1909-10), the writing becomes immediately humorous, jumps from philosophy to poetry. Alice brings, through her characterization, humor's question, the question that frees Gertrude Stein to celebrate in *Tender Buttons* the care with which everything so wrong is right, the question which frees her to become, in happy scandal, that jovial Madame Fattuski who lifts belly in Mallorca. Huck and Alice, these elusive figures of speech, these reluctant writers, enable Mark Twain and Gertrude Stein to slip away from the cramped and smothery intention of serious writing. In *Huckleberry Finn* and *Tender Buttons*, which set us adrift as readers, we begin to see how a spacious anti-Aristotelian, anti-patriarchal sense of the world, which does not fall discursively into the trap of counter-statement, of mirroring argument, might express itself in literature, how it would speak, given voice. That is the distinction of Mark Twain and Gertrude Stein as humorous writers: we see in their text how much, without lying, humor can contemplate.

So the humorous question emerges, and significant bricks, heavy bricks, have been hurled at it. "It takes courage," Kierkegaard writes in *The Concept of Irony* (1841), "when sorrow seeks to deceive one, when it would teach one to adulterate all joys into melancholy, all longing into privation, every hope into recollection, I say, it then requires courage to want to be glad; but it does not follow from this that every overgrown child with his insipid smile, his pleasure-drunken eye, has more courage than the man who bowed himself in sorrow and forgot to smile."[7] Humor is Kierkegaard's last word on irony, and it is ambiguous. There he is at the end of his dissertation, having rescued irony from Socrates and Schlegel, having looked through the negation of that irony, perceived the emptiness of its freedom, rethought it, dialectically negating its negation, and just here, as Kierkegaard delivers his notion of mastered irony, he is almost humorous. Irony no longer destroys the phenomenon by showing us it does not correspond to the idea, no longer destroys the idea by showing us it does not correspond to the phenomenon, but instead, properly regarded, is now an instrument to be used in clarifying and refining "truth, actuality, and content." This dialectical movement, which makes irony work in a way that resembles the activity of humor, brings Kierkegaard to a comparison of the modes, and here, necessarily, he stops short. Irony will admit the prospect of humor, even respect it, but it cannot in good faith step down from the privilege of its analytic discourse. Richter's romantic humorist witnesses the absurd disparity of finite and infinite, and is moved to humorous laughter, exhilarated by his sense of the world's nonsense. Kierkegaard's master ironist has no illusions about such emotional transformations of perspective. It is not possible to unknow what is known, the Naught, so the ironist may countenance humor, but always from a distance. Humor thinks at a lower level of consciousness, thinks in ignorance, speaks in the language of the shepherd, does not possess the knowledge of the Magi.

Even as Kierkegaard praises the "deeper scepticism" of humorous thought, its "deeper positivity," he satirizes the language of a contemporary Danish critic, H. L. Martensen, who, in his own criticism of irony, had advanced the notion of a Christian category of humor. It is, this doubled reference, a demonstration of the mastered irony Kierkegaard has just previously defined, for he does not deny the validity of Martensen's idea, he merely appropriates Martensen's phrasing, changing it slightly, to bring amending doubt into play. Martensen had hurled the "profundity" of his Christianized humor at the "cleverness" of irony, and herein Kierkegaard happily receives it.

> Finally, insofar as there can be any question of the "eternal validity" of irony, this can only find its answer through an investigation of the sphere of humour. Humour contains a much deeper scepticism than irony, for here it

is not finitude but sinfulness that everything turns upon. The scepticism of humour relates to the scepticism of irony as ignorance relates to the old thesis: *credo quia absurdum*; but humour also contains a much deeper positivity than irony, for it does not move itself in human-istic determinations but in the anthropic determinations; it does not find repose in making man human, but in making man God-Man. But all this lies outside the limits of this investigation, and should anyone wish food for after-thought, I shall then refer him to the review of Heiberg's *New Poems* by Professor Martensen (*CI*, pp. 341-42).

To this extent, turning Martensen about, Kierkegaard writes with good-humored irony about humor and achieves a truthful misrepre-sentation. It is what humor does as it rectifies the 'truth' of Ignatz's brick. In working out this particular effect, this illumination, the two modes seemingly coincide, and yet the practical difference of their separate styles is still there. The ironist remains poised in an aggres-sive discourse; the humorist always speaks from an excluded lan-guage. For that reason, because humor chooses to speak from the wrong discourse, to declare its vision in Huck's speech, in Krazy Kat's quaint parlance, in Gertrude Stein's loquacious double-talk, we are not accustomed to take its skepticism seriously. Where humor lies, it would seem, is exactly where Kierkegaard places it, outside the scan of irony, in a Never-Never Land beside intoxication, self-absorption, and ecstasy. There the humorist emulates the original God-Man, rights wrongs, redeems suffering, or, it may be, he draws us into a cozy delusion.

It takes courage to want to be glad, Kierkegaard writes, but. To humor oneself, to humor another, the ironist will quickly assert, means the worst kind of allowance, a condescending patience, the forging of a white lie, the gilding of the brick. We feel the brick. We have felt the brick and we know what the brick is. It is a brick. Cautionary tales exist in literature about the danger of listening to the humorist. Error is serious, is real, they remind us. To be in error is to suffer the wrong. Truth, serious truth, the oncoming brick, just past this humorous instance, is the pressing reality of what is. Ahab kicks Stubb in *Moby Dick*, and Stubb must then for the sake of his self-respect consider the kick. But first dinner, and then a doze. In his troubled sleep, Stubb beholds a wily merman who gives him the resolution of humor.

> " 'Look ye here,' said he; 'let's argue the insult. Captain Ahab kicked ye, didn't he?' 'Yes, he did,' says I—'right *here* it was.' 'Very good,' says he—'he used his ivory leg, didn't he?' 'Yes, he did,' says I. 'Well then,' says he, 'wise Stubb, what have you to complain of? Didn't he kick with right good will? it wasn't a common pitch pine leg he kicked with, was it? No, you were kicked by a great man, and with a beautiful ivory leg, Stubb. In old England the greatest lords think it great glory to be slapped by a queen, and made garter-knights of; but, be *your* boast, Stubb, that ye were kicked by old Ahab, and made a wise man of. Remember what I say; *be* kicked by him; account his kicks honors; and on no account kick back; for ye can't help yourself, wise Stubb.' "[8]

Herman Melville cuts these corners very fine. There is some truth in all this deception, and it is anchored to the bottom line, to the purest fatalism. *You can't help yourself. Invent the necessary lie.* Stubb humorously transforms the humiliation of the kick into what it is not, the honor of the kick, and will take the consequences. When the *Pequod* sinks, and all its gartered knights go down with it, wise Stubb might well be thinking: I should have taken Ahab's kick seriously. He has listened to the wrong humorist, the one who argues. Yet the merman is plausible, Ahab is large, and what else might humor have to say to Stubb? Once we step aboard the *Pequod*, we are in Ahab's fiction, and humor is hard pressed in this text. Ahab's fool is Pip. The humor that beholds Stubb's humor resembles Richter's sense of humor. It places small Stubb's resolution of the insult against great Ahab's response to his injury, and generates the deep silence of philosophical laughter. We need lies, Nietzsche tells us, in order to live. Humor, in this regard, is necessarily a short fiction, the hardest piece of work given to man, that for the nonce he believably beguile himself, make the wrong right, convert pain into pleasure, forgive error. To this extent, periodically, we are all humorists. We take the kick and love the brick.

2

What is the wrong that humor forgives? Herriman's cartoon exhibits at once the project of humor and its essential players. That bitterest of bricks, rejection, is promptly hurled and Krazy Kat is struck, always from behind, unexpectedly. Offisa Pupp strives to intervene, to stop the brick, arrest the thrower, and typically fails. For over thirty years, from 1910 to 1944, Herriman drew and redrew this single act in different scenes with different plots, without ever exhausting the force of its simplicity. We might call the brick Nemesis, or the Reality Principle—it is certainly a hard message, a brickbat, the word, *no.* The bricks in *Krazy Kat* vary in quality, substance, and accuracy. Ignatz experiments with a boomerang, pitches horseshoes, throws cuneiform tablets, brickish books (Plutarch), illuminated bricks, embossed bricks, plain bricks, anything that comes readily to hand. Anything can be a brick if the intention is right. The world, Ignatz tells Krazy Kat, is composed of sand and water. Ergo, battered, basted, baked, the brick. "Movillis," Krazy Kat muses, "stipenditz, killotzil." Three figures, three values, and the brick. We lose the play of the act if, to change paradigms, we reductively name Herriman's creatures Krazy Id, Ignatz Ego, and Offisa Super-ego, and yet the act of their exchange repeats as act repeats in the repetition compulsion. The question in *Krazy Kat* is the nature of the brick. Each character has his own interpretation of the brick, an interpretation that is at once his function and his fate. So, in this long-lived series, Herriman constructs the question panel by panel,

The Project of Humor

brick by brick. Here is the war within the self, the romance within the self, as play, a sophistication of child's play: hurt continually resolved by the sacred humor of the heart.

There is another context, another discourse, in which to set this scene of usurpation: how to make light of an egotistical ego in the passion of its scramble to write its name upon the world, this irked mousy self that, always foiled, is so easily hateful. "Look!" says

© 1974 King Features Syndicate Inc.

Freud's fond super-ego to the intimidated ego, "here is the world, which seems so dangerous! It is nothing but a game for children—just worth making a jest about!"⁹ The psychodramatics of this 'humorous' deception, so different from the other deceptions, those other defenses against suffering: intoxication, self-absorption, ecstasy, madness, inspired Freud to write twice in praise of humor, first in *Jokes and Their Relation to the Unconscious* and again in his essay "Humor," which is almost an encomium. It is to the ambivalent figure of Offisa Pupp, the watchful policeman, that Freud figuratively looks in his later essay. The act of humor, as he describes it, is that act of self-fathering wherein we give ourselves first perspective, then tolerance, and at last forgiveness. In the politics of the self, so to speak, knowing parent embraces known child. That the super-ego, who is otherwise a "severe master," should be the agent of humor, the consoling humorist, surprises Freud, for "in bringing about the humorous attitude, the super-ego is actually repudiating reality and serving an illusion" (*H*, p. 220). How does the super-ego displace its peremptory knowledge of the real? The humorist, Freud suggests, withdraws the psychical accent from his ego and uses it to puff himself up, to become properly parental. "To the super-ego, thus inflated, the ego can appear tiny and all its interests trivial; and, with this new distribution of energy, it may become an easy matter for the super-ego to suppress the ego's possibilities of reacting" (*H*, p. 219). So disguised, the super-ego is briefly benign, and speaks "kindly words" to the diminished ego. Nothing but a game for children, it says within the self to the self upon whom has fallen a load of bricks, nothing to it, just worth making a jest about.

Like the merman, this humorist lies. The bricks we thought were real, felt real, are not. And yet there is a sense of humor, lucid in the simplicity of Herriman's art, present even in Freud's writing, which seems dedicated to the very unmasking of that deception. This humorist captures himself in the "humorous attitude," falls into the text, dogfaced, dumb. I am lying, the liar now writes. Even if it is still reason unreasoning, still the super-egotistical humorist who speaks in that text, this best of liars has bravely put himself in a hard place. Here the difference between the parental humorist who writes as our interlocutor, as Mr. Mark Twain, to beguile and mollify, and the skeptical writer whose humorous sense of his or her authority is shaky, who enters the act of writing warily, becomes apparent. As Herriman delineates the love/hate triangle in *Krazy Kat*, draws the three quintessential figures, and sends coursing between them the flight of an ambiguous signifier, the empty/full, soft/hard brick, he exhibits the conceptual and psychological risk of a skeptically rendered humorous style. The brick seems, at times, to designate language itself. This is how Offisa Pupp reads the world, how Ignatz addresses it. There are crises of usurpation in Coconino County, ordeals of ambivalence, questions of adequacy, diverse constructions of the brick, and the very ground on which everyone stands is continuously shifty and supple in its krazy representation. "How I love to hate him," Ignatz says, a wit who loathes the flatfooted, admonitory Kop. Always looming, always overlooking, Pupp flashes the badge of authority. Like Freud's dubious forgiver, the Kop longs to humor Krazy Kat, to be humorous, so he attacks Ignatz, seeks to arrest him, and gets it all unerringly wrong. So, too, will Tom Sawyer, bustling knowledgeably into Huck's text. When the Puppish hold on the brick in humor is shaken, when he is seen as the problem, not the solver, then humor complicates, and the ending of it, the conclusion of the humorous text, becomes questionable. Humor seems now to emerge as an intelligence, a voice, from some other place in language. It speaks for a different system of values, a different way of knowing, and to this extent it speaks against authority, against the writer who is, however humorous, inescapably within the sphere of culture, in the foreknowledge of writing.

In *The Seven Lively Arts* (1924), which places Herriman's kat appreciatively beside Charlie Chaplin's tramp, Gilbert Seldes refers to Krazy Kat as a kind of Pan, the god of Coconino's rustic world, and there is some truth in the reference. There is, however, another Pan in American humor who plays directly upon the Arcadian lyre, who seems the more fitting Pan. He, too, 'speaks' within a humorous triad, and he gives us, along with his melodies, the other sense of Pan, *panic*. He will create panic, leap into the pursuit of unwary travelers — pretty maids, nubile ingenues, buxom matrons. What does humor have to say through the urgent showing of this acrobatic Pan? We have only to contemplate the manic light in Harpo Marx's eyes to see such humor at its absolute precipice: radiant Unreason shining with shameless desire. There is no return from this state of being. Harpo simply does not recognize the serious person, the serious situation, as serious. He can mimic seriousness, mirror it, but the concept does not exist for him. It belongs to a language he has refused to learn, or has yet to learn. His role in the comedy of the Marx Brothers is therefore curiously distinctive. He is not written. He has no lines to speak. So he is free, at large. He appears, and the haphazard narrative goes on around him. Yet he is never found in the purity of mime. His silence rather is a silence that is in relation to a particular brilliance of speech.

What is the distribution of energy in a Marx Brothers film? This question perplexed Arthur Sheekman and S. J. Perelman as they struggled to write *Horsefeathers*, and, so the story goes, they went to seek the advice of their irascible producer, Herman Mankiewicz. "In this sequence we're working on," Perelman explains, "we're kind of perplexed about the identity of the Marx Brothers—the psychology of the characters they're supposed to represent, so to speak. I mean, who *are* they?" The producer ironically replies, "One of them is guinea, another a mute who picks up spit, and the third an old Hebe with a cigar."[10] Perelman's question remains. Who *are* they? The same question, of course, is asked aboard the *Fidele* in Melville's *The Confidence-Man* of that other mute, that other guinea, that other fast-talking hustler, who magically appear and disappear, who would seem to share the same cabin and the same trunk. This much can be safely said: each of the Marx Brothers has a sign to mark his age and place in discourse. Harpo, whose gestural speech is preverbal, has a mop of infantile curls. Chico wears a juvenile cap, mispronounces words, mistakes their meaning, and gives us the broad comicality of learning language (viaduct—why-a-duck?). Groucho has the mustache. He is Captain Spaulding, the adult who possesses the mastery of words, the power of the joke. We scale the reaches of expression in this style. Chico typically mediates between the two extremes: the wordless manifestations of Harpo, the elaborate verbal treachery of Groucho. The brothers tolerate each other's antics because, however disparate, these comic styles share the same tumultuous origin, the spontaneity of desire. Harpo flings open his rumpled, seedy, voluminous trench coat to flash the near-nakedness of his ridiculous body, and that is exactly what Groucho's wit furtively achieves with the word, the flash of nakedness. Although he keeps his distance, Groucho cannot escape the reductive significance of Harpo's dumb-show, which at once underlines the single style and resolves its unity of effect.

Groucho's knowledge of the double meaning is therefore ultimately the knowledge of nonsense, nervous knowledge, and his repartee, his riffs, his routines, accelerate in delivery, driven by an exasperation. As he discovers innuendo, comes upon insinuation, the cigar wiggles and waggles, the eyebrows arch. It is already there, the other frame of reference: Margaret Dumont's unspeakable body stiffly upright in Mrs. Rittenhouse's stately gown. She greets, she introduces, she trills niceties. Her discourse flutters above and patters around Groucho's crouch-backed perspective. He sees the body in the form before we do, speaks it, and as Madame protests the revelation, Groucho is elsewhere, *zip* and *pow*. He never pauses over a meaning, because the meaning of language in this social world, this grown-up world, is the polite displacement of desire, defense, aggression, so this revealing wit keeps moving. But where? The body keeps turning up wherever a word is turned. There is no end to wit's pursuit. In *Animal Crackers* Captain Spaulding dictates a business letter to his secretary (Zeppo) that promptly becomes a slick meditation on the perversity of the sign.

> Zeppo: Now, uh, you said a lot of things here that I didn't think were important, so I just omitted them.
>
> Dumont: Well! . . . Whoa, Captain! Good Gracious! Oh, my!
>
> Groucho: So . . . you just omitted them, eh? You've just omitted the body of the letter, that's all. You've just left out the body of the letter, that's all! Yours not to reason why, Jamison! You've left out the body of the letter! . . . All right, send it that way and tell them the body'll follow.
>
> Zeppo: Do you want the body in brackets?
>
> Groucho: No, it'll never get there in brackets. Put it in a box.

All letters are disembodied messages, we might slowly think, but the absent body herein questioned undergoes rapid transformations, is this body and that body. In the text the referent is never there, but in spoken discourse the body is always unspeakably there (Mrs. Rittenhouse fluttering "Whoa, Captain!"). Groucho is fated to see what is omitted, what has been left out, in discourse, and also what is therefore there, in the blank. Jamison has purloined the letter, and Groucho is quick in his detection. Where's the body? Yet this is a ruse, for Groucho is the thief of meaning, the social criminal who points out unerringly the unsaid, the inhibition, and by the close of the dictation, the game almost up, he hastily destroys the evidence. No original, no copies, no message, no sender, no trace—the perfect crime. "I want you to make two carbon copies of that letter and throw the original away," Captain Spaulding instructs Jamison. "And when you get through with that, throw the carbon copies away. Just send a stamp, airmail. That's all. You may go, Jamison, I may go, too."[11] What Groucho anxiously knows about the missing message of the letter, Harpo sweetly is, the original, and this precisely is where they correspond, adult to child. Where *is* the body the letter leaves out? Who is not written? Groucho's wit refers to what is silent in social speech, silent beneath the *blague,* inside the rhetoric: the constant intention of primary narcissism, Harpo's unlettered child's body, Harpo's luminous expression. He is the value of a Marx Brothers film, the embodiment of its humor, the body in brackets, and yet what is to be done with him?

If the ending of a Marx Brothers film is always problematical, typically abrupt, the 'plot' carelessly resolved, a comical ending, where is Harpo's place in the frame when the entertainment is finished? He is, of course, parenthetically inside the script, given space and time from which he intrusively commands the attention of the other players, who tolerate him, who have the work of the story to do, lines to deliver, but he is as well fundamentally alone in the film, extrinsic, lineless, and therefore has no place to be in the final disposition. At the end of *Animal Crackers* Harpo has the 'real' painting, the stolen original, without ever realizing that it *is* the genuine picture. The two copies (one as good, the other not so good) have been identified and properly assessed by the pompous art critic "Roscoe W. Chandler," who, though an impostor, perhaps because an impostor, knows the real thing. Resolutions happily abound. It only remains for Harpo to surrender the 'real' picture so that it can be restored to its proper place. He does not surrender the picture. For now, at least, the picture is his, and no one is going to have the last word, not even Groucho. Harpo puts everyone to sleep, dancing about spraying ether, and when everyone has been put down, knocked out, silenced, he sprays himself and falls triumphantly asleep beside a slumbering blonde. *Animal Crackers* is *his* picture.

In the humorous text such palpable abandonment to the luxury of Unconsciousness is not possible. The spell of Harpo's speechless presence, this act that is the very performance of presence, a mute showing-forth of presence, is immediately distanced by an inscription. The challenge of Harpo's humor, that is seem not written, that it give always the illusion of spontaneity (no matter the number of takes), becomes an even greater challenge in literary humor where the it-seem-not-written must be written. When Harpo is written, he is distanced. This is, after all, lest we forget, a grown man in a wig. "If you've ever seen a Marx Brothers picture, you know the difference between him and me," Harpo 'writes' with Rowland Barber in *Harpo Speaks!* "When he's chasing a girl across the screen, it's Him. When he sits down to play the harp, it's Me."[12] The unserious Harpo, Him; the seriously harping Harpo, Me. The spell is therein broken. And yet in the illusion of the film, where Harpo's spell is certain and unswerving, we never make that distinction. The comedies play with the categories of high and low art, with painting and opera, with the tragic speech of Eugene O'Neill's drama, but these considerations are ultimately subordinate clauses in a larger conception: Harpo's perfect blindness to the existence of such values. He chases the girl, he plays the harp, and we do not see the difference. Harpo is not yet in the world where such differences (Him, Me) are figured, where burlesque begins. We behold his grinning lunatic face, that look Adolph Marx imaginatively realizes, and there is only radiant Unreason shining with shameless desire. It is krazy, not crazed.

"The poetic quality of a film like *Animal Crackers*," Antonin Artaud observes, "would fit the definition of humor if this word had not long since lost its sense of essential liberation, of destruction of all reality in the mind."[13] How indeed does *Animal Crackers* reveal the poetic quality of humorous thought? Artaud, it might be said, misreads the free-for-all of the brotherly exchanges, does not see through the commotion of the wreckage to the *primum mobile* of its humorous action. It is humorous assurance that lies at the heart of a Marx Brothers film, not the ironic freedom of negation. The reality destroyed in *Animal Crackers* is, after all, just the familiar reality, that reality imposed by social forms and conventional artistic modes. What is the psychology of the characters the Marx Brothers are supposed to represent? Harpo's silence, as we have seen, requires Groucho's speech, if not Chico's intermediate bumbling, to register its interruptive truth. In the triangulation of affect that leaps from brother to brother, from mute to guinea to Hebe, from child to youth to man, we make the circuit of a single psyche. Here is a mind turned humorously in upon the texture of its own reality. It thinks through Groucho and sees in the blank space between his lines the shine of its original body. It regards what might be called the insistence of Harpo's leg in the course of its conscious discourse. And this is our reflection, why Groucho turns so often to face the camera, harassed, exasperated, *our* brother. As we speak, sanely discoursing, we, too, find ourselves inexplicably holding Harpo's leg. He has come up beside us, silently, and lifted his bare leg into our hand. We have made a slip of the tongue. An inadvertent pun has turned up. When we make this discovery, grouchily, stopping in mid phrase, we look down and into the phrase, and there, beaming up at us, giving us the lie, is the gaze of humor.

Who speaks in *Harpo Speaks!*? Not Harpo. Who writes *The Autobiography of Alice B. Toklas*? Not Alice. Having painfully written *Huckleberry Finn*, Huck swears he will never write again. When he is driven once more to the task by the elder Mark Twain and forced to write sequels, Huck will only take dictation. The sequels concern the unfunny antics of Tom Sawyer. Those who speak humorously within the framework of a literary text, who offer the humorous question, are always in a certain state of peril. The interpreter of a humorous text is therefore well advised to follow Freud's example and keep an eye on the figure of the humorist in the text, this Offisa Pupp, the trope of control and closure in humor, for he is the complication of the humorous play, even as he deftly destroys the evidence of his presence. "If it is really the super-ego which, in humor, speaks such kindly words of comfort to the intimidated ego," Freud writes, "this will teach us that we have still a great deal to learn about the nature of the super-ego" (*H*, p. 220). So we locate the address of the humorist, but whether we have also found the expression of humor is open to humor's question. "En what dey got to do, Huck?" Jim asks. The humorous writer always establishes the figure of his or her authority in the text. He is G. G., Chief of

Ordnance, a baffled Kop in Coconino County, and in Gertrude Stein's writing that roundest of figures, the Aristotelian tradition, the Name of the Father. To this extent, the writer puts him- or herself into the play of the text. What must the writer do? He or she must let humor speak, voice its question, show its body, and risk, as a writer, that profound disruption. Because, after all, you can't learn a nigger to argue.

3

The humorous tradition in American literature begins effectively in the Jacksonian period, begins with Davy Crockett using his crooked grin to knock bears and coons down from the trees, with Jim Rice and Dan Emmett capering in their blackface minstrelsy, with James Russell Lowell and George Washington Harris, that odd couple, struggling to determine an appropriate structure for their style, and the importance of these early figures, their forms and routines, is considerable. It is where we begin, with the primordial comedy, with that distant sense of humor. Every writer who undertakes this subject is indebted to Constance Rourke's *American Humor, A Study of the National Character* (1931), that eloquent and still eminently useful exploration of the field. She describes the primary types, the elemental forms, and places humorous writing in our cultural history. It is the project of humor, however, that is before us—the problem of its resolution in the humorous style. Where Rourke's study of American humor explains its relevance in terms of the national character, the American *ethos*, this study examines the stylistic character of humorous writing in American literature.

To that end, we will look first at two humorously complicated Jacksonian texts: *The Biglow Papers* and *Sut Lovingood's Yarns*, to define a certain inhibition in humorous writing, a particular problem with the determination of writing (Papers) and speech (Yarns), and then consider Mark Twain's own struggle with the role of the humorist in *The Adventures of Tom Sawyer* and "Old Times on the Mississippi," a struggle that yields the resolution of *Huckleberry Finn*. Three styles are at the heart of this examination: Mark Twain's writing of Huck's speech, the parlance Herriman devised for *Krazy Kat*, and the playful hazarding of Gertrude Stein's poetic double-talk. Each style is located in an eccentric text, an improper discourse, and is turned from the uses of irony. Huckspeech, that distinctive style Mark Twain realizes in a single text and then never regains, transforms the Jacksonian mode of humorous writing and summarily expresses the hardest question in nineteenth-century American humor. For his part, Herriman is the first humorist in the twentieth century to articulate the skepticism of humorous intelligence in a thoroughly modernist idiom. Innocuous, sweetly tempered, *Krazy Kat* changes the frame of humorous reference. In the spelling of its text, the cartoon still invokes the orthography of nineteenth-century humor, and yet the site of its play and the nature of its symbolic illustration are new and strange. *Krazy Kat* effectively breaks from the locality of the traditional style, dislocates its regionalism, and creates instead a poetic space. Herriman's Coconino County is an abstraction of that other Coconino County. Gertrude Stein's specific relation to the humorous tradition is, at best, coincidental. Her *oeuvre*, so to speak, is large and diverse, and its intention is not 'humor' as we commonly understand it. Yet she understood better than any other writer of her generation the quality of the humorous play in cubism, the depth in its flat surface, and ingeniously appropriated its idiom. When we are inside *Tender Buttons*, moving across thresholds in her sentence, we are within a poetic conception of the world that is engendered from beginning to end by the humorous question. What is a carafe? It is a blind glass. What is substance? It is the stuffing in a cushion. These questions, strangely answered, reverberate, subsume the reader's question, and lure him or her into the wrongness of the text. The skepticism of humor herein reformulates, with great sophistication, the very statement of writing. Gertrude Stein composes, in brief, a seriously whimsical form of considered double-talk, ingenuous/ingenious, that is at once a criticism of definitive discourse and a liberation from it.

Although each style is distinct in its provenance and expression, there are conjunctions and continuities. The most important of these is the significance of voice in humorous writing. That is, of course, easily said: the early American humorists typically present themselves as the retellers of tales taken from the oral tradition, and yet there is more to this particular disposition than is immediately apparent. The phonocentrism of American humor discloses, predictably, a recurrent problem in the humorous style—the relation, the value, the position of speech in the text. Humor, Freud explains in

Jokes and Their Relation to the Unconscious, "scorns to withdraw the ideational content bearing the distressing affect from conscious attention as repression does, and thus surmounts the automatism of defense. It brings this about by finding a means of withdrawing the energy from the release of unpleasure that is already in preparation and of transforming it, by discharge, into pleasure."[14] In nineteenth-century American humor, the style itself iz the means of withdrawing the energy from the release of unpleasure. It achieves that transformation by the phonetic play of speech in writing, a disfiguring of the text. The immediate imposition of that generic sign of the Unserious, *iz*, instantly changes the lens in our attention to the text, lowers our gaze, and suffuses the "ideational content," the brick, whatever, with the warm glow of a tolerable miztake. Such is the function of that humorous style, its trick. It renders terrible things and awful feelings rongly, fixes them in the fiat of the low style: that nothing high, or tragic, or noble, nothing serious, can be expressed in the low style. Into the gravity of the sentence is laid the soft semblance of speech.

As Mark Twain takes up the style in *Huckleberry Finn*, it is a low style, restrictive, and its necessary prop is the device of misspelling. Until this moment the style appears as local as the idiom it strives to represent, and as simple as unlettered intelligence is supposed to be. Then it changes. Humor that is written, to put aside the eloquence of Harpo's silence, is written perforce in that very knowing discourse which properly serves the truth, not error. In effect, humorists must wrest their writing from proper writing, and this they do in a style that enhances speech values and sets these values against the prescriptive values of writing. As we shall see, this is at first a small stratagem for the humorist, an obvious device—phoneticized writing—but in this simple device lies the potent metaphor Speech, and here, in Huckspeech, the significant history of American humor begins. In *Huckleberry Finn* style is theme. How, then, does Huckspeech shape its beautiful wrong in the formality of the text, the text that demands the alienation of the letter-perfect? There sits the writer at his manuscript, all scrunched up in his chair, his face screwed, speaking aloud the words he painstakingly inscribes: *sivilize, nonnamous, considerble*. It is a hard thing to wrong writing for the sake of speech, to take up the cause of innocence and nonsense, cantabile, as Gertrude Stein does in *Tender Buttons*: "A no, a no since, a no since when, a no since when since, a no since when since a no since when since, a no since, a no since when since, a no since, a no, a no since a no since, a no since, a no since."[15] Affirmation is sung through the negative.

Humor deconstructs the formal knowledge of writing—and undoes the writer. All the important humorists in the nineteenth century write behind assumed names, an alias that is their alibi. To break the rule of writing, humorists had literally to disappear into their characters, lose themselves in the style, discount their literary value, and so they did. Of those who rote rongly in the Jacksonian period, who did phunny dialect-sketches in the decades after the Civil War, only Mark Twain is still before us, his alias, his alibi.

Notes

1. Samuel Langhorne Clemens, *Adventures of Huckleberry Finn*, ed. Hamlin Hill (San Francisco: Chandler Publishing Company, 1962), p. 110. All subsequent reference will be indicated *HF*. This text is a facsimile of the first American edition, published by Charles L. Webster Co. on February 18, 1885.

2. Robert Burton, *The Anatomy of Melancholy*, ed. Floyd Dell and Paul Jordan Smith (New York, 1927), p. 349.

3. Corbyn Morris, *An Essay towards Fixing the True Standards of Wit, Humour, Raillery, Satire, and Ridicule. To Which Is Added, an Analysis of the Character of an Humourist, Sir John Falstaff, Sir Roger de Coverly, and Don Quixote*, London, 1744. Cited in Stuart Tave, *The Amiable Humorist* (University of Chicago Press: Chicago, 1960), pp. 118-127.

4. Laurence Sterne, *The Life and Opinions of Tristram Shandy, Gentleman*, ed. Samuel Holt Monk (New York and Toronto, 1959), p. 376. All subsequent reference will be indicated *TS*. For an excellent discussion of the immediate influence of Shandean aesthetics on the comic writing of Washington Irving, see Martin Roth, *Comedy and America, The Lost World of Washington Irving* (Kennikat Press: Port Washington, N.Y., London, 1976).

5. *Horn of Oberon, Jean Paul Richter's School for Aesthetics*, trans. Margaret R. Hale (Wayne State University Press: Detroit, 1973), p. 92.

6. *Krazy Kat*, ed. Joost Swartz, 5 nrs. (Real Free Press: Amsterdam, 1974-76), 2:45. Each number in this well-produced series contains a representative sampling of Herriman's art in the different phases of its development. Swartz has also collected useful essays by Martin Sheridan, Coulton Waugh, Ed Ward and M. Thomas Inge. There is an American edition of Krazy Kat cartoons, *George Herriman's Krazy Kat*, with an introduction by e. e. cummings and a foreword by Barbara Gelman (Grosset & Dunlap: New York, 1977), but this text is now out of print and not generally available. cummings's essay is rather broad and somewhat condescending in its approach. What's interesting about it is cummings's straightforward assumption that Krazy Kat is feminine. Readers who wish to look up *Krazy Kat* have

The Project of Humor

the choice of either rummaging through the close-out bins in local bookstores for the American text or sending away to The Real Free Press for the five issues in that extant series. The address is Dirk Van Hasseltsstreeg 25, Amsterdam, Holland, the Netherlands.

7. Soren Kierkegaard, *The Concept of Irony,* trans. Lee M. Capel (Indiana University Press: Bloomington, 1968), p. 339. All subsequent reference is indicated *CI.* For an ironically humorous modern riposte to Kierkegaard's criticism of romantic irony, see Donald Barthelme's "Kierkegaard Unfair to Schlegel" in *City Life* (New York, 1970), pp. 83-93.

8. Herman Melville, *Moby Dick,* ed. Charles Feidelson (Indianapolis and New York, 1951), pp. 177-78.

9. Sigmund Freud, "Humor," in *Collected Papers,* ed. James Strachey (London, 1952), 5:220. All subsequent reference will be indicated *H.*

10. S. J. Perelman, *The Last Laugh* (New York, 1981), p. 160.

11. Cited in Joe Adamson, *Groucho, Harpo, Chico, and Sometimes Zeppo, A Celebration of the Marx Brothers* (New York, 1974), pp. 114-15.

12. Harpo Marx, with Rowland Barber, *Harpo Speaks!* (New York, 1961), p. 12.

13. Antonin Artaud, *Theater and Its Double* (New York, 1958), p. 142.

14. Sigmund Freud, "Jokes and Their Relation To The Unconscious," in *The Complete Psychological Works of Sigmund Freud,* ed. James Strachey (London, 1960), 8:233. All subsequent reference will be indicated *JRU.*

15. Gertrude Stein, *Writings and Lectures 1909-1945,* ed. Patricia Meyerowitz (Baltimore, 1974), p. 195.

II

Before Huck Writes

A chirographic and typographic bias still governs to varying degrees all but a tiny fraction of scholarship and criticism concerned with oral productions, and this fact itself deserves serious attention in any study of popular literature. The assertiveness of the chirographic and typographic bias, which accounts in great part for the hostile reviews of *Webster* III by virtually all subscholarly writers up to and including the level of the *New Yorker*, is highly informative, for it shows the massive and deep-set, subconscious defenses which writing sets up in the psyche to sustain the restructuring of personality which it brings about. Or, to put it another way, it shows how the acquisition of writing brings those who acquire this skill to structure their entire world view around a feel for the written word to the positive (but not often conscious) exclusion of the oral as such.

Walter J. Ong, S. J., "Literate Orality of Popular Culture"

1

Y ou kin spall an' punctooate thet as you please," Hosea Biglow writes in 1866, submitting a verse letter to the *Atlantic Monthly*. "I allus do, it kind of puts a noo soot of close onto a word, thisere funattick spellin' doos an' takes 'em out of the prisen dress they wair in the Dixonary."[1] It is the last entry in *The Biglow Papers* (1847-1866), No. XI. in the Second Series, "Mr. Hosea Biglow's Speech in March Meeting," and with it James Russell Lowell concludes the project, his excursion into humorous writing. A year later, in George Washington Harris's preface to *Sut Lovingood's Yarns* (1843-1867), Sut Lovingood protests, "Sumtimes, George, I wished I cud read an' write, jis' a littil; but then hits bes' es hit am, fur ove all the fools the woorild hes tu contend wif, the edicated wuns am the worst; they breeds ni ontu all the devilment a-gwine on."[2] Before the writing of *Huckleberry Finn*, these two characters, their names, their voices, express quintessentially the hazard of humorous writing.

Big? Low? Lowell could not make up his mind how he felt about the artistic integrity of the *Papers*, and particularly this humorous style, "thisere funattick spellin.' " "I do not think that Mr. Biglow can be fairly charged with vulgarity," Lowell chastely observes in his scholarly introduction to the *Papers*, "and I should have entirely failed in my design, if I have not made it appear that high and even refined sentiment may coexist with the shrewder and more comic elements of the Yankee character" (*BP*, pp. 279-80). Harris, on the other hand, is an unabashed spokesman for the license of speech, the eroticism of speech. In this regard he anticipates Philip Roth (and Lenny Bruce) by showing us, defiantly, that Huckspeech, grown-up, is fuckspeech. Sut likes good loving, but does not love the Good. At the end of his preface Harris looks straight at his mid-Victorian readers and tells them where to stuff their disapproval.

> "Make me a Notey Beney, George. I wants tu put sum-whar atween the eyebrows ove our book, in big winnin-lookin letters, the sarchin, meanin words, what sum pusson writ ontu a 'oman's garter onst, long ago—"
> "*Evil be to him that evil thinks.*"
> "Them's em, by jingo! Hed em clost apas' yu, didn't yu?"
> "Now, George, grease hit good, an' let hit slide down the hill hits own way" (*SL*, pp. 26-27).

The marvel is that a single style should easily contain in a single attitude, the humorous attitude, such extremes of feeling, such contradictory notions of the source and power of common speech. Lowell is a liberal Northerner, an eminent man of letters, who shows us through the style "homely common-sense vivified and heated by conscience" (*BP*, p. 200). Harris is a reactionary Southerner, an obscure and occasional writer, who shows us through the style the visual impact of Sicily Burns: "Such a buzzim! Jis' think ove two snow balls wif a strawberry stuck but-ainded intu bof on em" (*SL*, p. 69).

Before we examine this divergence of the myth, the metaphor, the meaning of speech in humorous writing, we need first to consider the style itself as a break. As we have seen, the sign of the humorous text in nineteenth-century American literature iz the funattick play of speech in writing. Humorists rong riting, impose *vox* upon *littera*, and this aspect of their writing, the misspelled sign, distinguishes them from comic writers (Washington Irving, Oliver Wendell Holmes), whose prose is always properly composed. The difrunce is immediate. Writing wrongs Speech. This simple logic directs the eccentric play of the humorous style. The humorist misspells to depict the textual "natur" of oral discourse, to score a tall tale as it is told, *vivace*, or, in character, in a topical letter, he misspells to show a naive writer humorously violate the rules of proper writing. When the "natur" of speech breaks into the *nature* of writing, there is fracture. So it is written: "Mistur Wilbur sez he to me onct, sez he, 'Hosee,' sez he, 'in litterytoor the only good thing is Natur" (*BP*, p. 491). And the style is constant, always the same, phone-logical, fonocentric. Whether the humor is Down East, the homespun rhyming of a Yankee farmer (Hosea Biglow), or Southwestern, the explosive yarns of an obscene backwoodsman (Sut Lovingood), the humorous text written in the Jacksonian period, or the text written in the post-Civil War period, the komposishuns of Artemus Ward or the allminax of Josh Billings, the same funattick play of speech in writing occurs, and the sign of that difrunce is immediate. Here, it says, iz humor.

Here, too, is the anxiety of the humorist, the anxiety of the writer who adopts this lowest of styles. "The misfortune waz, that the fust piece i wrote for the publik eye," Josh Billings (Henry Wheeler Shaw) confesses in 1873, "i waz so ashamed ov that i dare not trust it to good spelling, and so did it in bad to hide, and the piece waz lucky, having a run, and i kept on in the way ov wickedness and distorshun."[3] We are herein joshed, for Shaw took himself seriously as a humorist, and yet the confession is a confession. "Thare iz just az mutch joke in bad spelling," he writes, "az thare iz in looking kross-eyed, and no more" (*JB*, p. 126). So it would seem, and yet the first misspelled word in *Huckleberry Finn*, and the last, is *sivilize*. At the start the Widow Douglas "allowed she would sivilize me" (*HF*, p. 17), and at the end Aunt Sally is "going to adopt me and sivilize me and I can't stand it" (*HF*, p. 366). By invoking the sign of the style especially at the problematical close of the text, Mark Twain, it might be said, retains the humor of *Huckleberry Finn*, keeps the purity of Huck's speech intact, and effectively compresses the whole drama of the narrative into this single mistake, this repetition. We see the fault; Huck does not. If Huck is to write again, older and wiser, he must know how to spell the word, and in this correction, by this amendment, lose at once the pressing virtuosity of his speech, the imprint of his speech, and his humor. He would then be civilized. Misspelling releases the word from its imprisonment in the Dictionary, so Hosea Biglow tells us, and gives it a "noo soot of close," and therein lies the metaphor. *Sivilize.* It is a written word that has gone over to the side of speech. Riting now sensibly adheres to the sense of sound, draws itself closer to the presence of a speaking voice, and iz therefore realer, because such riting assumes what Walt Whitman assumed: that speech is the twin of vision, a sense. And this is what the humorist gives us through his style, the trace of that sense.

In this specific mode, humor necessarily alienates the 'civilized' writer, who is bound to the Dictionary. It speaks (graphically) for the priority of speech in discourse, for the value of speech (as she is spoken), so the writer who appropriates the style can never escape the sensible signifier of *sivilize.* Humor has its theses, and the first is that writing wrongs speech. Civilize me, the style sez, and I cease to speak. All the values we associate with good writing—rigorous intellection, compelling rhetoric, the surprise and complexity of luminous metaphors—are knocked flat by the humorous style. The humorist debases the privilege of writing. It is not that he resists these values, but that, strictly speaking, the style does not know them. Humor lacks a proper notion of Nature, this potent sign it always misspells. The humorist writes *in* Nature, not about it. Even before we read his material in the respective sketch or tall tale, aphorism or topical letter, the style has already presented the spectacle of its difference. And readers who see it, the "noo soot of close" on the word, are themselves abruptly liberated from the rectitude of writing, paroled. What thing in the nature of things can seriously withstand the confoundment of misspelling? The lesson Huck's line breaks, "sivilize me," is the lesson we all learn when we learn, for better or worse, how to spell *civilize.*

2

I will now throw the book at you. It means: full letter of the law, severest punishment. What, after all, are the most impressive institutions of orthodoxy for the nineteenth-century writer, but the Speller, the Grammar, and the Bible? These are the books thrown at Innocence and Ignorance at the primal crossing into culture, where one becomes literate, and they are thrown by those first pains in the neck: Parent, Teacher, and Pastor. Each text delineates a set of arbitrary 'truths,' commands a behavior, and abhors deviance as error. We can hear easily enough the slight childish tremor in Josh Billings's confession of his fault: "i waz so ashamed ov [it] that i dare not trust it to good spelling, and so did it in bad to hide . . . and i kept on in the way ov wickedness and distorshun" (*JB*, p. 126). The phunny fonocentrism of nineteenth-century American humor is struck through with nostalgia (idiom designates place, bespeaks region, the village) and condescension (the writer disfigures the speech of those who speak outside writing, exhibits them in the text), but the "distorshun" of the sign is the first thrust of humorous writing, and it takes us back, as it were, to the primal scene for all writers—to that crossing. It shows us, this phoneticized writing, that illiterate or semiliterate speech, speech that is outside the dictate of proper writing, is in error. The style is a perfect hinge that enables the humorist at once to evoke presence in his writing, signify the sense of sound, and show distance, for this iz obviously the discourse of an absolute other. So, as the writer summons a remembrance of innocence, he depicts ignorance. It makes a difference, Richard Bridgman argues in *The Colloquial Style in America*, whether the "writer's goal [in misspelling] was accuracy or buffoonery,"[4] but even Lowell, who took great pains to render dialect precisely, humorously brackets Hosea Biglow's writing by making this poetical farmer aware of the difference between speech values and literary decorum:

> You're 'n want o' sunthin light an' cute,
>   Rattlin' an' shrewd an' kin' o' jingleish,
> An' wish, pervidin' it 'ould suit,
>   I'd take an' citify my English.
> I *ken* write long-tailed, ef I please,—
>   But when I'm jokin', no, I thankee;
> Then, 'fore I know it, my idees
>   Run helter-skelter into Yankee. (*BP*, p. 480)

To this extent, it does not matter who is speaking in the humorous text, whether a pert rogue or an earnest yeoman, because the writer (as humorist) always begins with the concept of the first lesson: writing alienates speech. If we turn the concept up, from low to big, there is Lévi-Strauss, Wordsworth, Rousseau, Plato—and Lowell, writing as a professor, not a humorist: "It is only from its roots in the living generations of men that a language can be reinforced with fresh vigor for its needs; what may be called a literate dialect grows ever more and more pedantic and foreign, till it becomes at last as unfitting a vehicle for living thought as monkish Latin" (*BP*, p. 205). This we know, that 'good' writing keeps in close touch with the changing nature and direction of the spoken language. Lowell merely rephrases what Wordsworth expressed in the preface to the *Lyrical Ballads* when he attacked the diction of neoclassical discourse, that the simple language of the unlettered who live close to Nature is true and direct in its utterance. That is, Lowell uses a canonical trope to deride the usage of canonical tropes. Yet to learn to write, to letter, as a child, is to learn another system of signs, another discourse. To speak is not enough. We learn, in effect, that what we know (how to speak) must be supplemented, and that writing, the first formal supplement, first move from "natur," is a kind of power, a division of what is correct and what is incorrect, a division in Discourse of the world itself. As Lévi-Straus observes in *Tristes Tropiques* in that much-cited chapter "A Writing Lesson":

> Writing is a strange thing. It would seem as if its appearance could not have failed to wreak profound changes in the living conditions of our race, and that these transformations must have been above all intellectual in character. Once men know how to write, they are enormously more able to keep in being a large body of knowledge. Writing . . . might be regarded as a form of artificial memory, whose development should be accompanied by a deeper knowledge of the past and, therefore, by a greater ability to organize the present and future. Of all the criteria by which people habitually distinguish civilization from barbarism, this should be the one most worth retaining: that certain peoples write and others do not.[5]

This indeed is A Lesson, but there are turns to it, some of which are humorous. In the field the anthropologist distributes pencils and paper to the Nambikwara, a band of Brazilian Indians. They amuse themselves by drawing "wavy horizontal lines" on the paper, mimicking the 'work' of their observer. But the leader of the band is an ingenious 'student' who understands intuitively that writing is power, an appropriation, a currency:

> Each time he drew a line he would examine it with great care, as if its meaning must suddenly leap to the eye; and every time a look of disappointment came over his face. But he would never give up trying, and there was an unspoken agreement between us that his scribblings had a meaning that I did my best to decipher; his own verbal

commentary was so prompt in coming that I had no need to ask him to explain what he had written.

And now, no sooner was everyone assembled than he drew forth from a basket a piece of paper covered with scribbled lines and pretended to read from it. With a show of hesitation he looked up and down his "list" for the objects to be given in exchange for his people's presents. So-and-so was to receive a machete in return for his bow and arrows, and another a string of beads in return for his necklaces—and so on for two solid hours. What was he hoping for? To deceive himself, perhaps: but, even more, to amaze his companions and persuade them that *his* intermediacy was responsible for the exchanges. He had allied himself with the white man, as equal with equal, and could now share in his secrets. We were in a hurry to get away, since there would obviously be a moment of real danger at which all the marvels I had brought would have been handed over. . . . So I did not go further into the matter and we set off on the return journey, still guided by the Indians (*TT*, pp. 288-289).

So writing teaches something more than just the inscription of signs, especially to those who remain outside the knowledge of writing. What appears in this episode is not just the poignant imitation of the Nambikwaran chieftain, his desire to parade as one of the knowers, a white man, a writer, but also a "danger," the immediate threat of an extortion, a revenge. An axiom from the heart of the humorous tradition in American literature comes to mind, the motto of Johnson Jones Hooper's popular Jacksonian rascal, Simon Suggs: "Mother-wit kin beat book-larnin, at *any* game!"[6] Even, it would seem, the game of writing. In *Tristes Tropiques* the anthropologist, who has been 'stealing' the knowledge of the Nambikwara, recording it, writing it down, suddenly perceives that his 'writing' has been stolen, turned against him, and this reversal brings the writing lesson to a hurried close. The politics of this confrontation recurs in American humor, variously stated, always juxtaposing mother-wit (Speech) and book-larnin (Writing). In the text a native speaker, either illiterate or semiliterate, is graphically exposed, his speech misspelled, alienated, and it is typically to a literate narrator that he speaks, deceptively. Often these stylized routines are indeed no more than comic "misunderstandings and disputes over diction," as Bridgman describes them, a "staple of comic writing so long as dialects existed in the United States" (*CSA*, pp. 27-28), and yet the routine has a dramatic resonance that the humorist, if he chose, could forcefully exploit. The most important tall tale in the Jacksonian period, Thomas Bangs Thorpe's "The Big Bear of Arkansas" (1841), at once ironically subverts the myth of the Great White Hunter, the Bear Slayer, and the mythologist-narrator who credulously transcribes the hunter's ultimately bewildered account of his humiliation and defeat by this "*unhuntable bear.*" The only writing we can trust in this text is the writ of the Creation Bear, the inscription of his presence, his signature:

> "On a fine fall day, long time ago, I was trailing about for bear, and what should I see but fresh marks on the sassafras trees, about eight inches above any in the forests that I knew of. Says I, 'Them marks is a hoax, or it indicates the d--t bear that was ever grown.' In fact, stranger, I couldn't believe it was real, and I went on. Again I saw the same marks, at the same height, and *I knew the thing lived.* That conviction came home to my soul like an earthquake."[7]

Most tall tales turn back on the "stranger" who records them. He is there to 'sketch' a 'type,' to picture the bizarre, to record the curious speech and customs of the backwoodsman, to anthropologize; and the teller, the subject, 'satisfies' him. In *America's Humor* Walter Blair and Hamlin Hill trace these figures back to stock characters in Attic comedy; the *eiron* (ironist) and the *alazon* (blusterer), but to characterize the routine in such fashion, to regard Davy Crockett as an *alazon* or a *miles gloriosus*, tells us nothing about the nature of the particular exchanges in American humor.[8] In fact, the structure of the humorous sketch is triadic, for it is the humorist who comprises the scene, who 'speaks' in humor, who writes himself into the sketch, and in this exemplary sketch the Creation Bear is Thorpe's designation. It is from the high statement of those crude marks scrawled upon the sassafras trees that we are to read the sketch. Only the Bear has a sense of humor in Thorpe's tale. He 'forgives' the Bear Slayer. Desperately hunted, always elusive, omnipotent, he comes in finally to be killed (so the sketch may end), catches the hunter with his breeches down (he is taking a post-breakfast shit in the woods), and offers his bear breast to the hunter's dishonored shot, the limpest bang in nineteenth-century American literature. No hooded white phantom looms before us, nor does the marbled side of the White Whale roll away and down back into the Unseen. Here the Enigma simply presents itself: it is Anticlimax, a large black Nothing, and dogged Jim Doggett's poignant brag is the Nietzschean lie that covers it, almost. "I made a *bedspread of his skin*" (*BB*, p. 279), he uneasily tells us.

So Thorpe gives the tall tale its ultimate turn: a fooled writer records a native storyteller who is himself fooled; book-larnin' and mother-wit, the two sides of the typical exchange, collapse before an intelligence neither discourse can represent—the humorous knowledge of nonsense. That knowledge simply appears, like the bear, at the tale's end. It tells us that the tale in the sketch "The Big Bear of Arkansas" doesn't make sense. The tall tale is a lie that tells the truth about lying. To live in the "Creation State," Arkansas, in the state of "natur," not Nature, is almost unbearable, a reality of suffering that must be vanquished, and tall talk is the lie that humorously transforms that reality: "But mosquitoes is natur, and I never find fault with her. If they ar large, Arkansaw is large, her varmints ar large, her trees ar large, her rivers ar large, and a small mosquito would be of no more use in Arkansaw than preaching in a canebrake" (*BB*, p. 271). Those imposing marks on the sassafras trees, however, are "real," higher than the "hoax" of tall talk can reach, and they signify that unspeakable element of the Original Wilderness, the Creation State, which simply reduces the measure of signification, the measure of myth, to human babble. Each turn of the tale juxtaposes different systems of value and feeling in Jacksonian society: literate/illiterate, urban/rural, East/West, North/South, Farming/Hunting, but Thorpe's intent is to reduce these distinctions, these differences, to a primary alienation wherein writer and speaker glance covertly at one another, complicit, confused.

Few humorists in the Jacksonian period reach this point, or precipice, in their writing, because their sense of humor is readily constrained by the economy of the style. Too often the offense, the wrong, the pain, that is displaced in their writing is subsumed by the single error of riting rongly, and what is funny is simply the vulnerable simplicity of not-knowing: a travail of innocence, an exhibition of ignorance, the spectacle of raw speech captured by writing. Such humor characterizes types, sketches scenes, addresses topics, works from a distance, and does not sufficiently involve the reader in its exchanges. Because the humorist does not actively enter the play, what is set at naught, not taken seriously, is not in the first case that serious, and here we can observe, easily enough, the amiable appeal and cozy sentimentality of B. P. Shillaber's *Life and Sayings of Mrs. Partington* (1854) and William Tappan Thompson's *Major Jones's Courtship* (1843). Charm prevails in this particular mode of humorous writing, and both characters, dame and squire, are glazed in it. It is their eccentricity, a well-meaning and inoffensive eccentricity, that is the source of the humorous pleasure. Exemplary figures in Jacksonian humor, Mrs. Partington and Major Jones recall familiar figures in British humor, the odd characters drawn by Addison and Sterne, and then by Thackeray and Dickens. Shillaber in particular often caught the beguiling tone of this humor and wrote indeed with whimsical charm. About to drown a litter of unwanted kittens in a tub of water, Mrs. Partington has a flash of remorse: "Stop, Isaac, a minute . . . and I'll take the chill off the water; it would be cruel to put 'em into it stone-cold."[9] A drawing of Mrs. Partington, capped, shawled, and bespectacled, used as the frontispiece for the *Life and Sayings*, reappears as an illustration in *The Adventures of Tom Sawyer* (1876); Shillaber's garrulous old dame is now Aunt Polly, and into Aunt Polly she effectively vanishes. Humor that relishes the odd by domesticating it never escapes the moral universe of the parlor, and Mark Twain will show in *Huckleberry Finn* precisely how small that universe is. At the close of "The Big Bear of Arkansas," when narrator looks at narrator, perplexed, there is an anxiety that prefigures the anxieties provoked by Herman Melville's interrogation of humor in *The Confidence-Man* (1857), and there is anxiety in *Huckleberry Finn*. What this tells us perhaps is that the humorist who takes humorous writing seriously has somehow discerned the immensity of the wrong to be forgiven, the force of the pain to be discharged, and understood, as a writer, the hazard. How wrong is the humorist? That is always the question.

3

Before Huck writes, and goes wrong, how wrong is Lowell, how wrong is Harris? Apart from the overt politics of Lowell's humor, his sustained and clear-sighted attack on the South, his exposure of its various machinations to defend and extend the institution of slavery, there is another political struggle in the *Biglow Papers*, one that takes us back to the site of the Writing Lesson, and which reveals Lowell in the difficult act of deciding what constitutes humorous writing. Both Parson Wilbur and Hosea Biglow are opposed to the Mexican War and to slavery, they share the same moral conscience, and yet they are humorously juxtaposed. Lowell realizes that in humor the book must be thrown, so books are thrown at the start of the *Papers*, and Biglow is hit with the heaviest, the "acknowledged examples of English composition in verse" (*BP*, p. 17). The learned parson looks down on the rough writing of his rural parishioner, corrects the spelling, underscores Biglow's crude diction, and decides to give him a lesson in writing—even though, as we learn later, Biglow "*ken* write long-tailed, ef I please" (*BP*, p. 480). There is a right way to write, and a wrong way to write. Examples are given. "With this in view," Wilbur relates, "I accordingly lent him some volumes of Pope and Goldsmith, to the assiduous study of which he promised to devote his evenings" (*BP*, p. 17). The Writing Lesson constitutes one of the primary routines in humorous writing, and in it, latent, is a complicated transference of values. In *Huckleberry Finn*, as we have already observed, this routine is rendered with great sophistication. Huck will pick up the book thrown at him by the Widow Douglas (Who is Moses?) and Miss Watson, and throw it at Jim. Who is Sollermun? As Huck discovers, it is hard for a white boy to hit a black man with a Bible. Jim angrily tells him who Sollermun is—the capricious master of slaves. Much later, in *Portnoy's Complaint* (1969), Alex Portnoy will hurl at Mary Jane Reed the "Modern Library Dos Passos, a book with a hard cover,"[10] and then pelt her with *The Souls of Black Folk, The Grapes of Wrath, An American Tragedy, Poor White*, and *Notes of a Native Son*. Books and bricks fly in American humor. Yet Lowell never quite achieves the complication of a significant tension in his account of this exchange, a failure that sets forth at once his inability to wrong formal writing, to shift allegiances, and his underlying confusion about the nature and meaning of common speech. There is no troubling of the moral theme in the *Papers* (the political argument is sharply focused) and no actual conflict between Wilbur and Biglow, though an ostensible conflict is staged between pedantry and simplicity. Yet Lowell's piece-by-piece construction of the project (which spans several decades) tells us a great deal, if only by implication, about the problem of humorous writing.

Of all the nineteenth-century humorists, Lowell is the most writerly, an eminent poet, essayist, and, so far as that wit goes, an excellent professorial wit, the author of *A Fable for Critics* (1847), a still-bright piece of Jacksonian literary satire. To write in dialect, adopt the humorous style, was to write in a low style, and though the low style might be employed to undercut certain rhetorical excesses in the high style, it remained for Lowell invincibly a low style, and its proper place was the newspaper column. It is indeed the very humility of humorous writing that Lowell first sought to exploit when he published Biglow's letters, and the correspondence of his other yokel, Birdofredum Sawin, in the Boston *Courier*. He meant to relocate the argument against the Mexican War, to get away from the strident polemical tone of the Abolitionist press, from the logic-chopping and special pleading of the ongoing political debate, and let simple conscience speak. The argument is still there, Biglow's letter is at once an analysis and an indictment of "them nigger-drivin' States," but the device of the humorous style, its approximation of humble speech, its recurrent misspelling, effectively removes the edge of partisan righteousness from what Biglow sez. Unlike satire, which must look down on its subject, humor broadly issues from the 'heart,' and therefore has its place in the lower style—which is, as yet, an excursive style for Lowell, an extracurricular project. The humor of Biglow's writing is firmly fixed to a topic, it exists to serve a message, and yet from the start Lowell gives the style such figure and pace that the writing is simply lean and trenchant, as writing.

> Ez for war, I call it murder,—
> There you hev it plain an' flat;
> I don't want to go no furder
> Than my Testyment for that. (*BP*, p. 65)

Lowell had found a way to break through the thick obscure of Jacksonian rhetoric that hid the actual terms of the Mexican War. Biglow's letter is not *about* the distant war—it experiences that war in a New England village, responds to the experience, and relates the feeling. At the same time, even as Lowell fashioned his argument in the style, rote it rongly, he realized the colloquial force of the style, felt in his writing of it an exhilarating release from the demands of literary decorum. In his writing book, between two sections of drafted 'Biglow' verse, he begins briefly an unfinished poem: "Away, unfruitful love of books / For whose vain idiom we reject / The soul's original dialect. . . ."[11] When he had the disillusioned Sawin write home from the campaign in Mexico, Lowell introduced another perspective, and not just on the war, but on the "soul's original dialect." The political text is still primary, so obvious the writing has almost no personality, but again there is a jump to the line, a raucous energy just barely contained by the funny capping of the couplets. Sawin, we are told, writes his letters in prose. Biglow 'prepares' them for publication by versifying them. There is ultimately much rewriting that goes on in the *Papers*: Wilbur rewrites Biglow's letters, Biglow rewrites Sawin's letters, and, since Biglow can write competent English, he rewrites himself, choosing to place his thought in dialect. In Biglow's usage, the idiom is sweet; in Sawin's usage, it is rank. The constant revision of texts in the *Papers* is done for humorous contrast, but it also suggests Lowell's ambivalence about the discourse that lies on the far side of literate discourse, past *Nature* in "natur," for the flip side of its purest innocence is the rawest ignorance. In 1846, just beginning to write in dialect, Lowell merely appropriates the difference and applies it to the political question.

Birdofredum Sawin regrets, and ruefully describes the dumb thesis that enabled him thoughtlessly to enlist: "Thet Mexicans wor n't human beans."

Afore I come away from hum I hed a strong persuasion
Thet Mexicans wor n't human beans—an ourang outang nation,
A sort o' folks a chap could kill an' never dream on't arter,
No more'n a feller'd dream o' pigs thet he hed hed to slarter;
I'd an idee thet they were built arter the darkie fashion all,
An' kickin' colored folks about, you know, 's a kind o' national;
But wen I jined I wor n't so wise ez thet air queen o' Sheby,
Fer, come to look at 'em, they ain't much diff'rent from wut we be,
An' here we air ascrougin' 'em out o' thir own dominions,
Ashelterin' 'em, ez Caleb sez, under our eagle's pinions,
Wich means to take a feller up jest by the slack o' 's trowsis
An' walk him Spanish clean right out o' all his homes an' houses;
Wal, it does seem a curus way, but then hooraw fer Jackson!
(*BP,* pp. 79-80).

Sawin has come to realize that he, too, is a victim of the racist "persuasion." The order of his recognition is perhaps too programmatic, this *miles gloriosus* is a straw man, but then the action, so to speak, is in his language, not in his character. "A sort o' folks a chap could kill," he writes equably, and through the iteration of the homespun words, folks, feller, he discloses the curiosity, the strangeness, of the war. What *are* these farm boys doing in Mexico? How did they get there? "This 'ere's about the meanest place a skunk could wal diskiver" (*BP*, p. 77), Sawin observes, and, but for a space of time, he might be looking at the Mekong, with helicopters thumping overhead.

In either voice, Biglow's or Sawin's, the first shrewd, the second credulous, Lowell polemically renders the Speech of the Common Man—which is almost a style within the humorous style. Seba Smith had created such an epistolary figure in Major Jack Downing at the beginning of the Jacksonian period, David Ross Locke would follow Lowell with his vituperative Copperhead, Petroleum V. Nasby, and at the end of the century Finley Peter Dunne would give to Mr. Dooley his cynical interpretation of the Spanish-American War. In this small and enduring tradition, Lowell's writing is exemplary, rivalled only by Dunne's, and in the modern period by Langston Hughes's presentation of Jesse B. Semple's opinions in the *Chicago Defender*. Lowell and Hughes are in fact the definitive political humorists who write in dialect, the most sophisticated in their understanding of the subject and form. Almost a hundred years separate the *Biglow Papers* from *Simple Speaks His Mind* (1950), Lowell is emphatically white, Hughes beautifully black, and yet both texts are remarkably similar in stylistic approach and political angle. Big-low, be simple. The question before Lowell in 1846-47 was whether he could widen the low range of the simple style, and therein lies the tale, the attempted transformation of Biglow's dialect letters (Lowell's venture into popular journalism) into a book, the *Papers* (Lowell's literary enterprise).

The wonder of it is that Lowell should assemble all the constituting elements of high humor, possess in the style the essential *agon*, the rong, have in hand the trio of figures (Sawin-Biglow-Wilbur) whose interplay creates the humorous transaction and the anxiety of humor, and still fail so conspicuously to bring it all together. In part this is because Lowell himself never took the project that seriously— was even, to a certain extent, embarrassed by the popularity of the Biglow letters. His attempt to complicate them, to elevate the stature of the project, one suspects, was as much a defensive measure as it was an imaginative elaboration. An ambitious poet, a learned critic, Lowell suddenly found himself a successful humorist. The public preferred his junk, not his jewels. In both editions of the *Papers* Lowell begins the text with these two epigraphs:

> The ploughman's whistle, or the trivial flute,
> Finds more respect than great Apollo's lute.
> *Quarles's Emblems*, B.II.E.8.
> Margaritas, munde porcine, calcasti: en, siliquas accipe.
> *Jac. Car. Fil. ad Pub. Leg.* I

It is the thinking of Reverend Wilbur, that swine do not detect the value of pearls, and yet the joke betrays an attitude finally explicit in Lowell's introduction to the *Papers*, that to speak to King Demos, as Lowell puts it, the writer must put on cap and bells.

Even so, the problem of the *Papers* for the most part lies in Lowell's conception of the "soul's original dialect," the primary language of common speech. He could not resolve the paradox that the value of this first and immediate speech was at once big *and* low, and his confusion would lead him finally into a thicket of suspiciously ambiguous metaphors, to an aspect of original speech he would express without realizing. "No language after it has faded into *diction*, none that cannot suck up the feeding juices secreted for it in the rich mother-earth of common folk," Lowell writes in his treatise on the *Papers*, "can bring forth a sound and lusty book" (*BP*, pp. 205-206). And again: "Language is the soil of thought, and our own especially is a rich leaf-mould, the slow deposit of ages, the shed foliage of feeling, fancy, and imagination, which has suffered an earth-change, that the vocal forest . . . may clothe itself anew with living green" (*BP*, p. 206). The desire to exalt the idiom, and by extension the whole project of the *Papers*, is strongly expressed in the essay. Spoken language is alive, polymorphous, an organic process, an organic circuit—oral, anal—whereas "There is death in the dictionary" (*BP*, p. 206), in the linearity of writing. Yet Lowell's approach to the idiom is to regard it strictly as a *diction*, a trove of expressions, figures—items that require a glossary where presumably they suffer a death. The contradiction is everywhere. Spoken language, in whatever guise: "spoken dialect," "popular idiom," "colloquial speech," is the Good, and yet to catch after it, writers must write down, alter *their* diction, prefer heart to head, instinct to reflection, risk bad or vulgar writing, bring Good Speech into the script that must fault it.

So earthy language is the soil of thought. Lowell rephrases Wordsworth. Primary language articulates primary desire, is closer to reality. Writing follows after, fixes, is at once a mediation, an interruption, and a repression of that immediate utterance. "True vigor and heartiness of phrase," Lowell writes, "do not pass from page to page, but from man to man, where the brain is kindled and the lips suppled by downright living interests and by passion in its very throe" (*BP*, p. 206). Into this passage which treats suppled lips and passion in its very throe, which celebrates the oral tradition, Lowell slips a single lame colloquial term, "downright." He is on the right phonocentrical track, it would seem, but he doesn't go anywhere. The treatise begins by justifying the license of humorous writing, expands, as we have seen, into fulsome praise of the vitality of the idiom, sanctifies the colloquial style, and then breaks into a rambling dissertation on the curiosities to be found in Bartlett's *Glossary of Words and Phrases Usually Regarded as Peculiar to the United States*. Without ever indicating a change of topics, Lowell turns the issue of humorous writing into the question of a colloquial style. They are different issues with different questions. As a theoretician of colloquial writing, Lowell is not impressive. At no point does he take up the hazard and difficulty of transforming raw speech into cooked composition, or discuss the problem of devising an appropriate form. And not everything spoken in the first language, told in the oral tradition, which is green and growing, can be written.

Undoubtedly Lowell could have profited from a close reading of *Leaves of Grass*, more than from his perusal of Bartlett. On the same track in his approach to Language (as the soil of thought), Walt Whitman not only goes around the bend in 1855, he goes off the cliff—that is, he originates a theory of discourse, and its first assumption is the absolute identity of speaker and writer. Lowell remains within the staid conventions of a Romantically sublimated version of phonocentrism. Preferred Speech is an emanation of Presence, but the quality of that Presence (and the motive for the preference) remains happily abstract. Therefore the humorous triumvirate of Sawin-Biglow-Wilbur is without the drama of a significant exchange. Each figure represents a level of writing, if not a mode, and the three simply co-exist as marks on a stylistic rule. Sawin is ignorant, the closest to illiterate speech; Wilbur too learned, the farthest from ordinary speech; while Biglow constitutes a rough middle mode. To express himself strongly, Biglow chooses to allow speech values to dominate his written discourse—within the formal structure of verse. That is, as he admits the value of speech, he admits the value of literary form. No one mode does violence to the other since each is translatable. Sawin submits his crude prose for Biglow's versification, Biglow submits his verse to Wilbur for editing and emendation, and the only effective question is substitution. Sawin writes that he has "seen a *scarabaeus pilularius* big ez a year old elephant," and Biglow footnotes "it wuz 'tumblebug' as he Writ it, but the parson put the Latten instid. i sed tother maid better meeter, but he said tha was eddykated peepl to Boston and tha would n't stan' it no how" (*BP*, p. 78). The humorous style merely places a "noo soot of close" on the word, and the rong is nearly circumscribed.

Where, then, is the real wrong that makes the situation for humor? It is there, but thoroughly baffled. Everything Biglow writes in dialect can be respelled without significant loss of meaning. The sense of the idiom, of spoken language, taken into writing does not reorient or even disturb the formal and structural priorities of conventional writing. It offers at best different words, different expressions. Using the idiom, a writer can picture phonetically a speaking voice. Yet in all this experimentation Lowell does not for a moment rethink the hierarchy of styles with its classification of appropriate tone and subject. He does not think big in the low style. Biglow's writing in dialect is a kind of writing that Lowell intermittently explores, assuming a character distant from the authorial self of his own writing, and his condescension is constant.

> When I began to carry out my conception and to write in my assumed character, I found myself in a strait between two perils. On the one hand, I was in danger of being carried beyond the limit of my own opinions, or at least of that temper with which every man should speak his mind in print, and on the other I feared the risk of seeming to vulgarize a deep and sacred conviction. I needed on occasion to rise above the level of mere *patois*, and for this purpose conceived the Reverend Mr. Wilbur, who should express the more cautious element of the New England character and its pedantry, as Mr. Biglow should serve for

its homely common-sense vivified and heated by conscience. (*BP*, p. 200)

A small problem in an obscure text. The writer in this humorist
flinches, needs to "rise above" the "perils" of vulgarity, and so at
length the parodied editorial *persona* dominates, becomes the determining narrative voice, the explainer who at once circumscribes the
rong riting and carries the charge of the writer's skill as a writer.
Mark Twain would begin here in *Tom Sawyer* as a genial, avuncular
narrator beseeching tolerance for the ecstasies of Tom's egotistical
pranks. Like Lowell's condescending parson, the narrator of *Tom
Sawyer* is omnipresent, directing our gaze, setting the scene, orches-
trating our response, the very image of that Freudian super-ego who
speaks such "kindly words" to the ego. And there is, of course,
another humorous text in American literature in which an idiomatic
rural versifier is overtaken by a zealous editor whose commentary
overtakes the verse—*Pale Fire*; Nabokov, however, has an understanding of the editorial presence that is simply beyond Lowell.
Wilbur *is* another self, an accursed self (a publishing consciousness,
a pompous style, located somewhere between Cotton Mather's and
Lowell's), and he is there to be confronted, either crazily embraced
in all his superliterate monstrosity (as Kinbote is in *Pale Fire*) or
denied. If, as a humorist, Lowell were to rise above the parson,
where, as a writer, would he be?

The Reverend Homer Wilbur, A. M., Pastor (so the title-page
reads) of the First Church in Jaalam and (Prospective) Member of
Many Literary, Learned, and Scientific Societies, is in charge of
Biglow's verses. To come upon the humor of Biglow's first verse
letter, which rhymes "nater" with "tater," we must first work
through the joke of Wilbur's usurpation of the text. Only after
Wilbur's Note to the Title-Page, his *curriculum vitae*, a long anecdotal
introduction, an example of Wilbur's own pastoral verse, an ex-
tracted essay on Yankee dialect, a dissertation on Biglow's lineage,
some press notices, a *proemium* and *operis specimen* in Latin, does
Biglow's plain voice speak in the *Papers*. Wilbur is the pedagogical
book-hurler, the authoritarian brick-thrower, but the missile of his
verbum somehow never strikes Biglow hard enough to make a rong.
He is, after all, a recognizable New England type, the self-important
pedantic parson, and as such Lowell treats him fondly. Biglow

respects his learned pastor, calmly accepts his tutoring, but knows when and how to go his own way. That the minister exploits him in the collected *Papers*, surrounds Biglow's modest verse with massive commentary, writes long interpolative self-advertisements, does not concern the simple farmer. But Wilbur is worse than this genial caricature makes him out to be. He is for Lowell something of a tar baby. His prose style, Wilburese, is an index of the worst features of Lowell's own writing. It is a fussy, self-preening academic style in love with allusion and the Latinate, and Lowell wrings it wryly, so wry, so arch at times, that he falls into the very mode he is parodying. "There is scarce any style," the verbose minister observes, "so compressed that superfluous words may not be detected in it. A severe critic might curtail that famous brevity of Caesar's by two thirds, drawing his pen through the supererogatory *veni* and *vidi*" (*BP*, p. 151). By the slightest of turns, parson becomes professor, and Lowell intrudes, shows his face, as if to signal his sustaining presence.

Here, then, is Lowell's problem as a humorist: to unstick himself from the propriety of Wilbur's sentence. Since both right and rong writers oppose the Mexican War, oppose slavery, oppose the evasive course of Northern politics, only their styles, their modes of expression, can be opposed in the *Papers*. To move from the narrow confines of his political subject, Lowell had to confront these styles as conflicted values in the psychology of his own writing. As a scribbling parson, Wilbur is an innocuous character, a perfect foil, but he is also the embodiment of the "Universal Schoolmaster" Lowell stridently attacks in his treatise, a censorious self *in* the writer who repressively screws writing tight to the principle of rectitude, *le mot juste*. Lowell, who was himself a schoolmaster, a professor at Harvard, proposes to satirize this voice, this self, the right writer, by showing how straight and true the rong riter can be, but the juxtaposition, the upset of values, never occurs. What speaks through Wilbur is Lowell's own uneasiness about writing in dialect, this rigorously unserious style, and to that extent, obviously, the rong of Biglow's writing (a small rong in any case) is not forgiven. At best, an exception is made. Wilbur is Lowell's inhibition in writing Biglow, and though the inhibition is mocked, Lowell adheres to it.

So it is that the introduction to the 1866 *Papers* is written in Wilburese. True humor, Lowell declares, "is never divorced from moral conviction" (*BP*, p. 201). And there is indeed no loose levity in Lowell's humorous writing. Here, then, is one extreme in the style before Mark Twain writes it as Huck's speech, and it discloses a particular anxiety. What value is there in writing that must not be serious as writing, which must be written in a low, plain, earthy style—soiled? In Lowell's humor, the writer enters the text as an editor, as self-parodist, and yet all the same the writer certifies the comprehensive intelligence of the humorist. If we turn now to the other extreme, go from *Papers* to *Yarns*, the question of the style dramatically re-presents itself. Speech is so served in Harris's writing that his text is almost unreadable. In the *Papers* idiom is a raw material to be constantly mined (and converted) by an alert literature, but in the *Yarns* idiom shows its recalcitrance, its exclusivity. What we immediately encounter in Harris's humorous writing is the issue of repression. How wrong is Harris as a humorist? Too wrong for Edmund Wilson. The *Yarns*, he tells us in *Patriotic Gore*, constitute "by far the most repellent book of any real literary merit in American literature."[12] Nothing funny here, Wilson insists, just Southern horror.

4

An idiom, after all, defines itself *against* the standard language, is turned inward to bespeak a local world, a specific community, and when written down, when published at large, this difference is typically bracketed. Idiom is always the known, and never the knower. Literary or scientific discourse 'captures' it. In the *Yarns* Harris strives to render the sense of Sut's speech accurately, to capture its fibrous crudity, its rough stuff, but this readiness to reproduce textually a dialect, Harris saw from the start, also requires a tolerance for the knotty topics of that speech: sex and violence. "George," the writer who introduces Sut's tales, does not judge them. What this means to Sut, who is always singling "George" out to explain himself, is that Sut is given to feel a tacit complicity, a secret understanding that subverts the usual politics of such exchanges. "George" is not here to throw the book at Sut. Harris's slight placement of "George" in the text is therefore as deliberate as Lowell's preemptive positioning of the editorial Wilbur. Because "George" is only peripherally in the text, the scan of Sut's humor is broad, almost the totality of the text, and yet "George" is not merely a neutral recorder. Sut's stories are rhetorically turned toward

"George," toward the tolerance of his sophisticated comprehension, toward the destiny of a fair transcription. Harris works *on* the page, *in* print, with this phenomenon. Rong riting is pictorial. It visibly disrupts the serial flow of the conventionally lettered line. Before a page of Harris's text the scanning eye falters: here is a fractured maze of misspelling in which, periodically, we discern short stretches of "George's" writing, glimpse the familiar. Of all the humorists in the nineteenth century, Harris is the most insistent, the least compromising, in portraying the otherness of the illiterate.

The sketch "Mrs. Yardley's Quilting" provides a small disquisition on the difference of that difrunce. Harris begins predictably by juxtaposing native speaker and observing writer, with the show of the incongruity, and then, in Sut's voice, he briefly considers the elements of his art.

> "Thar's one durn'd nasty muddy job, an' I is jis glad enuf tu take a ho'n ur two, on the straingth ove hit."
> "What have you been doing, Sut?"
> "Helpin to salt ole Missis Yardley down."
> "What do you mean by that?"
> "Fixin her fur rotten cumfurtably, kiverin her up wif sile, tu keep the buzzards frum cheatin the wurms."
> "Oh, you have been helping to bury a woman."
> "That's hit, by golly! Now why the devil can't I 'splain myself like yu? I ladles out my words at random, like a calf kickin at yaller-jackids; yu jis rolls em out tu the pint, like a feller a-layin bricks—every one fits. How is it that bricks fits so close enyhow? Rocks won't ni du hit."
> "Becaze they'se all ove a size," ventured a man with a wen over his eye.
> "The devil yu say, hon'ey'head! Haint reapin-mersheens ove a size? I'd like tu see two ove em fit clost. Yu wait ontil yu sprouts tuther ho'n, afore yu venters tu 'splain mix'd questions." (*SL*, p. 114)

"George," the writer as bricklayer, does not respond to the question of fit. Undoubtedly he knows the distinction between homology and analogy and sees the flaw in Sut's figure, but what he thinks is not given. The poor-sighted bystander who opines that bricks fit "Becaze they'se all ove a size" speaks the simple truth. It is also true that in "George's" educated discourse words are shaped to fit the requirement of forms, and that in writing they are set in types from left to right, evenly assembled paragraph by paragraph, page by page. But the order such discourse makes of the world, of the nature of things, is not necessarily the "natur" of things. Rocks in the field, spoken words "at randum," and "reapin-mersheens" of the same make, do not "fit clost." A text is a brick-by-brick wall of words, an obstruction, and nearly every "skeer" that Sut relates, each prank, each practical joke, has in it an explosion of things, the crashing of some decorum, whether the simple hypocrisy of the constable and the preacher, bearers of the Writ, or simply a structure.

The best of the 'yarns' deal with the "natur" of sexual desire: "Blown Up With Soda," "Sicily Burns's Wedding," "Parson John Bullen's Lizards," "Mrs. Yardley's Quilting," "Rare Ripe Garden Seed." Sut's narration of these affairs is raw, offensively rednecked. What *do* men talk about when they are relieved of the proprieties of the parlor? What *is* the richest vein in the oral tradition? These are essentially masculine stories and they are principally about wanting to blank women or blanking women, or being blanked by them. There is really no other way to put it. "A tetch ove the bridil," Sut asserts, "an' they knows yu wants em tu turn, an' they dus hit es willin es ef the idear wer thar own. I be dod rabbited ef a man can't 'propriate happiness by the skinful ef he is in contack wif sumbody's widder, an' is smart" (*SL*, p. 118). So the talk goes. Yet there is more to these sketches than just boast and brag. Fear, for example, and disgust. Each of Sut's tales is about a "skeer." Life in this place, in rough, rural Tennessee, is lived near the frontier, close to the amoral dark of the Hobbesian wild where life is short, nasty, brutish—and skeer'd. Sexual energy, as Sut sees it, is simply the clarification of what is animal in the human—and in the *paysage* he depicts the fever of rut is constantly simmering near the brawling point. That, too, is scary. Harris knows this place in a double sense: what it is and how it scares us.

In *Patriotic Gore* Wilson explains that Sut means South, the *mean* South, and he belabors academic critics who blithely treat the sadistic ferocity of Sut's "skeers" as folklore. "As for the 'fun' of Sut Lovingood," he observes, "it is true that Harris explained his aim as merely to revive for the reader 'sich a laugh as is remembered wif his keerless boyhood,' and that he liked to express his nostalgia for the dances and the quiltings of his youth; but even in one of Harris's pre-Lovingood sketches that deal with one of these, the fun seems mainly to consist of everybody's getting beaten to a pulp, and in the Lovingood stories themselves, the fun entirely consists of Sut's spoiling everybody else's fun" (*PG*, pp. 513-514). Wilson is precisely the reader Harris requires. It is before the fascination of such moral disgust that Sut 'performs' his "skeers." That is, Wilson reads the Sut who is in the tale and forgets that Sut is the teller of the tale. The "skeer" is often sadistic, always perverse, and typically it is the violent interruption of a social function: camp meeting, wedding, wake, quilting party, but there *is* functional meaning to Sut's perversity. Just as we look in at what the sketch reveals, at the picture of these backward folk, look in with scholarly prurience, just as we observe the 'primitive' emerge, as the dance and the fornication are about to begin, Sut's prank rips the scene apart and scatters the pieces.

So Sut is wrong, the spoiler of fun, a wronger of the tale, as wrong as the South itself, the damned and foolish South, as wrong as Harris could make him, and ugly, too. In his back-country Tennessee, in the tale he tells, Sut looks indeed very much like the mythological figure of the trickster, that strange intermediate being who, in Winnebago legend, is apt to punish himself for gluttony by searing his anus, who behaves crazily on the threshold between the bestial and the human as a form or state of consciousness that has not as yet extended its full control over the behavior of the body. "The overwhelming majority of all so-called trickster myths in North America," Paul Radin writes in his definitive study of the myth, "give an account of the creation of the earth, or at least the transforming of the world, and have a hero who is always wandering, who is always hungry, who is not guided by normal conceptions of good and evil, who is either playing tricks on people or having them played on him and who is highly sexed."[13] Among the Siouan tribes in the late nineteenth century, where animism makes its last ghostly stand, the trickster had his cult. Indians took on as a religious vocation a life of absurd opposition. A "Wrong-Way" walked forward backward, washed with dirt, made a happy face to show anger, an angry face to show happiness, and in general was maddening to himself and to others, and was therefore deeply respected. Tricksters exist in most cultures as perverse creatures in folklore, and there is at least one "Nat'ral Born Durn'd Fool" in every neighborhood, the teaser, the contrary, who, in other neighborhoods, easily enough, is the criminal, the psychotic.

Harris knew nothing about the value the Winnebago and Sioux placed upon the trickster, yet he relished Sut's trickery, and brought it unabashed into the text. To do this, obviously, he had to wrong himself as a writer, make the significant move that Lowell was unable to make, "enter into the *feeling of the opposite*."[14]

The phrase is Pirandello's, who holds that the comic is mere *"perception of the opposite."* Imagine, he asks us, a grotesque old lady who has dyed her hair and done her face to look like a young girl. If 'I' can get past the first glance to imagine the pity of her terror, or the poignance of her motive, "then I can no longer laugh at her as I did at first, exactly because the inner working of reflection has made me go beyond . . . the initial stage of awareness: from the beginning *perception of the opposite*, reflection has made me shift to a feeling of the *opposite*" (*OH*, p. 113). Pirandello has in mind the humor of Cervantes and Dostoyevsky, holy humor, but what if the feeling of the opposite is the feeling of an unholy opposite? The act of humor is no longer an empathetic feeling from above for an *other* who is nobly wrong or pathetically ridiculous, but is instead now a 'black' feeling, the inverted humor of black humor. We confront in such a humorist an identification with otherness, with the opposite, that is truly disquieting; we must deal with a sense of humor that seems alien, or wrong. Tolerance has gone too far, or so it would seem, too much is 'allowed.' The interlocutor, our insurer of the ground of humor, is out to lunch: the minstrel show has lost its formalizing center, and who now will bring the caper of this humor back to a proper ending? We certainly do not trust the "Uncle Bill" who narrates *Naked Lunch*: "And some of us are on Different Kicks and that's a thing out in the open the way I like to see what I eat and visa versa mutatis mutandis as the case may be. *Bill's Naked Lunch Room.* . . . Step right up. . . . Good for young and old, man and bestial."[15] The humorist who humors has become the humorable, has joined the minstrels, become a trickster. So "George," that almost blank reteller of the tale, fades into Sut, and *we* must humor Sut.

The axis of humor is turned, and not everyone finds this funny. In *The Rise and Fall of American Humor* (1968), Jesse Bier directly links the work of the Southwestern humorists, notably Harris's writing, to the "sick humor" of Lenny Bruce, a humor that Bier finds repellent. It is a "radical hysteric humor that screams instead of laughs," he writes, "and the four-letter amoralism is no less cheap than any hypocritical moralism it attacks."[16] This much is certain: Lenny Bruce knew exactly what Harris knew about the edge in dialect, the sharp edge of its "difrunce," and realized, too, that for the elect, the educated, an idiom cannot deliver the high style of serious knowledge, and therefore can never constitute a poetic language.

> But it's just his sound. That's why Lyndon Johnson is a fluke—because we've never had a president with a sound like that. Cause we know in our culture that "peeple who tawk lahk thayat"—they may be bright, articulate, wonderful people—but "people who tawk lahk thayat are shitkickuhs." As bright as any Southerner could be, if Albert Einstein 'tawked lahk thayat, theah wouldn't be no bomb:
> "Folks, ah wanna tell ya bout new-cleer fishin—"
> *"Get outta here, schmuck!"*[17]

Harris is an important reference in the study of Mark Twain's fiction (Mark Twain wrote a review of the *Yarns*), if only because Sut swings easily into Pap Finn, and Harris also figures in William Faulkner's novels where the Suttish character appears in several of the Snopeses, but his actual place in American humor is beside William Burroughs and Lenny Bruce. No multilingual V. K. Ratliff (our mellow interlocutor in *The Hamlet*) is present in the *Yarns* to comprehend Sut, to turn him as an object to study, to do his voice. Like Burroughs, like Bruce, whose feeling for the opposite is from the other side, Harris makes speech break into writing. It is the first swerve of the humorous style before Mark Twain writes *Huckleberry Finn*, a jump in the style toward the Unfunny.

The abrupt chaotic violence that is at the center of Sut's tales is at once an insistent theme in the *Yarns* and a reflection of the style. A bull is loose inside the house where a wedding party is taking place, a party to which Sut, a spurned lover, has not been invited. The bull is an angry manifestation of Sut's wounded sexual vanity—and the expression of his expression:

> I think he wer the hottes' and wus hurtin bull then livin: his temper, too, seemed tu be pow'fully flustrated. Ove *all* the durn'd times an' kerryins on yu *ever* hearn tell on wer thar an' thar abouts. He cum tail fust again the ole two

story Dutch clock, an' fotch hit, bustin hits runnin geer outen hit, the littil wheels a-trundlin over the floor, an' the bees even chasin them. Nex pass, he fotch up agin the foot ove a big dubbil injine bedstead, rarin hit on aind, an' punchin one ove the posts thru a glass winder. The nex tail fus' experdishun wer made aginst the caticorner'd cupboard, outen which he made a perfeck momox. Fus' he upsot hit, smashin in the glass doors, an' then jis' sot in an' stomp'd everything on the shelves intu giblits, a-tryin tu back furder in that direckshun, an' tu git the bees ofen his laigs.

Pickil crocks, perserves jars, vinegar jugs, seed bags, yarb bunches, paragorick bottils, aig baskits, an' delf war—all mix'd dam permiskusly, an' not worth the sortin, by a duller an' a 'alf. (*SL*, pp. 79-80)

At the quilting party all the finished quilts are hung on lines outside the house, where they make walls of patterns, forms: nine diamond, gridiron jacket, star, Irish chain. Sut sends a frightened horse rampaging through the lines, tearing the quilts, entangling them, and finally carrying them all off on its wild plunge. "Two months arterwards," Sut relates, "I tracked the route that hoss tuck in his kalamatus skeer, by quilt rags, tufts ove cotton, bunches ove har (human an' hoss), an' scraps ove a gridiron jackid stickin ontu the bushes, an' plum at the aind ove hit, whar all signs gin out, I foun a piece ove watch chain an' a hosses head" (*SL*, p. 121). In that ruckus Mrs. Yardley is trampled to death.

Each tale takes apart the tale, and Sut, the perfect fool who tells the tale, makes a poetry of that destruction, for his account of the wreckage is as intricate and detailed as a fine description of some elaborate artifact. Here is a vandal who admires his handiwork, who has a certain aesthetic distance from the ruin he creates. There has always been, after all, a fascination in American art with the destruction of things. Our history begins with the swing of an axe. Harris's stampeding bulls and careening horses produce "skeers" that anticipate the modern spectacle in film of car chases and car carnage. We like to look at the event of demolition, feel the release of all that power, see things fly. Sut's rendering of the action is acutely visual, and he delights in special effects: the large motion of the maddened bull and the small movement of small things. We watch the "ole two story Dutch clock" fall, burst, spill its workings, "the littil wheels a-trundlin over the floor, an' the bees even chasin them." Everything that crashes from the upset cupboard is carefully seen: "Pickil crocks, perserves jars, vinegar jugs, seed bags, yarb bunches, para- gorick bottils, aig baskits, an' delf war" (*SL*, pp. 79-80). We are indeed a short technical distance in these "skeers" from the kinetic bedlam of silent film comedy. As a pioneering craftsman in this mode, Sut takes an artistic pride in the beauty of his collisions. His set-ups are often the entire tale, a careful piece-by-piece construction of props and devices, which then briefly explode at the end. His "skeers," or stunts, are designed, and yet open to improvisation: ". . . an' that minds me tu tell yu what I thinks ove planin an' studdyin: hit am ginerly no count. All pends, et las' on what yu dus' an' how yu kerries yursef *at the moment ove ackshun*" (*SL*, p. 63). What Sut does there, create and break, create and break, is the intention of Harris's adversary style. It is a church-going Presby- terian, a devoted family man and a prominent citizen of Knoxville, who asks: what *is* low, stupid, vile, in this lowest of styles? In the *Yarns* the humorous style is itself breached. What *is* unspeakable in Jacksonian literature? Suttishness. Lunch, naked, on the table. The grisly voice of Caliban. How well Harris entered into the feeling of the opposite can be appreciated from still another angle. The con- triver of these destructive pranks was the owner of a metalworking shop that made or repaired everything from medical instruments to watches, a skilled machinist who later became the superintendent of the Holston Glass Works.

Back in the woods, near the Ducktown mines in eastern Tennes- see, the "life and vigor and originality" of the "popular idiom," to use Lowell's words, speaks from a different source in the human heart. Of Sicily Burns, whose strawberried breast we have already contemplated, Sut says: "I be durned ef hits eny use talkin, that ar gal cud make me murder ole Bishop Soul, hissef, ur kill mam, not to speak ove dad, ef she jis' hinted she wanted sich a thing dun" (*SL*, p. 70). It is desire, the will to impose presence, and not conscience, that animates Speech in the *Yarns*, that makes Harris's style thrust its entangled misspellings against the conformity of the proper text. In Sut's speech, which is the amoral language of a "Nat'ral Born Durn'd Fool," Harris becomes the trickster: he gives us full in the face the perversity of the mean South, he blows things up, devises panics, is the wrecker, and is wrong, but the fundamental trick of this discourse, its prime subject, is the trickery of the body. If the lesson of the Writing Lesson is the disembodiment of discourse, the trick of displacement, an illusion of mastery, then humor, as Harris writes it, returns the trick by giving us in writing through a sense of speech, an illusion of voice, the body as the unsubdued and unruly trickster, first and last trickster. In the *Yarns* Speech takes as its primary significance the visceral reality of the body, a reality far removed from the romanticized body, which steps so beautifully and easily into writing. Speech, or its preferred cognate, the "popular idiom," is not here "rich leaf-mould" fertilizing the ground of a colloquial style, as Lowell would have it, but a starker utterance from a different place in the "vocal forest" where men and women live close to cowshit and horsepiss, and the talk is tough.

Sut's speech is about the absurd body, that which is always out-side the civilizing designation of writing, and which continually gives polite discourse the lie. His own ugly body is a tumult of conflicted desires, and when, rarely, he beholds a beautiful body, it burns him. It is the hot body of Sicily Burns. Yet one must be careful not to become an appalled Gulliver in this reading of Sut because Harris's Yahoo is knowingly Yahooing. "The effect of images of flayed and butchered animals, of diseases and verminous insects, of fatness and thinness, of occasionally seductive women," Milton Rickels writes in his biographical study of Harris, "fills the *Yarns* with a sense of ever-present flesh. The dark chaos of flesh emphasizes Sut's solitary condition. There is no meaning to discover or to recover in this dark atmosphere but the feeling of flesh. At the broadest, the human condition is isolated, ugly, dying, without transcendental mean-ing."[18] Rickels is himself too broad in this observation, if only because *this* "ever-present" body, however imprisoning, however betraying, is just a brick that Sut hurls at us, humorously. The trickster is at play between the two states of existence, between that "dark atmosphere" and "transcendental meaning."

How to scare awake a comatose hillbilly boy, a "dredful fat, mean, lazy boy, 'bout my age" (*SL*, p. 63), is the formidable task Sut sets himself in the tale, "Old Skissism's Middle Boy." Sut ties the sleeping boy to his chair, binds this inert, passive, somnolent, repulsive body, and then proceeds "tu practize" on it. What follows is a perfect elaboration of Harris's practice as a humorous writer. With all the pride of a makeup artist, the contriver of special effects, Sut creates a monster. "I painted his face the culler ove a nigger coal-burner, scept a white ring round his eyes; an' frum the corners ove his mouf, sorter downards, slouchwise, I lef a white strip. Hit made his mouf look sorter like ontu a hoss track an' ni ontu es big. He wer a fine picter tu study, ef your mind wer fond ove skeery things." It is a torture, but with a surreal twist; a torture in which the body, this blank unconscious body, is a dummy. Sut continues: "I screw'd ontu each ove his years a par ove iron hanvices, what his dad squeezed ole clocks, an' crac't warnuts wif, an' they hung down like over-grow'd year-rings; I tied a gridiron tu wun ankil, an' a par ove fire tongs tu tuther" (*SL*, pp. 64-65), and on and on, bugs down his back, a rat in his britches, until at last the "skeer" penetrates the thick oleaginous slumber of young Skissism, and he awakens—is skeer'd awake. In the technical sense, all that Harris does here is to admit into the oral tale the physical comedy that later becomes so familiar in film: the acrobatic escapes of Harold Lloyd, the tortures of the Three Stooges, driverless cars hurtling down busy streets, a thumb in the eye, collapsing walls, and yet Harris's conception of this scene is radically different. The *Yarns* do anticipate, visually, the knockabout of short comic films, but we would have to see a Harold Lloyd or a Three Stooges 'short' charged with political and cultural reference, done with a nastily drawling voiceover, assuming our complicity, in order to achieve the full effect of Sut's "skeer." Jesse Bier is right in *The Rise and Fall of American Humor*: the line is straight from Harris to Lenny Bruce. The same body is in their speech.

"Hole that ar hoss down tu the yearth." "He's a fixin fur the heavings." "He's a spreadin his tail feathers tu fly. Look out, Laigs, if you ain't ready tu go up'ards." "Wo, Shavetail." "Git a fiddil; he's tryin a jig." "Say, Long Laigs, rais'd a power ove co'n didn't yu?" "Taint co'n, hits redpepper."

These and like expressions were addressed to a queer looking, long legged, short bodied, small headed, white haired, hog eyed, funny sort of a genius, fresh from some bench-legged Jew's clothing store, mounted on "Tear-poke," a nick tailed, bow necked, long, poor, pale sorrel horse, half dandy, half devil, and enveloped in a perfect net-work of bridle, reins, crupper, martingales, straps, surcingles, and red ferreting, who reined up in front of

Pat Nash's grocery, among a crowd of mountaineers full of
fun, foolery, and mean whisky.
This was SUT LOVINGOOD. (*SL*, p. 33)

Rocks and bricks alternate on the page, and through the tension of
their jointed construction, the creature of that tension, Sut appears.
It is about as much of "George" as we ever get in the *Yarns*, this
introduction that recognizes in Sut's ugliness, in this grotesque body,
the shine of genius.

5

Out of the diversity of humorous writing in the Jacksonian period,
its constructions of rock and brick, two exemplary figures thus
emerge: Parson Wilbur and Sut Lovingood. Each is what the other is
not, contraposed projections within the writer's self. Here is a Writer,
too learned, too literate, too fussy, inescapably orthodox, laboring
at his escritoire, miserably serving the cause of the high style, always
a preacher, the horror of Lowell's artistic life, and there is an illiterate Speaker, an "onregenerit" speaker who prefers alogical modes,
enjoys fragmentation, delights in dirty talk, in body speech, who will
tolerate narrative if it is loosely composed, but who refuses absolutely the lesson of the Writing Lesson. A principle of killing order, a
principle of destructive play. Neither Lowell nor Harris could bring
the two principles, the two characters, into significant relation in
their humorous writing.

Before we turn now to the question of Huck's speech in *Huckleberry Finn*, Mark Twain's rocky going, his understanding of the
humorous style, we might note, if only in passing, that as Mark
Twain worked intermittently on the novel, he began in 1879 to
compile selections for his anthology, *Mark Twain's Library of Humor*
(1888). The project led him back to an extensive rereading of Jacksonian humor and, as Walter Blair has shown in *Mark Twain & Huck
Finn*,[19] he began almost immediately to appropriate material from
that reading. Bits and pieces, notably from William Tappan Thompson's *Major Jones's Courtship*, appear in *A Tramp Abroad* (1880)
and in *The Prince and the Pauper* (1882), and more importantly he
drew directly on the work of the Southwestern humorists when, in
the latter sections of *Huckleberry Finn*, he came to depict the
antebellum South as the mean South. But Mark Twain's sociological

depiction of the mean South is not his strongest suit in *Huckleberry Finn.* It is rather the continuous ordeal of Huck's writing that is before us, the question of the style, the question of the humorous lie. Then, as now, humorists stole profusely from one another—routines, stories, jokes—but what could not be stolen, and still cannot be stolen, is that unique sense of pain which, by sleight of hand, a stroke of genius, becomes a deep and disquieting sense of humor.

There is another work of Jacksonian humor that has a severe application to the writing of *Huckleberry Finn,* a narrative that brings us roundabout the pestilential vapors of Cairo. Mark Twain did not know it, excerpts from *The Confidence-Man* do not appear in any of the post-Civil War anthologies of American humor, and yet the novel speaks with perfect command about the anxiety inside humorous thought. What it says brings us back, ironically, to where we started, to the project of humor, that simple transformation of suffering Herriman draws in *Krazy Kat.* Melville's simpleton, seemingly mute, stands before us demonstrating a slate on which he writes, one after the other, the commandments of love: "Charity thinketh no evil . . . suffereth long, and is kind . . . endureth all things . . . believeth all things . . . never faileth."[20] He produces, that is, a passage from I Corinthians 13, the krazy heart of Christian wisdom. Misanthropes appear; another sign is presented, *No Trust*; brickbats are thrown at the mute, at a poor crippled darky; and so the great ship of fools is launched, moves out upon the Mississippi where it will pass, in the happenstance of the similar time frame, a certain small raft bearing its own freight of fools.

The World's Charity, the Omni-Balsamic Reinvigorator, the Samaritan Pain Dissuader—these are several of the projects, the products, contrived and sold aboard the *Fidèle.* Considering Mark Twain's record as a compulsive investor, the bizarre schemes he 'bought' throughout his life, it might be said, if only to cross references, that he would have bought everything offered on the *Fidèle,* beginning with those dubious shares in the Black Rapids Coal Company. He was, in that sense, the original mark. Melville's purpose in *The Confidence-Man* is to say this of the genial humorist: mark twain, discern duplicity. This humorist baffles suspicion, deflects the fact, takes the wily sense of the merman's discourse in *Moby*

Dick to the highest level of sophistic persuasion. The question for us is whether he represents Melville's sense of humor.

When Frank Goodman and Charlie Noble, these boon companions, these falsely funny fellows, sit down to exchange confidences, the disquisition on humor begins. Goodman has already established his authority: "Ah, now . . . irony is so unjust; never could abide irony; something Satanic about irony. God defend me from Irony, and Satire, his bosom friend" (*CM*, pp. 192-93). That is indeed the humorous position on irony, and Goodman, dressed in this chapter as a gorgeous dandy, articulates the position brilliantly, driving the ironist out of his argument into his mood, stripping irony of its reasoning power, characterizing it as mere melancholy, a bad humor. Goodman's logic simply follows the suasion of desire. He speaks for the pleasure principle and is so plausible that his gun-toting adversary is finally driven to desperate cursing. With smiling Charlie Noble before him, Goodman changes his position, and with wicked irony turns humor into a joke.

> Humor is, in fact, so blessed a thing, that even in the least virtuous product of the human mind, if there can be found but nine good jokes, some philosophers are clement enough to affirm that those nine good jokes should redeem all the wicked thoughts, though plenty as the populace of Sodom. At any rate, this same humor has something, there is no telling what, of beneficence in it, it is such a catholicon and charm—nearly all men agreeing in relishing it, though they may agree in little else—and in its way it undeniably does such a deal of familiar good in the world, that no wonder it is almost a proverb, that a man of humor, a man capable of a good loud laugh—seem how he may in other things—can hardly be a heartless scamp" (*CM*, pp. 231-32).

A contradictory brick is promptly hurled at this suave interpretation of humor. Our gaze is directed to the figure of a "pale pauper-boy" standing in a pair of monstrous boots, and from this poignant figure we derive a good loud laugh. "Look—ha, ha, ha!" So adept is this mock humorist in his changes of meaning, his changes of identity, so inexorable is the temporal course of the day, the passage of the sun, that the simple logic of all this symbolism, twisted and knotted, would seem to dictate the presence of a single calamity, a single tale obsessively told: the loss of a sense of humor, the arrival of darkest despair. And yet, by the very doctrine of coappearance (the sacred requires the profane, vice versa, et cetera), the mock humorist is fated to divulge the true humorist. Frank Goodman will ponder Shakespeare, the Shakespeare who creates Autolycus in *The Winter's Tale*. He is a "queer man," Goodman avows, impressed. Every character, each situation, in Shakespeare's drama is multiple, various, turnable, inconsistent. We see things as they are. Goodman's professional respect for the wily Shakespeare, which is diversely stated, recalls Kierkegaard's opinion of Shakespearean irony. "When Shakespeare relates himself ironically to his work," Kierkegaard wrote, "this is simply in order to let the objective prevail. Irony is now pervasive, ratifying each particular feature so there is neither too much or too little, so that everything receives its due, so that the true equilibrium may be effected in the microcosmic situation of the poem whereby it gravitates towards itself." For this to happen, Kierkegaard advises, the "poet must himself be master over irony" (*CI*, p. 336). The argument in *The Confidence-Man* is strenuously considered in that state of vigilant supervision. Each assertion reveals a question, each question is held in a balance, measured, so that everything receives its due. The armed misanthrope will suddenly stare at the benign cosmopolitan, see through him, declare him a Diogenes, identify the 'meaning' of the cosmopolitan's lulling discourse, but no, with a twist of apt denial, Melville foils the decoder, leaves the "discomfited misanthrope to the solitude he held so sapient" (*CM*, p. 195). If it is true that a scathing ironist sheds his humorous guises in this text, outfit after outfit, lie after lie, still there is another outfit, no end of costume, no end of the possible. There are kinds of humor, high and low, in *The Confidence-Man* just as there are different modes of irony, and each interpretation of reality is severely rated. The ironist, for example, cannot himself escape the clinging, resistant logic of life-preserving humor, which hopes, desires, believes, which turns back on him, on his spurious name, Goodman, spiting spite. A master over irony, that is a kind of humorist.

The Confidence-Man refers to the treachery of the tall tale, uses certain formal elements of the Southwestern sketch, but the reference is distant, the usage rarefied. Although many Jacksonian readers thought of Melville as a humorist, the entertaining writer of *Typee, A Peep at Polynesian Life,* he did not properly enter even that literature. In the School for Humorists that Mark Twain attended, Melville was not required reading. Yet Melville's question—*what does a humorist do?*—asked in an ironic text, asked in obscurity, will reappear in Mark Twain's fiction, and the response is *Huckleberry Finn.*

Notes

1. James Russell Lowell, *The Biglow Papers* (Boston and New York, 1898), p. 490. All subsequent reference will be indicated *BP.*

2. George Washington Harris, *Sut Lovingood's Yarns,* ed. M. Thomas Inge (New Haven, 1966), p. 25. All subsequent reference will be indicated *SL.*

3. Cited in David B. Kesterson, *Josh Billings* (New York, 1973), p. 126. All subsequent reference will be indicated *JB.*

4. Richard Bridgman, *The Colloquial Style in America* (Oxford University Press: New York, 1966), p. 62. All subsequent reference will be indicated *CSA.*

5. Claude Lèvi-Strauss, *Tristes Tropiques,* trans. John Russell (New York, 1968), p. 291. All subsequent reference will be indicated *TT.*

6. Johnson Jones Hooper, *Simon Suggs' Adventures and Travels* (Philadelphia: T. B. Peterson, 1848), p. 53.

7. *Humor of the Old Southwest,* ed. Hennig Cohen and William B. Dillingham (Boston, 1964), p. 275. All subsequent reference will be indicated *BB.*

8. Walter Blair and Hamlin Hill, *America's Humor, From Poor Richard to Doonesbury* (New York, 1978), pp. 309-318. In this recent historical survey of American humor, which is generously inclusive, Blair and Hill make several ambitious attempts to escape the parochialism of the typological approach first established by Constance Rourke in her pioneering work, *American Humor, A Study of the National Character* (1931). They trace certain structures in Jacksonian humor back to the routines found in Attic comedy, undertake morphological studies of recurring jokes, sketch in, helpfully, a European context for American humor, and yet at no point do they clearly distinguish between humorous and comic modes. So everyone is here, from Benjamin Franklin to Gary Trudeau, but their difference, this distinction, is often lost in the crowding.

9. B. P. Shillaber, *Life and Sayings of Mrs. Partington* (New York, 1854), p. 109.

10. Philip Roth, *Portnoy's Complaint* (New York, 1970), p. 235.

11. Lowell, *The Biglow Papers* [*First Series*], ed. Thomas Wortham (Northern Illinois Univ. Press: DeKalb, 1977), p. 244.

12. Edmund Wilson, *Patriotic Gore* (New York, 1966), p. 509. All subsequent reference will be indicated *PG.*

13. Paul Radin, *The Trickster, A Study in American Indian Mythology* (New York, 1972), p. 118.

14. Luigi Pirandello, *On Humor* (University of North Carolina Press: Chapel Hill, 1974), p. 113. All subsequent reference will be indicated *OH.*

15. William Burroughs, *Naked Lunch* (New York, 1966), p. xlvi.

16. Jesse Bier, *The Rise and Fall of American Humor* (New York, 1968), p. 301. Bier's contentious reading of American humor is unfortunately caustic. He believes "We are in great part humorless as never before" (p. 305), which is, of course, a humorless position, and debatable. Yet Bier's study is particularly good in the careful attention it gives to the significance of Artemus Ward, and he writes cogently on the comedy in American film.

17. *The Essential Lenny Bruce,* ed. John Cohen (New York, 1967), p. 97.

18. Milton Rickels, *George Washington Harris* (New York, 1965), p. 116.

19. Walter Blair, *Mark Twain and Huck Finn* (University of California Press: Berkeley, 1962), pp. 240-48.

20. Herman Melville, *The Confidence-Man: His Masquerade,* ed. H. Bruce Franklin (Indianapolis and New York, 1967), pp. 6-7. All subsequent reference will be indicated *CM.* For another approach to the humor of Melville's irony, see Richard B. Hauck, *A Cheerful Nihilism: Confidence and 'the Absurd' in American Humorous Fiction* (Bloomington: Indiana University Press, 1971). An excellent comparative study of Melville and Mark Twain is found in Warwick Wadlington, *The Confidence Game in American Literature* (Princeton University Press: Princeton and New York, 1975).

III

White Lies, Bluff Reefs

In this mortuary volume I find Nasby, Artemus Ward, Yawcob Strauss, Derby, Burdette, Eli Perkins, the 'Danbury News Man,' Orpheus C. Kerr, Smith O'Brien, Josh Billings and a score of others . . . whose writings and sayings were once in everybody's mouth but are now heard of no more and are no longer mentioned. Seventy-eight seems an incredible crop of well-known humorists for one forty-year period to have produced, and yet this book has not harvested the entire crop—far from it. It has no mention of Ike Partington . . . no mention of Doesticks, nor of the Pfaff crowd, nor of Artemus Ward's numerous and perishable imitators, nor of three very popular Southern humorists whose names I am not able to recall, nor of a dozen other sparkling transients whose light shone for a time but has now, years ago, gone out.

Why have they perished? Because they were merely humorists. Humorists of the 'mere' sort cannot survive.

The Autobiography of Mark Twain

1

There is Cardiff Hill, Pleasure's deferred, distant Haunt, a "Delectable Land, dreamy, reposeful, and inviting." Here, immediate, present, punishing, is Work's Space: "Thirty yards of broad fence nine feet high!"[1] *Tom Sawyer* effectively begins with the question of how we get from here to there; how, humorously, we transform work into play, pain into pleasure, and what, in the dazzle of all this displacement and substitution, is actually gained or really lost. Mark Twain liberally applies a wash of humorous intelligence to Tom's fence, depicts a lie that poses the play of whitewashing as the work of humor. On the other side of this smartly gleaming fence, the brightest thing in *Tom Sawyer,* is Mark Twain's meditation on the epistemology of humorous writing, "Old Times on the Mississippi," and beyond that, *Huckleberry Finn* and the issue of Huck's speech. The question of humorous transformation will reappear in these texts, and in Huck's telling so complicate Mark Twain's sense of humor that, ironically, he will lose it. A genie, the genius of humor,

White Lies, Bluff Reefs

always secures Tom's pleasure in *Tom Sawyer,* works for him, provides for him, but where is he, that good genie, when Huck needs him? Huck has only Tom at the end of *Huckleberry Finn,* the homunculus of a humorist, to get Jim from here to there, from slavery to freedom, and Tom's script is not funny. Before Mark Twain reaches this impasse, there is first the obstruction of that "far-reaching continent of unwhitewashed fence" (*TS,* p. 15), plank after plank of painful reality. Tom looks to avoid his sentence, hard labor on Saturday morning in early summer, and in the flair of his solution, just there, Mark Twain leaves the sign of his question.

We know how Tom solves his problem. He whitewashes the whitewashing of the fence. So bright is this lie that the finished fence might indeed stand as the culmination of the scene, the masterpiece itself, a perfect, almost blinding abstraction, white on white, lacking only a signature. If we think of the whitewashing episode, that is how we see it, as a single act, the triumph of head work over hand labor. Yet this illustrious swindle in Chapter II, which seems complete, actually begins a sequence that will reach its proper close in Chapter IV with Tom, the thief of meaning, interrogated before a classroom of his peers, caught barefaced in a lie. Read in its Aesopian entirety, from event to moral, the sequence appropriately warns its youthful readers that even splendid liars are finally apprehended, and at the same time, read differently, the fable establishes the manic-depressive pattern of Mark Twain's ambivalence in *Tom Sawyer.* Every gilt-edged triumph awarded Tom in the novel is immediately tarnished, turned into a question. The humorist, as it were, desires to write *Tom Sawyer* as a pleasing success story, keeps trying right up to the very end, but someone in his text is always present, to the side, signifying failure.

Huck does not appear this particular morning to stand in line for his turn with the brush. Tom has the scene all to himself. He begins lowdown in a hard place (Jim, briefly gulled, has been sent flying by Aunt Polly's slipper), and here it is, then, that "dark and hopeless moment" when one takes the daunting measure of an unavoidable task, addresses the misery of profitless convict labor, the end of which is a vast thirty yards distant. The fence, after all, is a brutal affair, almost a wall, so long and so high you can't see over it or around it. Tom is up against it, in a fix that prefigures the greater extremity of Huck's plight on the moored raft in *Huckleberry Finn.* Huck also has an ugly task to perform, one that will rob him of his self-respect, and no way out of it. For Tom this stupid work violates his deepest sense of himself as master, hero, lord of the land. It is nigger-work, and the idea of "free boys" tripping by him, seeing him compelled to work, slaving away, horrifies him. The "very thought of it burnt him like fire" (*TS*, p. 16). Here, epiphany! With knowing appeal to childish egotism, Tom transforms the work of painting into the art of painting, turns nigger-work (manual) into white man's work (conceptual). What *is* painting but the application of brush to surface? All these little boys, who have already glimpsed the limiting wall of necessary labor, busily play at work. Here comes Ben Rogers, chug-a-chug, playing steamboat, impersonating that most admired of adult workers, the pilot, whose work simply gives him the free play of his native skill. He will step readily into Tom's fiction. Tom is painting a scene, struggling with a conceptual problem, seeking to be faithful to his vision. This is obviously work at the highest level, for all its low look, and we are at an early suspenseful stage. Tom sweeps his brush "daintily back and forth," steps back to note the "effect," places a "touch here and there," then steps back to criticize the "effect" again. He tells Ben, who is hypnotized by Tom's panto-mime of authority: "I reckon there ain't one boy in a thousand, maybe two thousand that can do it the way it's got to be done" (*TS*, p. 18). And there ain't, really. So plausible is Tom's act, his performance of the *artiste* at work, which looks like play, the onlook-ing boys contend for the privilege of doing his chore, and pay for it.

Tom has discovered a "great law of human action," and the humorist spells it out for him. If Tom "had been a great and wise philosopher, like the writer of this book, he would now have compre-hended that work consists of whatever a body is obliged to do, and that play consists of whatever a body is not obliged to do" (*TS*, pp. 19-20). Yet Tom's application of the law is questionable (a theft of meaning, a theft of labor), and so, too, is the tolerance of the humorist who virtually tells us he is repeating, differently, Tom's act, Tom's trick. For in practice this "great law of human action" simply depends on credulity, on innocence or ignorance, and the fun of it surely is that it produces superadded profit for Tom, tangible wealth: apple core, kite, dead rat, piece of string, twelve marbles, et cetera. The "law" enables Tom to steal the labor of his friends, and to that extent (Tom, after all, owns the fence, the paint, the brush) the "law" resembles the meanest of tricks in the nineteenth century, the production of surplus value. Tom has discovered the perfect crime.

There is, in the round, such a marvelous economy of effect in this exchange. Everyone is satisfied. Tom gets his work done for him, the fooled boys have their fun, Aunt Polly's fence is painted, and no one, save God, the Truth, the humorist, and possibly the reader, is the wiser, or a loser.

> "It's all done, Aunt."
> "Tom, don't lie to me. I can't bear it."
> "I ain't, Aunt; it *is* all done."
> Aunt Polly placed small trust in such evidence. She went out to see for herself; and she would have been content to find twenty per cent of Tom's statement true. When she found the entire fence whitewashed, and not only white-washed but elaborately coated and recoated, and even a streak added to the ground, her astonishment was almost unspeakable. (*TS*, pp. 20-21)

Here, then, is the whitewashed fence in *Tom Sawyer,* proudly exhibited, and it is *too* white, *too* painted, painted and repainted, and there, presumably at the farthest end of the fence, the painter has added a streak to the ground, a run-on line that takes us back into the texture of *Tom Sawyer,* which is *too* white, too condescending in its plea for tolerance of Tom's misdoing, and which tells us the episode does not end here. In the humorous lie we whitewash the wrong, whitewash the hurtful brick, we cover over reality, and take a deep and joyous satisfaction in the feat. Even as Mark Twain shows us the trick of whitewashing the fence, as he celebrates the ingenuity of Tom's deception, there is a larger act of whitewashing at play in the text. The run-on line that astonishes Aunt Polly in *Tom Sawyer* is a loose end. It points us toward a different understanding of humor in *Huckleberry Finn,* toward the lunacy of Tom's last trick, his last whitewashing, which Huck can not properly judge. And this trick, a whitewashed Nigger Jim, which we see and judge, returns us to the whitewashed fence, to this forgiven and pardonable trick.

Obviously there is another side to this fence, another side to *Tom Sawyer.* The immediate significance of the scene spills over into the next several chapters. Tom attempts to repeat the trick of white-washing the fence, to get something for nothing, but here the power of illusion, Tom's fiction, abruptly collapses before an inconvertible reality. He didn't paint the fence; he won't study the Bible. Tom exchanges his hoard of commodities (licorice, fishhook, white alleys) for a currency of coupons used in school as a reward for Bible recitation. Lie engenders lie, dissimulation is added to dissimulation, until Tom has cornered the market in duplicity and cashes his coupons in for the biggest prize, the Bible itself. But the two languages, the language of economics and the language of morality, are not translatable. Put to the test, asked to name the first two apostles summoned by Christ, Tom is struck dumb, exposed. He knows only about David and Goliath, small and large, smart and stupid. Of Jesus and his unmitigated suffering, of Jesus and His Gang, Tom knows nothing. The boys in the classroom who have grimly watched Tom stand in undeserved splendor to take the prize, who have bitterly realized they were the "dupes of a wily fraud, a guileful snake in the grass" (*TS*, p. 34), now get to witness with delight his consternation—but we don't. "Let us draw," says the humorist, "the curtain of charity over the rest of the scene" (*TS*, p. 36). So ends, dubiously whitewashed, the whitewashing episode.

Humor *is* charitable. The appeal of the humorist is direct: *Tom, c'est moi, c'est toi! See in these adventures an egotism you will recognize.* Tom lies, the humorist lies, and we lie. It is a truth Mark Twain bravely reveals in *Tom Sawyer*, a proof of candor he hoped would set the book apart from its genre. "It is *not* a boy's book, at all," he protested in a letter to William Dean Howells in 1875. "It will only be read by adults. It is only written for adults." But by then Mark Twain had already himself sensed that there was something wrong in the lyrical perfection of *Tom Sawyer*. He writes in the same letter: "I perhaps made a mistake in not writing it in the first person." Howells had suggested that he continue the narrative, take Tom as a *picaro* into early manhood, but what Mark Twain now realized was that he had to reopen the question of the humorous lie, and this time talk it, not write it. He had a different project, so he wrote to Howells: "By & by I shall take a boy of twelve & run him on through life (in the first person) but not Tom Sawyer—he would not be a good character for it."[2] It is indeed to redress a wrong, the lie in *Tom Sawyer*, the lie of *Tom Sawyer*, that Huck begins to speak in his book.

For some readers of *Tom Sawyer* nothing can be wrong in the text. Because the narrative is distanced by a "burlesque-indulgent perspective," starts from the implicit premise "once upon a time," so it is argued, *Tom Sawyer* does not properly have a psychological dimension. "Tom's play *defines the world as play*," James M. Cox writes in *Mark Twain: The Fate of Humor*, "and his reality lies in his commitment to play, not in the involuntary tendencies which are often attributed to him."[3] To the extent that the plot of *Tom Sawyer* yields the happiest of endings, an absolute preservation of ego-fantasy, this definition of Tom's reality is apt. "Y-o-u-u- *Tom!*" The novel beings with the call that ends play, that call at once caring and constraining, mother's call, the parental call, to come in, to clean up, to defer an immediate pleasure. Cox's interpretation wonderfully stresses the importance of the humorous transaction in *Tom Sawyer.* It is what the book is about, he insists, the infallible conversion of pain into pleasure. Tom eludes the call, evades the fence; has the curtain drawn over his humiliation in school; pays no heed to sermon, speech, and lecture; escapes all that, even the menace of Injun Joe; and enters play.

> Play is the reality principle in the book. What makes Tom Sawyer seem more real than the adults who submit to his power is his capacity to take his pleasure openly in the form of make-believe while they take theirs covertly under the guise of seriousness. Tom's virtue lies not in his good heart, his independence, or his pluck—none of which he really has—but in his truth to the pleasure principle which is the ultimate reality of the enchanted idyl. The very enchantment results from the indulgent perspective the author assumes toward the action. The narrator's indulgence is none other than the pleasure he takes in disclosing the play world. (*MTFH,* p. 147)

Nothing is wrong in such an enchanted idyl. Play excludes Aunt Reality, Judge Reality, Injun Joe Reality, and finally all those readers who are unwilling to enter Tom's play.

Yet the value Cox assigns to play in *Tom Sawyer* is suspect, if only because the play in *Tom Sawyer,* as play, is so problematical. It is certainly not an unstructured spontaneous play that Tom desires, nor the principled play of folk games where roles are prescribed and usually shared, but a particular play that is as revealing and compromised as the play of adults, as the play of the humorist who narrates *Tom Sawyer.* For Tom the pleasure of play is in the manipulation of it. He directs the play, controls the players, and always comes into the play referring to the authority of a script: *it is written* that we do this or that. The scripture of Tom's "adventures" reveals the character of his personality. Only if we accept play as magical, exempt, a privileged form of human activity, does *Tom Sawyer* stand as an "enchanted idyl," like *Peter Pan*. It *is* what the humorist asks of us, our indulgence, our belief in the humorous transformation, and yet his exposure of the procedures and the politics of the play, of the *modus operandi* of humor, is so exact, so discriminating, that each game, each instance of play, is effectively a psychodrama—and not at all embryonic in its expression of desire. Tom's play for Amy Lawrence and then for Becky Thatcher, his playing them off against each other, drives Becky to the desperate stratagem of devising a picnic, a playful picnic that will lead the principal players into the labyrinth of the cave. The realism of *Tom Sawyer,* its underlying seriousness, is to be read in such passages, and here, for example, Mark Twain will allow himself that humorless adjective, *vicious.*

> Tom decided that he could be independent of Becky Thatcher now. Glory was sufficient. He would live for glory. Now that he was distinguished, maybe she would be wanting to "make up." Well, let her—she should see that he could be as indifferent as some other people. Presently she arrived. Tom pretended not to see her. He moved away and joined a group of boys and girls, and began to talk. Soon he observed that she was tripping gaily back and forth with flushed face and dancing eyes, pretending to be busy chasing schoolmates, and screaming with laughter when she made a capture, but he noticed that she always made her captures in his vicinity, and that she seemed to cast a conscious eye in his direction at such times, too. It gratified all the vicious vanity that was in him; and so, instead of winning him, it only "set him up" the more and made him the more diligent to avoid betraying that he knew what she was about. (*TS*, p. 124)

Tom's play is the imaginative play of romantic fiction. Every wish and longing is realized. He would like to be dead so he could enjoy the remorse of his mourners. He would like to be engaged in the heroic enterprise, to slay the dragon (or minotaur), win the Fair Lady, and all the treasure. He wants to be rich, famous, and beloved. To get from here (reality) to there (romance). Tom's fiction, after all, is childish fiction, boyish imagining, pubescent fantasy, and it is self-centered, imperious, manic. We see the children at play. They are playing the game of romance. Tom's performance has in it the charge that drives all theatrical performers—*look at me!*—and also the consequent anxiety. For this fiction does not adequately represent the *other*, has no place in its play for the conflicting claims of the *other*. The *other* is either dominated (Huck) or eliminated (Amy Lawrence). As for the rest, the other *others*, they are spectators. Huck has the last word in *Tom Sawyer*, but it is his submission to the dictate of Tom's script: "I'll stick to the widder till I rot, Tom; and if I git to be a reg'lar ripper of a robber, and everybody talking 'bout it, I reckon she'll be proud she snaked me in out of the wet" (*TS*, p. 221). Tom's lie, Tom's play, Tom's fiction, will reappear in *Huckleberry Finn*, disenchanted, as robbery. The question that is thematically implicit in *Tom Sawyer*, smuggled in and posed before the fence, is at last dramatically explicit. How innocent *is* Tom's play? How innocent is his lie? What happens to stolen meaning?

2

The humorist who asks this question unavoidably turns the question back upon himself. How much can he know in his text and still be humorous, before slipping into the change of irony? In the simple act of humor we make of a large thing a small thing, defer logical thinking, reject the dubious help of irony, and take flight from seriousness. "Look," says Freud's fond super-ego to the intimidated ego, "here is the world, which seems so dangerous! It is nothing but a game for children—just worth making a jest about" (*H*, p. 166)! The expectation of a pleasure founded in the relief of play determines the course of humorous writing, gives it a specific function, and imposes on the humorist the obligation of performance. If a humorous text is not funny, does not yield pleasure, it is nothing. "Although my book is intended mainly for the entertainment of boys and girls," Mark Twain writes in the preface to *Tom Sawyer*, "I hope it will not be shunned by men and women on that account, for part of my plan has been to try pleasantly to remind adults of what they once were themselves, and of how they felt and thought and talked, and what queer enterprises they sometimes engaged in" (*TS*, p. 5). So the humorist is caught up by the imperatives of the humorous act, "to try (pleasantly) to remind adults of what they once were," and he works in a style that appropriately demeans the seriousness of writing and belittles authoritative modes of critical discourse. He parodies, writes burlesques, concocts tall tales, adopts the humorous style, and he depicts the play of innocence and/or ignorance. The humorist who takes himself seriously therefore writes in the double sense Mark Twain indicates in his preface. *Tom Sawyer* is an "entertainment" for boys and girls, but adults will also find something in it, a reflection. The humorist must make of his small thing a large thing, write big in the low style, contrive a boy's book for adults, and stay within the humorous style, a style that professes the value of innocence.

Innocence, of a kind, is the veritable thesis of Mark Twain's early work. It is what the humorist knows, his material, and it is wisely what he shows us—Innocence, in all her situations. The American tourists in *The Innocents Abroad* (1869) who scramble about Europe and Palestine in search of significant experience and souvenirs are incorrigibly innocent. They strive to be serious, they study to be informed, they labor to behold, but what they are told seriously to see is not quite there, and so, inevitably, their pilgrimage to the center and origin of their culture places them before the fake and the genuine, before the Tomb of Adam and the Sphinx. Both monuments are defaced: the first by a false rhapsody and the second by sacrilege. "While we stood looking, a wart or an excrescence of some kind appeared on the jaw of the sphinx. We heard the familiar clink of a hammer and understood the case at once. One of our well-meaning reptiles—I mean relic-hunters—had crawled up there and was trying to break a 'specimen' from the face of this the most majestic creation the hand of man has wrought."[4] The journey to the Source ends with an act of vandalism. In *Roughing It* (1872) the men who run the territorial government of Nevada, who dig for silver, who shoot at each other, are all invincible youths, callow to the core. The grandiloquent Colonel Sellers who dominates the scene in *The Gilded Age* (1873) is a large poignant child in an adult body whose bluster and bravado are easily demystified. *No one ever grows up*—this is the early sense of Mark Twain's humor.

We overlook grand adventures in these first several narratives: The Return to the Old World, A Journey into the Wilderness, The Way to Wealth, but no *rite de passage* occurs in the narration. There are different adventures, the scenery changes, but the scene and the adventurer remain the same. Here is Reality, there is Romance, and the Innocent, whether Abroad or out West, indefatigably tries to connect them. He alway fails, but he has typically a load of 'literary' style, pails of purpled prose, to lay on over the failure, and this is principally what we see in the travel books—the incessant sweep and stroke of the traveler's 'literary' brush. We see, through burlesque, the necessary fiction that smooths over discontinuity and difference. For Mark Twain this single act, this painterly writing, is a synecdoche, the characteristic gesture of his generation. The age is gilded, the fence is whitewashed, and what is laid on, thickly, is the myth of innocence.

The humorist (not just Mark Twain) has an unerring eye for the action of that performance. Indeed the humorist's play with the concept of innocence is so constant and variable that the underlying complexity of the concept, as the humorist sees it, is often overlooked. *Innocence* is there in the humorous text like *play,* as a pure figure of the simple. For Mark Twain, as he turned in his fiction from Colonel Sellers to Tom Sawyer (who had in his own life the continual study of his crackpot brother, Orion Clemens), the idea of 'growing up' as the entrance into another discourse, another *I,* a serious discourse, a knowing *I,* is the fantasy of children, the myth they create. That is in part their innocence. And the innocence of adults lies in their belief that they have achieved the passage, learned to read and write, lost their innocence, lost their childishness. The humorist always discerns the child in the adult, the adult in the child, and humorously exonerates the reversal. All of Colonel Sellers's implausible schemes come to naught in *The Gilded Age.* The young Hawkinses who have come to Washington under his tutelage to seek their fortune are corrupted and broken. Yet Colonel Sellers remains inviolable, somehow unscathed by the criminality that enmeshes everyone else in the novel. There is no death for this salesman. To the very end he sings the same old song. He will give up land speculation for a legal career: "There's worlds of money in it!—whole worlds of money! Practice first in Hawkeye, then in Jefferson, then in St. Louis, then in New York! In the metropolis of the western world! Climb, and climb, and climb—and wind up on the Supreme bench. Beriah Sellers, Chief Justice of the Supreme Court of the United States, sir!"[5] He dreams, in brief, of the world Tom Sawyer inhabits, that world where wishes are fulfilled, where all lies are innocent, and the best liar the biggest hero.

Those humorists who complicate the intelligence of their writing, who put humor at risk in their work, begin invariably at just this point, by criticizing the first principle, *Innocence.* And who can forgive a humorist this unpardonable act, this breach of trust? It is a delicate situation when the humorist begins to bring up the big guns in his text, when he begins to pose a question, begins to confuse the simple message of his humor, innocent play, with other messages, and it is precisely for this reason that Mark Twain poses as the Chief of Ordnance in his admonitory *Notice* in *Huckleberry Finn.* Nothing serious here, folks. No motive, moral, or plot. We are given notice: the humorist has disappeared. The serious question about humorous knowledge is not imposed on the character of Innocence from without, by a thinker, by commentary, but rather is generated within the style, so that, humorously, the question of innocence is innocently posed. "Tom's most well, now, and got his bullet around his neck on a watch-guard for a watch, and is always seeing what time it is, and so there ain't nothing more to write about, and I am rotten glad of it, because if I'd a knowed what a trouble it was to make a book I wouldn't a tackled it and aint't agoing to no more" (*HF*, p. 366). Tom has his 'glory,' Jim is at last 'free,' and now Huck looks for closure, for completion. He is tired; the sentence trips forward, almost slurred: *a—a—a.* The style itself speaks, and it tells us everything it will not say. The face of Innocence, typically distanced by the humorist who composes it, who celebrates it, is suddenly, by virtue of his absence, brought up close.

A seriously written humorous text, it might be said, must end with the ending of innocence. It is hard to write, Huck discovers, to write and relive experience. Next he must learn to spell *sivilize.* The problem of this resolution, and the sense of Mark Twain's stylistic discovery, recurs in humorous writing. There is Woody Allen's Isaac running desperately through the streets of Manhattan to recapture his Youth, his blonde, beautiful Aryan youth. He also runs to recover the balance of the film itself, to rejoin Humor (Woody Allen) and Romance (Mariel Hemingway) in *Manhattan* (1979), and therein lies the question. As a serious writer of humorous romances, the scenarist/director of entertaining films we are to regard thoughtfully, Allen faces the same problem that confronted Mark Twain in *Tom Sawyer*. What are the limits of the humorous style? What can be said of love and death in humor, and how is it to be said? How to write big in the low style? In Allen's films the problem is complicated by the obvious 'humor' of Woody Allen's figure, that diminutive frame, those large spectacles, the disheveled boyishness, which generates, without the aid of funny lines, its own droll melancholy. The wistful appeal of this figure is as much a hazard as a help to Allen in the making of his romances. Here is the physiognomy of innocence, an immediate signification: the *ingenu,* and yet, as Allen has sought to complicate his humorous writing, this selfsame *ingenu* has had also to serve as a *raissoneur,* be innocent here and knowing there. The effect of this contradiction, the doubled role, is a self-centering of narrative that recalls the problem of perspective in Mark Twain's early work. A knowing MarkTwain presents an innocent Mark Twain, a knowing Woody Allen presents an innocent Woody Allen, and in that genial complicity, this preservation of type and tone, we have the constant reassurance that we are in the presence of Humor. No significant harm can ever befall the *ingenu,* this childish fellow, because he is too innocent to be wrong. Yet the humorist's sense of the wrong, of the *ingenu,* must become equivocal before he can rethink the adequacy of his humor. The problem is at once conceptual and stylistic, and it appears specifically in Allen's romantic films. The literary humorist who writes the burlesques and parodies in *Getting Even* (1972) and *Without Feathers* (1976) works contentedly in the restriction of those modes.

The self-centered ending of *Manhattan,* a close-up of Woody's worried face, returns us abruptly to the risk of Mark Twain's venture in *Huckleberry Finn.* Allen cannot bring himself to break the image of Isaac's innocence, which is the essence of Woody Allen's act, and yet this is exactly what Mark Twain does in *Huckleberry Finn:* he breaks our belief in Tom Sawyer's innocence by showing us how trapped, how bound and blind, Tom is in it. Tom has elbowed his way into the final frame of Huck's picture, and there Tom is, the would-be hero of Huck's life story, "his bullet around his neck on a watch-guard for a watch," gesturing at himself, checking out the time, explaining. When the *ingenue* regards the *ingenu* at the end of *Manhattan,* she sees the same winsome Isaac we are supposed to see, the child-man, and indeed, in the final fade, Woody's unsacrificed

Isaac is all we do see. There is no problem in the perspective. The breakthrough for Mark Twain, obviously, is his recourse to Huck's speech, his absolute departure from the controlling diction of the humorist. In Huck's steady gaze, his literal telling, Tom is on his own, and here, it might be said, Mark Twain achieves that Kierke-gaardian moment of mastered irony. We look ironically at this strutting Tom, but the irony is held within the humorous feeling of Huck's style. The earlier mode of humorous writing, easily enough, is cynical. A humorist simply refers to the blind spot of egotism, the innocence of self-love, and shows—through lapses in the rationality of our discourse, through fissures in the complicated surface of our rhetoric, our 'style,' through the pratfalls taken and the obvious lying that contradict the poetic elaboration and refinement of our life struggle—shows, through this transparence, that we are the merest of babes demanding attention, seeking approval, needing recognition. Look at me! Admire me! This is the play of Tom Sawyer, and his innocence, and it is why the humorist can draw us into complicity before the whitewashed fence. Whitewash is what we do, as we go along in life, justifying it. *Tom Sawyer* mirrors the intent of humor—*te absolvo,* a washing of the spirit, a whitening of self-love, exculpation—but in that generous reflection of self, the man in the child, our innocence in Tom's innocence, Mark Twain glimpsed still another child who did not fit into Tom's play, into Tom's innocence, whose speech the humorist could not sufficiently write. Huck appears; he is the other *ingenu,* and he brings into the "enchanted idyl" of the narrative the semblance of a loose end, a run-on line, a problem, and when at last he is ostensibly incorporated, brought into the final integration of *Tom Sawyer,* snaked in out of the wet, there is the question of the sequel. What follows innocence but knowledge?

There is, then, another knowledge in humor to draw upon when belief in the absolution of whitewashing begins to fade. The farther back Mark Twain went in time, moving from the exploits of those big children in *Innocents Abroad, Roughing It,* and *The Gilded Age,* to the child Tom Sawyer, the more complicated and problematical became his conception of humor, innocence, and play. And this passage in his humorous thinking coincides with his emergence as a writer serious enough to appear in the *Atlantic Monthly.* Here, so he wrote to Howells in 1874, he could at last draw a breath as a humorous writer. The readers of the *Atlantic* did not require "a 'humorist' to paint himself striped & stand on his head every fifteen minutes" (*THL*, p. 34). Almost from the start, writing in the glow of Howell's confidence, the 'humorist' began to search in his forms for what was not funny, what was not humorous performance.

The dialect sketch "A True Story," which appeared in the *Atlantic* in November, 1874, dramatically reveals the new turn in Mark Twain's humorous writing. It presents a familiar exchange: an urbane interlocutor, Mr. C—, introduces a native speaker, a black mammy, "Aunt Rachel," who is, so he comfortably tells us, a "cheerful, hearty soul." Her pealing laughter regales the after-dinner company seated on the porch in the summer evening, and Mr. C— then asks the dumb question: "Aunt Rachel, how is it that you've lived sixty years and never had any trouble?"[6] What follows is not a tall tale, an ironic exaggeration, but a "true story," bitter and hard. "I was bawn down 'mongst de slaves," Aunt Rachel tells the company, "I knows all 'bout slavery, 'case I ben one of 'em my own se'f" (*SWMT*, p. 60). Her story, briefly told, is an epic of suffering, separation, and exile, and it breaks the rationalization of the frame tale. The interlocutor does not return to sign the sketch off, to frame its humor. Aunt Rachel's cry hangs in the air, on the page: "Oh, no, Misto C—, I hain't had no trouble. An' no *joy*" (*SWMT*, p. 63)! Howells paid Mark Twain handsomely for "A True Story." As he later recalled in 1907, he wanted to show Mark Twain "the highest recognition of his writing as literature." Henry Houghton, publisher of the *Atlantic,* also "believed Mark Twain was literature" (*THL*, p. 23) and went along with Howell's scheme. So Howells and Houghton invested sixty dollars in the venture. *Mark Twain is literature,* this is the shared thesis as Mark Twain writes *Tom Sawyer* and begins "Old Times," which is written specifically for the *Atlantic,* for literature.

In Howells's discovery that Mark Twain's humorous writing could be taken seriously, there is, of course, a recognizable condescension. By the definition of his mode and his public, the humorist is not a 'serious' writer. Mark Twain's peers in the humorous profession, notably Artemus Ward, Josh Billings, and Petroleum V. Nasby (David Ross Locke), saw themselves primarily as entertainers whose material was convertible, for publication and performance. Howells would encourage Mark Twain, but the Mark Twain he took to the Whittier

White Lies, Bluff Reefs

Birthday Dinner in 1877 was the humorist, the performer, and not Mark Twain the writer. There, as everyone knows, the humorist disgraced the writer. Introduced as "a humorist who never makes you blush to have enjoyed his joke; whose generous wit has no meanness in it, whose fun is never at the cost of anything honestly high or good" (*THL*, p. 103), Mark Twain stood before the grizzled Fathers of the New England literary establishment—Ralph Waldo Emerson, Henry Wadsworth Longfellow, Oliver Wendell Holmes, and James Greenleaf Whittier—and told a vulgar story. The scandal of a disrespectful humorist mocking the solemnity of poets and essayists in their own preserve is not at issue here. It is rather the anxiety in Howells's introduction. This is a high humorist, he reassures the assembly, not a low humorist. Then came the performance, lowdown, irreverent, malicious, and Howells could only imagine, as he wrote to Charles Eliot Norton, that a "demoniacal possession" overtook Mark Twain. Still the rong a humorist does to litterytoor can always be righted, and Mark Twain would later make his abject apologies to the perplexed celebrants of Whittier's birthday.

Big? Low? Where does the writer place the 'humorist' in the hierarchy of writing? What is the rank of the humorist, his dignity? The ambivalence Lowell felt as a 'humorist' in the *Biglow Papers* is written *into* the texture of its humor. To write humor, to evoke voice, Lowell steps down from the eminence of literature, and in the Boston *Courier,* the lesser space for a writer, he takes up anonymously the low style. Here, then, is Mark Twain stepping up out of the low humorous style into the eminence of literature, into the *Atlantic,* and the same anxiety about values and intention is stylistically present in his writing. Even as Mark Twain addressed the significance of the brush stroke in *Tom Sawyer,* he was at work on "Old Times," and to follow the direction of his thought in this crucial phase in his development, we now have to place beside the whitewashing episode a comparable scene from "Old Times." What *is* the rank and dignity of piloting, Mark Twain asks in the *Atlantic,* and who *are* these magisterial pilots who 'know' the river? If the pilot knows anything, he knows the difference between the white lie of a wind reef and the black truth of a bluff reef.

> ". . . Why, what could you want over here in the bend, then? Did you ever know of a boat following a bend upstream at this stage of the river?"

"No, sir, —and I was n't trying to follow it. I was getting away from a bluff reef."

"No, it was n't a bluff reef; there is n't one within three miles of where you were."

"But I saw it. It was as bluff as that one yonder."

"Just about. Run over it!"

"Do you give it as an order?"

"Yes. Run over it."

"If I don't, I wish I may die."

"All right; I am taking the responsibility."

I was just as anxious to kill the boat now, as I had been to save it before. I impressed my orders upon my memory, to be used at the inquest, and made a straight break for the reef. As it disappeared under our bows I held my breath; but we slid over it like oil.

"Now, don't you see the difference? It was n't anything but a *wind* reef. The wind does that."

"So I see. But it is exactly like a bluff reef. How am I ever going to tell them apart?"

"I can't tell you. It is an instinct. By and by you will just naturally *know* one from the other, but you never will be able to explain why or how you know them apart."[7]

Nearly every critic who discusses "Old Times" stresses its importance as a treatise on writing. Although Mark Twain's narrative "ostensibly concerns the technical knowledge acquired by a pilot," Henry Nash Smith points out in *Mark Twain, The Development of a Writer* (1962), "the imagery and diction broaden the issue into an analysis of the whole scope of conventional aesthetic theory."[8] It is an exemplary approach to the text. Mark Twain couples his precise exposition of river knowledge in "Old Times" to an attack on rhetorical modes of representation, and strives withal to create an appropriate style. "It is a middle style," Smith writes, "the voice neither of Jim Blaine nor of the genteel tourist who viewed the crater of Kilauea, but of a man familiar with the world of common-place things who assumes that the reader lives in the same world" (*MTDW*, p. 81). And yet, as Edgar J. Burde suggests in his recent article, "Mark Twain: The Writer as Pilot," there are certain ambiguities in the clarity of both Mark Twain's analysis of conventional aesthetic theory and the reach of his new style. As Mark Twain undertook the project, Burde demonstrates, he "developed complex and contradictory feelings about piloting."[9] These feelings are projected upon the two Master Pilots, Bixby and Brown, who come ultimately to represent in Mark Twain's imagination different aspects of his narrative method. In Bixby's knowledge, Burde argues, Mark Twain saw "a way of mediating between a number of conflicts that he would never cease to find emotionally and intellectually disturbing: between the claims of subjective and objective knowledge, between absolute truth and empirical fact, between the past and the present" (*MTWP*, p. 883). Bixby's intuitive mastery of river knowledge therefore becomes an artistic ideal in Mark Twain's writing, an esemplastic power he fitfully sought to appropriate in his own literary reconstruction of the river. Brown, on the other hand, is a literalist, the pilot who lacks poetic intensity, whose recall simply lists remembered data. As Burde describes them, Bixby and Brown are almost (though he does not use the terms) Metaphor and Metonymy, pilot-factors who speak from different spheres in Memory.

It is a provocative reading of "Old Times," though Burde must anticipate the compositional failure of Part II in *Life on the Mississippi,* the later text, to support the figurative equivalence of Bixby and Brown in "Old Times." His proof of Mark Twain's anxiety about piloting (and writing) largely comes from sources outside the proper text. It is not finally the individual pilots who matter in this first memoir, but their science, their knowledge. The point of "Old Times," after all, is Mark Twain's artistic assumption of the pilot's lore. *Tom Sawyer* is ultimately glazed in a veneer of fantasy, its innocence as a boy's book preserved, but in "Old Times" Mark Twain humorously strips the cub pilot of his innocence. To know the difference between reefs is a matter of life or death. The two scenes, Tom's whitewashing of the fence and the cub pilot's mastery of the river's "language," designate the turn in Mark Twain's conception of himself as a humorous writer. Just as there is a double deception in *Tom Sawyer,* Tom's trick and the humorist's, so there is a doubled disenchantment in "Old Times." This much Mark Twain knew: the pilot knows the river, is before it, in touch with it, and the writer who knows what the pilot knew at once encompasses that knowledge and is alienated from it.

3

"Speech," Jacques Derrida writes in *Of Grammatology,* establishing the awful Scale of Supplements, "comes to be added to intuitive presence (of the entity, of *essence,* of the *eidos,* of *ousia,* and so forth); writing comes to be added to living self-present speech; masturbation comes to be added to so-called normal sexual experience; culture to nature, evil to innocence, history to origin, and so on."[10] The terms *eidos* and *ousia* do not frequently appear in Mark Twain's text, but a homespun version of that Scale and an intense feeling about supplementarity, superimposition, and adding on, do exist in his fiction. It is what the tall tale does to the tale—add on, enhance, exaggerate, all the while slyly telling us this is what it is doing, what all tales do. In Mark Twain's lexicon, *ousia* is the omnipotent, moving River, out there as the flexing *natur* of Nature, and in here as *eidos,* Memory and Consciousness, surface and depth and constant direction. The river flows out there between its banks, turning here, turning there, but always flowing south toward the Gulf, and it flows similarly in the pilot's mind toward his End. To the River (actual and symbolic) is added that merest of filaments, the float of a raft, the "free and easy" talk of Huck and Jim, the proximity of "living self-present speech." This is the closest we come in Mark Twain's writing to the *natur* of things, the exposure of their nakedness to the element of the water, and the medium is Huck's speech, written. Then there is the blundering bulk of the steamboat, either wreckage in *Huckleberry Finn,* the half-sunk *Walter Scott,* or wrecking, the juggernaut that comes down on the raft at the end of Chapter XVI, but which in "Old Times" is quite another thing, a large social construction deftly guided by dead-certain pilots who know the swerve and depth of the river. Raft and steamboat are relations to the river. Huck is down here, powerless, humbled by the force of the river, barely able to steer the raft, and the pilot is up there, aloft, empowered, proud, directing a vessel that is at once a small factory and a city. The contrast yields easily enough a paradigm in which we can locate the relation of the writer to his river.

The River is Huck's source: he is "snaked in out of the wet" at the end of *Tom Sawyer* and his first lesson in *Huckleberry Finn* is the story about Moses and the Bulrushers, the story of being landed, being born into an identity, the wrong one, a story he contemptuously rejects as being about "dead people." Huck's name, after all, is

Finn. Others have said as much: Huck is a fin in a waste of water, and by the story's end, having assumed other names, he will be Finn again. The River is his source; it is the site where he enjoys Being, where his experience is fluent. There is only the interposition of the raft, which the River idly bestows upon him, and this is his craft, his conveyance, clumsily guided, foolishly risked, almost lost, seemingly destroyed, but always reappearing, and then at last forgotten. We barely notice the raft, its changes, its transformations, this refuge which becomes a prison. It is the type of Huck's style, its unseen trope, the craft of his craft, elemental discourse simply functioning to signify, never calling attention to itself, just there, used, instrumental, and finally abandoned, used up. The raft, which means one thing to Jim, another to Huck, makes possible the playing forth of their drama. It is a material they work on, fix up, enhance (a lantern, an extra steering oar), and it is a way of life, liberating and confining, that becomes increasingly absurd. As we shall see, raft life, for all its biracial bonhomie, still holds implicit the black truth of an unspoken rift, a difference Huck will not at first acknowledge.

Confronting the River as his subject, his material, Mark Twain strives to evoke a sense of its ambiguous presence in "Old Times" and *Huckleberry Finn,* and at the same time keep before us the importance of the respective craft, whether steamboat or raft. The river is that which bears all, is sheltered in its own law, and always wrapped up in itself. So it passes through Mark Twain's fiction, concealing, revealing, always the same, but the "worlds" fashioned from it, upon it, are different. What the raft outlines, what it illumines, is the issue of Huck's style, this barely guided writing which passively follows the course of the river and tells each event in its totality. It, too, arises from a *Natur,* the nature of speech, the spoken language, and reflects the earthiness of the idiom in its diction, its syntax. And yet this writing is conflicted. Huck admires the "world" Tom Sawyer's 'style' creates, so he turns continually from Jim the raft-tender, the secret sharer, from their "world," to Tom for guidance, for motive, moral, and plot. Tom enters *Huckleberry Finn* by steamboat. He travels by steamboat. The raft will not budge for him; the river will not receive him. After all the perilous diversion of his play with Jim's fate, Tom, shot in the leg, reaches the raft, is on it, and immediately takes charge: "Man the sweeps, and set her loose" (*HF,* p. 344)! But the raft remains fixed, does not move, could not move. "He raised considerble row about it, but me and Jim stuck to it and wouldn't budge; so he was for crawling out and getting the raft loose himself; but we wouldn't let him" (*HF,* p. 345). Raft and raft-style are herein configured, and what shows through at the end of *Huckleberry Finn* is not the confusion of its themes, or the denial of its imperatives, but slippery, two-faced truth.

Rift, raft, reef. Huck is happiest when he is afloat, going nowhere. That is, when the river dissolves into a pure plenitude, when it is quiescent, simply the field or flow in which he exists. Only the raft, so given over the the river, can render this feeling. Only a writing, so given over to speech, can represent this feeling. The river that passes through "Old Times" is always problematical, reefstruck, clamorous, and what makes it so different, so distant, is the steamboat. On the raft, in his idiomatic prose, Huck feels the river. These instances always mark his regression toward finnytude, Huck's return to the primal lap, and they are, as we shall see, beautiful delusions only briefly sustained. In the steamboat, aloft, passing down instructions to the engineer, the pilot knows the river, and laments his loss of poetic feeling. Before his scrutiny the 'beautiful' river continually relapses into plain steamboat language, into discursive pilot prose. "The passenger who could not read it [the river] was charmed with a peculiar sort of faint dimple on its surface . . . but to the pilot that was an *italicized* passage; indeed, it was more than that, it was a legend of the largest capitals, with a string of shouting exclamation points at the end of it; for it meant that a wreck or a rock was buried there that could tear the life out of the strongest vessel that ever floated" (*OT,* pp. 91-92). The steamboat establishes the textuality of the river. It requires that the Mississippi be written (lettered or shaped in the pilot's mind) so that it may be read and translated into the terminology of the steamboat. "My boy," Bixby tells the cub pilot, "you must get a little memorandum book; and every time I tell you a thing, put it down right away. There's only one way to be a pilot, and that is to get this entire river by heart. You have to know it just like A B C" (*OT,* p. 75). This writing of the river, this reading of the river, constitutes the science of piloting, a complicated science that crucially involves the perception of *Gestalt,* the ability to figure the rift that appears in the river. So it is for the pilot, the question of the reef, the response of his craft. So it is for the writer who recuperates that earlier power of insight, finds the figure in his material, and applies it to his craft.

The River and the Steamboat, Nature and Culture, these two large imponderables in the literature of European and American Romanticism, are briefly resolved in "Old Times" by the deft mediation of piloting. As a humorist, Mark Twain had come upon a new subject: knowledge. At work on the second episode, "I Want To Be A Cub-Pilot," he wrote to Howells in 1874: "Its newness [the subject of piloting] pleases me all the time—and it is about the only new subject I know of" (*THL, p. 33*). Howells is there promptly to encourage him: "The piece about the Mississippi is capital—it almost made the water in our ice-pitcher muddy as I read it, and I hope to send you a proof directly." Yet he also recognized a certain tension in Mark Twain's exposition, a "hurried and anxious" note in the writing. "If I might put in my jaw at this point," he wrote, pointedly reminding Mark Twain of his appeal as a colloquial writer, "I should say, stick to actual fact and character in the thing, and give things in *detail*" (*THL, pp. 32-33*). The request is for vivacity, for local color, the freshness of a sketch, and yet serious topics had emerged in "Old Times." To an extent, in a different tone, in a distant style, Mark Twain was counting the same gains and losses Wordsworth had considered in "Lines, Composed a Few Miles above Tintern Abbey, on Revisiting the Banks of the Wye during a Tour, July 13, 1798." He, too, was looking at that "Mighty world/Of eye and ear,—both what they half create,/And what perceive."[11] Howell's advice speaks directly to this issue in Mark Twain's memoir, the problem of its direction. "Don't write *at* any supposed Atlantic audience, but yarn it off as if into my sympathetic ear" (*THL, p. 33*). Don't think, Howells effectively argues, feel. Yet "Old Times" is about thought, the *science* of piloting.

From the start Mark Twain wanted to change the title from "Old Times," which indeed suggests local color, the nostalgic recitation of place and person, and which might have brought to his mind, inappropriately, Harriet Beecher Stowe's *Oldtown Folks* (1869). "Let us change the heading," he proposes, "to '*Piloting* on the Miss in the Old Times'—or to '*Steamboating* on the M in the Old Times'—or to '*Personal* Old Times on the Missi'" (*THL, p. 33*). The new titles point to the "new subject," the new direction, which is away from history, from the pictorial effect of sketches, toward science, the activity of knowing. "Any muggins can write about Old Times on the Miss. of 500 different things," Mark Twain protests, "but I am the only man alive that can scribble about the piloting of that day—and no man has ever tried to scribble about it yet" (*THL,* p. 33). The "detail" Howells wanted is in "Old Times," and it is appealing, but the strength of the memoir lies in its abstraction. All the details, even the personalities of the pilots, refer to an immanent structure, a relation of three elements: River, pilot science, Steamboat. The title remains the same in the *Atlantic,* this is a piece by Mark Twain the humorist, but the memoir explores other reaches, turns in upon itself. The cub pilot at first confuses his texts, the scribbling of "things" in his notebook, Bixby's data, for the enigmatic scripture of the actual phenomena. He looks *to* Bixby, not *at* the river. We compound his mistake if we look for a revelation of the Mississippi in "Old Times," for the vivid picture, and fail to see that it is the abstract "shape" of the river, its structural function, and not the river itself, that is important.

Write the details of the river down in a book, Bixby tells the cub pilot, and then throw the book aside. Memorize the river as a throng of particulars and then forget their specificity. In all this contradiction Bixby redirects the cub pilot's gaze. Similarly Mark Twain redirects our gaze. This is a lesson in rereading the river, in rereading Mark Twain's text. The cub pilot must put aside his romantic preconception of the river, realize the limitation of empirical knowledge, which is merely collective, and above all he must stop predicating the Mississippi. Instead he must let the river speak, let *it* reveal what it conceals. There are its letters, its signs, which the Master Pilot then composes into sentences. These sentences are commands that guide the passage of the steamboat. Bixby is strong on this topic. The discourse of the river is *for* the steamboat. A Master Pilot never studies the river for itself, never loses himself in the mystery of its presence. He knows, moreover, that what he knows of the river is never *au courant,* however intensely memorized, because this Heraclitean river is never the same. What he has memorized down river and up river, by day and by night, in changing atmospheres, serves him simply as a ground against which change and difference appear, figure. He knows the ABC of the river as it was, as it should be, only to recognize how the dissembling present river is not the river he knows. So Bixby admonishes the cub pilot: "Always steer by the shape that's *in your head,* and never mind the one that's before your eyes" (*OT,* p. 84). Yet this reading, this way of perceiving the river, which discards the adequacy of direct observation, if not the principle of identity, A=A, is also limited. It drills the pilot's memory in the Same so that he will sharply see those interpolations of Difference, but on the Mississippi reality and appearance often share the same sign, a particular agitation of the river's surface. The wind reef is a "bluff," a sham, and the bluff reef is real, a reef. The cub pilot asks, "How am I ever going to tell them apart?" The Master Pilot replies, "I can't tell you. It is an instinct" (*OT,* p. 91). Bixby's withdrawal as the Master begins with this admission.

And here, across this unexplained rift in the text, the cub pilot suddenly speaks as a Master Pilot. "The face of the water, in time, became a wonderful book—a book that was a dead language to the uneducated passenger, but which told its mind to me without reserve, delivering its most cherished secrets as clearly as if it uttered them with a voice" (*OT,* p. 91). The pilot becomes an interpreter of the rift; he looks upon the rippling water, at the suspect reef, and comprehends the profound Unreason of the Mississippi. What follows is the much-quoted passage wherein the pilot says farewell to "the grace, the beauty, the poetry" (*OT,* p. 92) of the river. An innocence, which seems mostly an ignorance, is lost. The river has told him he can't know what he knows, that he himself, if only in the working of his memory, is like the river, a totality of forces mostly hidden, subvocal, subliterate, but incessant, perfect. "And how easily and comfortably the pilot's memory does its work; how placidly effortless is its way; how *unconsciously* it lays up its vast stores, hour by hour, day by day, and never loses or mislays a single valuable package of them all" (*OT,* p. 92)! Clever pilots, dull pilots, somnambulistic pilots, have equal access to this rich, resonating current of being—and to the oral tradition it inspires. For the pilots are continually telling each other about the river, discussing its changes, pooling their information. Mark Twain celebrates the pilot's feat of memorization in "Old Times," but with a significant reservation. The pilot's memory is brilliant *"only in the matters it is daily drilled in"* (*OT,* p. 111). It works for the steamboat, does not transcend that usage, and to this extent, as a science, it is bound to a specific historical phase, is perishable. The tale is briefly told at the close of "Old Times." So expert on the river at discerning the proper reef, the pilots are finally blind to the yawning rift that opens beneath them when they monopolize the profession, close rank, and seal their river knowledge in locked boxes on the various wharves. The science of piloting, as well as the practice, begins to decline in its intensity and value. Most of the pilots still understand the river, are good readers of its nuances, but what they do not adequately understand is the technology and commerce that places steamboats at their disposal. The pilots take their craft as a given, focus their gaze upon the river, and forget that it is the ephemeral steamboat that makes the eternal river speak to them.

Yet the brief moment of the pilot's absolute command on the Mississippi, the brief relevance of his science, is splendid, and Mark Twain, as we have seen, realized from the start the depth of its significance. If the pilot's knowledge of the river is ultimately mystical, magical, a wonder of memory and intuition, an act of faith, still that knowledge had to be translated into a discourse applicable to the engineered mass of the steamboat. Mythical thought, Lévi-Strauss's *pensée sauvage,* which knows the river intimately as a dwelling-place, which imaginatively "shapes" the river into a symbolic reality, speaks distinctly and efficiently to the boiler room, to that other world of turning gears, driving pistons, specialized labor (white scanning gauges, blacks shoveling coal), and the steamboat, a construction of scientific thought, energetically responds, thrusts itself *this* way upon the water. In the seam between Nature and Culture, between the silent dark river and the brightly-lit chuffing steamboat, the pilot mediates, adjusts force to force. He takes sightings, and he makes soundings. His science brings into rapport contradictory knowledges, each with its own distinctive precision, its own values, and the result is true direction, proper response. The steamboat depends on the pilot, trusts that he will be in touch with Nature, see through its cunning surface, and it rewards him by placing him there, high on the hurricane deck, by giving him a formidable coat with impressive buttons, and the right of swagger. Knowledge is here command. He has only to speak, and it is done. The pilot's labor does not alienate him. It glorifies him. His only superior is the River, is Being, is the Unknown. The steamboat is but the mechanism of the social world, a tiered, complex form of social exchange driven by a Comtean paddlewheel, which he guides. A pilot lives in both worlds:

the river out there is *in* his head, and he stands invincible on the hurricane deck.

Such is the myth of piloting, the myth of pilot science, almost a tall tale, and yet there is a flaw in the balance of this arrangement of forces, in this particular mediation. The pilot's eye, like his memory, is fixed on a practical experience of the river. He does not see beyond the specific watery track he must traverse, or realize the immensity of what the river still conceals, because to speak it, to sound *that* river, marking twain, he would have to leave his lexicon, learn another discourse. The pilot's memory is narrow, Mark Twain takes pains to remind us, narrow and mostly mechanical. Brown is an example, a pilot whose prosaic stream of consciousness is humorously spilled before us as a muddy flow of dull stories. The science of piloting conjoins two worlds, natural and civil, but the visionary extent of the privilege does not occur to the pilot. At the end of "Old Times" Mark Twain first presents the myth, "Rank and Dignity of Piloting," and then the flaw, "The Pilot's Monopoly." For a brief moment the pilot stands before us in his glory, "the only unfettered and entirely independent human being that lived on the earth" (*OT*, p. 116), and then History, that other fast-running river of social time and change, abruptly sweeps the pilot away, "in the twinkling of an eye, as it were" (*OT*, p. 130). The question of Mark Twain's own direction in "Old Times," so often the topic in his enthusiastic letters to Howells, reappears in this juxtaposition. What exactly is asserted, and to whom, when Mark Twain asserts with such hyperbolic force the rank and dignity of piloting? "Old Times" is a memoir in a popular genre, the reminiscence of a simpler time before the Civil War, and to that extent, as Howells shrewdly realized, just right for the *Atlantic,* yet obviously there are bigger fish in these waters, larger themes, which emerge. As the pilot stands in relation to the river, so the writer stands in relation to his writing. And all the while the river (as *ousia,* as *eidos*) ceaselessly generates texts: sentimental texts, dire texts, the literary text.

The turning point in "Old Times," as we have seen, is the running of the reef. When the pilot masters the lie of the wind reef, he loses forever the poetic texture of the river. He sees that Nature lies, a rift opens in the concept of natural beauty, a rift opens in his objective knowledge of the river, whereupon an innocence is lost. It is the pilot's finest moment, since what he loses aesthetically, what he loses cognitively, he regains instinctively, an appropriate sense of the river, an ability to surmount deception. In such crisis, bearing down on a dangerous crossing, thought fails, simple perception fails. The pilot is open to the river, open to himself. Mystery, *aletheia*. And then, across this moment, across this rupture, a new text, a technical text, structures the river for the beholder, severely designates it. "No, romance and beauty were all gone from the river. All the value any feature of it had for me now was the amount of usefulness it could furnish toward compassing the safe piloting of a steamboat" (*OT,* p. 93). Pilot science brings the pilot to this compass, and no further. His pride, therefore, depends to a large extent on his relative blindness. Don't look at the river out there, Bixby scolds the cub pilot, heed only the necessary river you've learned. The pilot sees what he sees truly enough for safe piloting, but he does not see how his vision is compassed, how the relation of the steamboat to the river spells the river out for him. Nor does he translate his reef research into psychological acumen, turn the lesson of his rift study back upon the working of his memory. Knowing the river does not make the pilot wise.

There is indeed a curious double vision in "Old Times." It is the writer who encompasses the science of piloting, who sees around it, and takes the measure of the pilot's achievement. Because he is distanced from the river, and painfully aware of the social form that guides his own discourse, the writer sees the parenthesis that brackets pilot science. The steamboat appears in the first episode; it is a large floating Vanity Fair, and it makes the science of piloting possible. In the final episode the steamboat disappears, displaced by the train and the tugboat, by other forms of transportation, and pilot science becomes a dead science. The pilot's river knowledge, his *rite de passage,* yields now simply a principle which the writer appropriates for his purposes. Yet the former pilot also takes the measure of the writer, considers the activity of writing, allows Mark Twain to turn back on his own text. Pilot science in its critical phase is, after all, rift study, an exact reading of what is different, what is discontinuous, in the known river. The pilot in his vessel on the river is obligated to know the truth and act upon it. The writer also faces in his material, in the unreeling spool of his memory, in the flow of his conscious thought, an enigmatic spread of meaning. He, too, must approach the contradiction of the rift, those crises where latent meaning lies hidden in manifest meaning, but where the pilot crosses, the writer modifies. Here Mark Twain briefly twists the analogy. "We write frankly and fearlessly, but then we 'modify' before we print." He goes on, pressing the point, showing his manacle: "In truth, every man and woman and child has a master, and worries and frets in servitude; but in the day I write of, the Mississippi pilot had *none*" (*OT*, p. 116). So the former pilot compels the present writer to make a sad admission. Other fettered writers may simply write on, comfortably ensconced in their chains, but *this* writer was once a pilot, once free, and *he* knows the extent of his alienation, his distance from the reality of the river.

What, then, is modified in "Old Times"? The profanity of the steamboatmen is given in dashes. We do not see the rich local color of actual life on a steamboat. That curtain remains drawn. No one deals a card in "Old Times," or lifts a skirt. But the world below the hurricane deck, that vivid gallery a pilot knew when he was off watch, is not really in the purview of Mark Twain's "new subject." Mark Twain, the former pilot, has in mind a broader reference when he stresses the inhibition of those other guides who steer craft in the public domain, the editor who utters "only half or two thirds of his mind," the clergyman who never speaks the "whole truth" (*OT*, p. 116) in his sermons, the writer who modifies. The small case of expunging profanity is always a mock issue for Mark Twain, a blind for his awareness of larger concessions to the popular style, in which lies the polite discretion of the *Atlantic* style. *You whitewash reality*, this is the pilot's accusation, *you seek to please a master, that Other who gives you recognition.* Near the end of "Old Times" Mark Twain effectively returns to the question he had exposed in *Tom Sawyer*, but this speaker is not an entertainer, the humorist who genially admires the play of deception. It is a river scientist who begins his sentences with "The reason is plain" (*OT*, p. 116), and "In truth," who is responsible only to his data, to what his subject shows.

Here, between *Tom Sawyer* and *Huckleberry Finn*, writing his first long piece as a *"subtile* humorist" for the *Atlantic*, just here Mark Twain writes about *knowledge, direction, rank,* and *dignity.* The memoir painstakingly retraces a crossing, the cub pilot's *rite de passage*, and the writing of it is itself, for the writer, a similar crossing. Ten years before, in 1865, Mark Twain had confessed to Orion Clemens that he had "a 'call' to literature, of a low order—i.e.

humorous,"[12] and here he is, the low humorist risen, literary, a serious writer no longer playing the fool, the innocent. Howells would nominate this new Mark Twain in the *Atlantic,* call him a *"subtile humorist,"* and point out the "growing seriousness of meaning in the apparently unmoralized drolling"[13] present in his work. Yet the pilot identity Mark Twain assumes in "Old Times" to differentiate himself as a humorous writer, to assert his authority, also serves to distance him from the suspect role of a 'serious' literary writer. To this extent the pilot is simply a rhetorical figure Mark Twain manipulates in order to assert the pure eccentricity of his art. In the guise of the pilot, Mark Twain steers his craft over wind reef and around bluff reef, between his Scylla and Charybdis, the conflicting demands: to be funny, to be serious. "You could have drawn a seine through his system," he writes of Bixby, who has just exhausted himself swearing at a blundering trading scow, "and not caught curses enough to disturb your mother with." What immediately follows is Bixby's sober injunction: "There's only one way to be a pilot, and that is to get this entire river by heart. You have to know it just like A B C" (*OT*, p. 75). In such swift and deft motion, Mark Twain's discursive prose achieves what Henry Nash Smith calls the "middle style," not vernacular, not rhetorical, but a style that humorously holds both elements in an opportune tension.

Everything, then, is doubled in "Old Times," reflected. The pilot speaks to the innocence of the cub pilot, and deprives him of it. He speaks to the knowledge of the writer, and makes the writer rattle his chain in the pages of the *Atlantic.* At another place in "Old Times," river borne, patiently sounding deeps and shallows, reading reefs, the pilot speaks directly to the artist about his art. As Mark Twain summons him, so he summons Mark Twain. He is severe, not unlike the tutelary wraiths who appear in classical literature, and he re-presents the river to Mark Twain, he re-poses the science of piloting, the river as text, a text already-written. The river now again begins to flow, to signify, and Mark Twain has the *praxis,* the science, to read it. He has only to get closer to it, off the steamboat, as it were, and find a new relation to it. "The piloting material," he writes to Howells early in 1875, "has been uncovering itself by degrees, until it has exposed such a huge hoard to my view that a whole book will be required to contain it if I use it" (*THL,* p. 41). Such excitement. It is indeed Mark Twain's relation to his work, which uncovers itself by degrees, that is at issue in this important period before he begins to write Huck's speech.

River, Memory, Material: it is always there, pouring, present, and if the form, the vessel, the craft, the prow that cuts into it, grounds itself on a reef, "you've only to leave it alone and it will fill up again in time, while you are asleep—also while you are at work at other things and are quite unaware that this unconscious and profitable cerebration is going on."[14] In 1906, dictating his autobiography, Mark Twain would return to the metaphorical charting of "Old Times," to that triadic structure of River-Pilot-Vessel, and re-summon the pilot as his guide, his exemplar. Just as the river is already-written, a text to be read, A B C, so the book writes itself, uncovers itself, is already spoken. The pilot-writer simply mediates, interprets the river, translates his reading into steamboat language, formalizes it. But this mediation is always precarious. Something will happen. Something will break the trance of the writer's knowledge. Mark Twain indicates his present "literary shipyard" where some five projects lie "neglected and baking in the sun." "As long as a book would write itself I was a faithful and interested amanuensis and my industry did not flag," he reports, "but the minute that the book tried to shift to *my* head the labor of contriving its situations, inventing its adventures and conducting its conversations, I put it away and dropped it out of my mind" (*AMT*, p. 288). On the river, in the mind, there are reefs and there are rifts. Although his specific reference is to *Tom Sawyer*, Mark Twain roughly describes here the interrupted composition of *Huckleberry Finn*, that most difficult of river passages: where he writes raftily, loose upon the tide, pilotless, powerless. Significant rifts occur in this book, displacements of the raft, those instances where the narrative broke off and Mark Twain put the manuscript aside, and the question in *Huckleberry Finn*, the problem of these rifts, is always whether the narrative, once it starts up again, is refloated, goes over the reef-rift, or around it.

That Mark Twain could at last bring such intricate topics and difficult issues within the compass of a humorous style, rethink humorous knowledge, and draw an appropriate expression from the style, is the wonder of his achievement at this critical moment in his career, this crossing. He had written the whitewashing episode in 1872, sketching it out in London. In effect, the scene precedes his work on the final version of *Tom Sawyer*. It is still perhaps the most widely known passage in his work, the very signature of his humor. Yet between 1872 and 1876, Mark Twain's sense of humor changes. "Wherein does its greatness lie?" Lionel Trilling asks of *Huckleberry Finn.* "Primarily in its power of telling the truth."[15] After *Tom Sawyer,* that boy's book written for adults, whitewashing as the model of humorous thought is no longer applicable. The science of piloting, that study of reefy rifts, now becomes the intelligence of Mark Twain's humorous writing.

Notes

1. Mark Twain, *The Adventures of Tom Sawyer* (New York and London, 1976), p. 15. All subsequent reference will be indicated *TS.*

2. *Selected Mark Twain—Howells Letters, 1872-1910,* ed. Frederick Anderson, William M. Gibson, Henry Nash Smith (New York, 1968), pp. 48-49. All subsequent reference will be indicated *THL.*

3. James M. Cox, *Mark Twain: The Fate of Humor* (Princeton, 1966), p. 147. All subsequent reference will be indicated *MTFH.*

4. Mark Twain, *The Innocents Abroad* (New York, 1966), p. 458.

5. Mark Twain and Charles Dudley Warner, *The Gilded Age* (New York, 1964), p. 428.

6. *Selected Shorter Writings of Mark Twain,* p. 52. All subsequent reference will be indicated *SWMT.*

7. "Old Times on the Mississippi," in *Selected Shorter Writings,* p. 91. All subsequent reference will be indicated *OT.*

8. Henry Nash Smith, *Mark Twain, The Development of a Writer* (Cambridge: The Belknap Press, 1962), pp. 77-78. All subsequent reference will be indicated *MTDW.*

9. Edgar J. Burde, "Mark Twain: The Writer as Pilot," *PMLA,* 93 (1978), 880. All subsequent reference will be indicated *MTWP.*

10. Jacques Derrida, *Of Grammatology,* trans. Gayatri Chakravorty Spivak (Baltimore and London: Johns Hopkins Univ. Press, 1976), p. 167. All subsequent reference will be indicated *OG.* The doleful contradiction into which Derrida at first places Rousseau in the *Grammatology,* writing against writing, becomes comic when Derrida exhibits it in Rousseau's pedagogy. Here, in the writing-lesson, whose lesson is alienation from feeling, Rousseau is exposed, struggles in his insufficient thinking with the problem of imitation, and, before relentless Derridean interrogation, can only fudge the issue. *"For Rousseau the concept of the child is always related to the sign. More precisely, childhood is the non-relation to the sign as such.* But what is a sign as such? There is no sign as such. Either the sign is considered a thing, and it is not a sign. Or it is a reference, and thus not itself. According to Rousseau, the child is the name of that which should not relate in any way to a separated signifier, loved in some way for itself, like a fetish. This perverse use of the signifier is in a certain way at once forbidden and tolerated by the structure of imitation. As

White Lies, Bluff Reefs

soon as a signifier is no longer imitative, undoubtedly the threat of perversion becomes acute. But already within imitation, the gap between the thing and its double, that is to say between the sense and its image, assures a lodging for falsehood, falsification, and vice'' (pp. 204-205). The schoolmaster in *Emile* is, of course, spared the questioning of such a brightly demonic pupil. We can see, easily enough, that conceptual tension in Mark Twain's imagination as he renders the difference in Huck and Tom, a difference at once established in Rousseauistic terms (Huck has yet to grasp the ruse of metaphor, get a genie from the rubbed lamp) and ironically compromised. For even as Huck names himself a child in the text, the retrospection of his writing places him elsewhere. He has followed the bad example of Tom Sawyer, followed Tom into the Supplement, and become a writer.

11. *The Complete Poetical Works of William Wordsworth,* ed. A. J. George (Boston and New York, 1904), p. 92.

12. *My Dear Bro: A Letter from Samuel Clemens to His Brother Orion,* ed. Frederick Anderson (Berkeley: Berkeley Albion, 1961), p. 6.

13. William Dean Howells, *My Mark Twain* (New York and London, 1910), p. 121.

14. *The Autobiography of Mark Twain,* ed. Charles Neider (New York, 1961), p. 289. All subsequent reference will be indicated *AMT.*

15. Lionel Trilling, *The Liberal Imagination* (New York and London, 1978), p. 101.

IV

Huckspeech

> Due allowance being made for the sounds of language, *writing aloud*
> is not phonological but phonetic; its aim is not the clarity of mes-
> sages, the theater of emotions; what it searches for (in a perspective
> of bliss) are the pulsional incidents, the language lined with flesh, a
> text where we can hear the grain of the throat, the patina of conso-
> nants, the voluptuousness of vowels, a whole carnal stereophony:
> the articulation of the body, of the tongue, not that of meaning, of
> language.
>
> Roland Barthes, *The Pleasure of the Text*

> My souls, how the wind did scream along! And every second or two
> there'd come a glare that lit up the white-caps for a half a mile
> around, and you'd see the islands looking dusty through the rain,
> and the trees thrashing around in the wind; then comes a *h-wack!*
> bum! bum! bumble-umble-um-bum-bum-bum-bum — and the thunder
> would go rumbling and grumbling away, and quit — and then *rip*
> comes another flash, and another sockdolager. The waves most
> washed me off the raft, sometimes, but I hadn't any clothes on, and
> didn't mind.
>
> Mark Twain, *Adventures of Huckleberry Finn*

1

First, then, to close the two words: Huck's speech, written as
spoken, talked into prose, becomes Huckspeech, a new style in the
humorous mode. It signifies, in whichever text it appears, *Ursprache*,
Original Language, First Presence of Self-Consciousness, the almost-
voice of an almost-child, wary innocence, an almost-innocence. It is
written at once in the vulgate, as *common* speech, and in the vernacular, which it assumes in the purest sense of its original meaning,
as the homely speech of home-born slaves. That is, Huck speaks a
familiar speech spoken all around us at all times, the speech of the
illiterate, the speech of the preliterate, of the poor, and of children,
which, in its proper place, is charming, but which is also, in other
places, in the schoolroom, in courts of law, inadequate, wrong, the
excluded language of the vulnerable, the ignorant, the innocent. It

96

is emotionally rite and socially rong, a paradox Huck enters when he begins to write his story down, as he would speak it, and the mistakes appear. Speech wrongs writing. Writing wrongs speech. In *Huckleberry Finn*, to use Hosea Biglow's happy phrase, but in a double sense, Huck tries on a "noo soot of close," and the fit is often tight, often smothery. Huck's speech is thus written, miswritten, and becomes Huckspeech, Mark Twain's raft style.

To keep us straight before Huck's funny *felix culpa*, Mark Twain, the sophisticated composer of Huck's naive style, makes certain we perceive his authority as a linguist. There are several dialects spoken in the style: "the Missouri negro dialect; the extremest form of the South-Western dialect; the ordinary 'Pike-County' dialect; and four modified varieties of this last." It is his last word in *Huckleberry Finn*, this brief *Explanatory* which assures us that Huckspeech, which might otherwise seem a loose approximation of the idiom, is in fact worked, composed, *written.* "The shadings have not been done in a haphazard fashion, or by guess-work; but pains-takingly, and with the trustworthy guidance and support of personal familiarity with these several forms of speech" (*HF*, p. 7). So we are to appreciate the music of the style, the exactitude of its intonation, but for Huck, who writes it, speech, *his* speech, is simply the expression of his feeling, the only language he has, and bereft of aesthetic value. It is the speech of the slave, the abject, those outside, and Huck has had sufficient schooling to know that from the inside, to know at least the meaning of *sivilize.* Jim clarifies the term for him, but so, too, does Pap Finn, who will knock the book from Huck's hand, and curse him for his "starchy clothes." It is a nervous tic, this first and last misspelling, *sivilize.*

In *Tom Sawyer,* where Huck is still very much the pig son of his swinish father, Huck's speech is regarded as a seduction, and prohibited. Why are you late? the schoolmaster demands of Tom, and when Tom confesses that he stopped to talk to Huckleberry Finn on the way to school, the teacher is aghast. " 'You—you did what?' 'Stopped to talk with Huckleberry Finn' " (*TS,* p. 51). A severe whipping immediately follows. Huck is "cordially hated" by the mothers of St. Petersburg, who dread his influence, who fear contamination. Pap Finn sleeps with the hogs in the tanyard, and Huck himself sleeps in "empty hogsheads," is the "son of the town drunkard," is "idle, and lawless, and vulgar, and bad" (*TS,* p. 45), is Pap's piggish boy. Huck's speech is necessarily unclean. The character described in *Tom Sawyer* has indeed a lively career elsewhere in contemporary manuals of sexual hygiene where he appears as the archetype of the evil companion. When J. H. Kellogg (who would later discover the cornflake) cites the thirty-nine "Suspicious Signs" of self-abuse in *Plain Facts For Old and Young* (1879-1886), the listing reads as an index of Huckish traits: lassitude, love of solitude, shambling gait, use of tobacco, easily frightened, sleeplessness, confusion of ideas, unchastity of speech. In *Huckleberry Finn* the Widow Douglas and Miss Watson throw the appropriate books at Huck, the Bible and the Speller, and Huck appropriately judges their "book-larnin" with the wry skepticism of his "mother-wit." It is the Writing Lesson, a familiar routine in American humor, and Huck is typically recalcitrant, but the issue of the exchange is problematical. The lesson is learned. In *Tom Sawyer* Huck's illiteracy is the sign of his freedom; he does not go to school, he does not submit to the arbitrary imposition of rules, he possesses the license of speech, but he has come in from out the wet in *Huckleberry Finn,* and he does learn to write. Huck even becomes a good student, winning a "little blue and yaller picture of some cows and a boy" for "learning my lessons good" (*HF,* pp. 40-41). The lesson is learned, and in writing, looking outside back at the river, at the raft, Huck discovers the magnitude of the lesson.

The simple distinction of vulgar speech and polite writing that constitutes the "funattick" play of humorous writing in the Jacksonian period, a distinction that juxtaposes the stiff, self-conscious, professorial writing of a Parson Wilbur and the rough yarn of Sut Lovingood's unruly speech, is exquisitely complicated in Huckspeech, confused. Perched in writing, barely in writing, Huck is torn between the two systems of value, the two discourses, between Jim and Tom, between Pap and the Widow, and it is the perfect anxiety of this conflict that makes the style of *Huckleberry Finn* different, a transformation. Huckspeech emerges from the humorous style, the style of Lowell and Harris, of Artemus Ward and Josh Billings, overtakes it, reveals its phunny phonocentrism as unfunny alienation, and this is the pain, the hurtful brick, that hits Huck at the start of his narrative, that makes the project of its humor doubtful. In another sense, contextually, the style reflects in its tension Mark Twain's own anxieties as a writer and a humorist. It is, after all, the Mark Twain of

Tom Sawyer, that affable whitewasher, who is immediately summoned into Huckspeech, judged a liar, and then forgiven. *Huckleberry Finn* effectively begins with a critical reading of *Tom Sawyer,*
with a certain knowledge of its mystification.

> You don't know about me, without you have read a
> book by the name of "The Adventures of Tom Sawyer,"
> but that ain't no matter. That book was made by Mr. Mark
> Twain, and he told the truth, mainly. There was things
> which he stretched, but mainly he told the truth. That is
> nothing. I never seen anybody but lied, one time or
> another, without it was Aunt Polly, or the widow, or
> maybe Mary. Aunt Polly—Tom's Aunt Polly, she is—and
> Mary, and the Widow Douglas, is all told about in that
> book—which is mostly a true book; with some stretchers,
> as I said before. (*HF,* p. 17)

Huck has read the book, examined this humorous representation
of the adventures of boyhood, and seen what it leaves out, what it
evades. His critique of Mark Twain's writing is the critique of the
pilot in "Old Times." Writers 'modify' the truth. What, then, does
Mark Twain stretch, 'modify,' in *Tom Sawyer?* Things. "There was
things which he stretched, but mainly he told the truth." Huck
understands the necessity for 'white' lies, having witnessed in the
great world the prevalence of deception, and yet *this* narrative is
reliable. So Huck begins, asserting the difference of his text. So Mark
Twain begins, setting Huck free. And the first thing Huck does, at his
safe distance, is to give his liberator the lie. It is a hazard, the withdrawal of authority. The humorist is excluded, and so, too, is the
work of his humor, stretching the truth. If we are to look at *Huckleberry Finn* as a humorous text, we must then distinguish its humor
from the humor of *Tom Sawyer.* Mark Twain's functional shift from
third to first person signifies a corresponding shift in his sense of
humor. Huck is alone in the liberation of his plain style. It is a large
irony, and a severe task. Everything that is repressed in *Tom Sawyer,*
or humorously manipulated, returns in *Huckleberry Finn,* amplified
—these "things," but by the end of Huck's opening passage, having
invoked the truth as his criterion, Huck is without the defenses of
humor, bare to his experience.

The humorist, of course, is still there in the text, but he appears in
the diminished figure and reckless activity of Tom Sawyer. He is

present not as the happy resolver of difficult situations, as the complicit liar, but as a part of the problem, the source of Huck's confinement. That humor which professes the innocence of Tom's play speaks falsely in Huckspeech. It can only speak through its favored creature, Tom, and what an awful constraint it is, to have Tom as a mouthpiece. As we have seen, Huck begins his story by carefully separating himself from the fiction of *Tom Sawyer,* and yet Tom is immediately present to lure him back into the humorous world of make-believe, the safe world where the Dark-Man is always at last locked up, sealed off, killed. We might again ask, after Freud, who speaks in Tom's discourse. It would seem to be the consoling Superego, urging substitution, displacement, sublimation, the Good Genie, except that in Huckspeech the superegotistical voice is fatally compromised. What the humorist says here inevitably appears as contradiction, the sign of danger, not security. "But Tom Sawyer, he hunted me up and said he was going to start a band of robbers, and I might join if I would go back to the widow and be respectable" (*HF,* pp. 17-18). It is the humorist's consummate trick: no villainy in this villainy, no wrong in this wrong. The overt question of Huck's adventure is whether he can humorously forgive himself, having actually overturned the categories of right and wrong. Within the intersubjective drama of the style another question emerges, whether Huck can forgive Tom's sense of humor.

So Huck begins inside the risk of narrative; so Mark Twain begins an inside narrative. A double set of brackets incloses the proper text of *Huckleberry Finn,* the first and last *sivilize* (the unregenerate expression of preliterate consciousness) and Tom's first and last usurpation of Huck's writing, these reimpositions of motive, moral, and plot, the 'literary' play of his fictions. In Huckspeech Mark Twain appropriates the structure of the humorous style, but not to yield its humor—to question it. The style is placed over the earlier style, like a semi-transparent overlay, and what we see is the subtle disparity, a telling incongruence, how this routine, seemingly so like the other routine, is still different, elaborated. Just as the Widow Douglas teaches Huck about Moses and the Bulrushers, so Huck, after the 'adventure' on the wrecked steamboat, teaches Jim about the wisdom of Sollermun. Mark Twain draws upon familiar forms in both exchanges, on the Writing Lesson and its corollary number in the minstrel show. Here the learned throw books at the unlearned,

Parson Wilbur hurls Goldsmith and Pope at Hosea Biglow, and the Interlocutor's stiff question gets a supple response from Mr. Bones. In *Huckleberry Finn* Tom is the principal book-thrower, brick-hurler. " 'Do you want to go to doing different from what's in the books, and get things all muddled up' " he demands. " 'Don't you reckon that the people that made the books knows what's the correct thing to do' " (*HF*, p. 27)? When Huck teaches Jim about Sollermun, he repeats the lesson of authority he has learned. He throws the book at Jim, but promptly it comes back. " 'Doan talk to me 'bout Sollermun, Huck, I knows him by de back' " (*HF*, p. 112). What indeed is the mastery of the Book, the dead letter, over Life? What book will explain to Jim the master/slave relationship, the right of kings to have harems, the right to separate children from their parents? Jim easily deflects Huck's presumption of authority, but he is at the mercy of Tom's books, those romances of captivity and escape, which immure him. Each consequent turn of the exchange in the narrative lessens its humor and increases its seriousness. Within the brackets, the closure of Huck's writing, is the river, the raft, Jim, the scene of Huck's initiation. The knowledge he gains there is played against the lesson he learns in the Writing Lesson, and Jim is the teacher, and Jim's lesson is the hardest.

2

The constant crisis in *Huckleberry Finn* is the urgent issue of direction, of destination. What does Huck want? Where is Huck going? The question of direction is also the crisis of *Huckleberry Finn*, since each literal and thematic interruption of the narrative constitutes a significant rift in the text, and each rift is an ordeal for Huck, an ordeal for Mark Twain. What is the course of *Huckleberry Finn* as a humorous text? Its composition, begun, deferred, written in spasms of energy, indicates the imaginative stresses Mark Twain experienced as a practicing humorist. Any close reading of *Huckleberry Finn* must take into account the bricolage of its construction, its crooked seams, its changing conception of itself. Mark Twain wrote roughly the first sixteen chapters in 1876, breaking off just as Huck and Jim struggle toward Cairo, the missed point of Jim's liberation; then the bulk of the middle section in 1879-1880, including Huck's soliloquy on the truth of Jim's meaning; and finally in 1883 the controversial ending. The truth of Jim's meaning, which figures so largely in the politics of *Huckleberry Finn,* which keeps Huck from writing the bad letter, passes through these three sections as the Brick of bricks. Jim is hard perdurable pain, the spook of guilt, unresolved, omnipresent, that figure of suffering which is outside the authority of writing, which, when written (by Tom), can only be wronged. Because Huckspeech is barely in writing, a styleless style 'open' to speech values, to the idiom, to slave talk, Jim 'speaks' in the style, but, as we shall see, mostly between Huck's lines. He is a large brick, indeed the largest brick in American life, and thrown right through the book.

Bang. The task of the humorist, we know, is to wring the bliss of love from the pain of the brick. This transformation is what humor is for. And indeed Huck never ceases to love Jim, never ceases to love Tom. Yet the humorist is not in *Huckleberry Finn* to work this transformation for us. The style excludes him. He can only speak through Tom's foolery, as the poorest of whitewashers, the unfunny humorist. The burden given to Huck is therefore too heavy for his simple discourse to bear, too big for this low style. In the *Biglow Papers,* it will be remembered, Lowell "feared the risk of seeming to vulgarize a deep and sacred conviction" (*BP,* p. 200) and created Parson Wilbur to convey in appropriate discourse his principled attack on slavery. For Mark Twain, however, the very limitation of the low style is opportune. Such is the beauty of Huckspeech as a humorous style, that it continually breaks down, fails to generate pleasure from unpleasure, fails to find the necessary fiction. Up a tree, Huck watches the Shepherdsons shoot at the wounded Grangerford boys, one of whom is a child. "It made me so sick I most fell out of the tree. I ain't agoing to tell *all* that happened—it would make me sick again if I was to do that." Huck can only endure the slaughter, see it as it is, suffer it. "I ain't ever going to get shut of them—lots of times I dream about them" (*HF,* p. 154). And how, humorously, to get around the throbbing headache of what to do about Jim. Bricks fly in Huckspeech, and hit, and hurt, a fact which makes Huck long for the comfort of Tom's 'style,' for Tom's manipulative ebullience. Tom will resolve the problem of Jim for us, give us the right ending, but the ending is written in Huckspeech, and Huckspeech is always fated to get this humorous resolution rong. So Jim's ordeal, Huck's guilt, this big brick, comes through the text, misses Tom, who doesn't even see it, slips through Huckspeech, and perversely strikes us as a problem.

Jim is the wrench, the sudden turn, that takes *Huckleberry Finn* out of one humorous mode into another, one not yet mapped or charted, from simple to serious humor. It is a question of direction, a question that could not occur to Tom, but which is for Huck the only question, intricate, delicate, deep, and to which, paradoxically, the text itself is the response. Conjoined on the raft, by the raft, headed South to get North, Huck and Jim are going in different directions. Jim is going to Cairo, into the socio-political world, into *Uncle Tom's Cabin,* or Francis Grierson's *The Valley of Shadows,* where he will find work, try to make sufficient money to buy his family out of bondage, perhaps even associate with Abolitionists. "I owns mysef," Jim declares on Jackson's Island, "en I's wuth eight hund'd dollars" (*HF,* p. 73). Miss Watson's perfidy has taught him to calculate, and Cairo, the free state, is Jim's destination. This is not where Huck wants to go, and it slowly dawns on him, gradually comes to him, that Cairo is where he is going. "We would sell the raft," he reports in Chapter XV, "and get on a steamboat and go way up the Ohio amongst the free States, and then be out of trouble" (*HF,* p. 115). The "miserableness" of this scheme is soon apparent. With his goal in sight, Jim loosens up; he is free in his speech; he talks openly about his intentions; he speaks as a determined and clear-headed adult, and Huck, alarmed, suddenly beholds their difference. Jim is self-present in his speech, in himself, for himself, and this is not funny, familiar slave talk, nor does this Jim take into account Huck's priorities, Huck's needs.

The raft is for Huck the end of his journey, the place where his "free and easy" river world is regained, but for Jim raft and river are primarily the means of his deliverance elsewhere. It is not as Huck figured it: " 'They're after us' " (*HF,* p. 92)! *They* are only after Jim. It is rather as Jim figured it: "He said that when I went in the texas and he crawled back to get on the raft and found her gone, he nearly died; because he judged it was all up with *him* anyway it could be fixed; for if he didn't get saved he would get drownded; and if he did get saved, whoever saved him would send him back home so as to get the reward, and then Miss Watson would sell him South, sure." Huck faithfully records in italics the careful and suggestive distinction Jim makes, *him,* and almost, at that point, understands *him.* "Well, he was right; he was most always right; he had an uncommon level head, for a nigger" (*HF*, p. 109). Above Cairo Huck at last completely understands the significance of Jim's flight. The nigger mask is down. "He wouldn't ever dared to talk such talk in his life before" (*HF*, p. 124). It is the most chilling moment in *Huckleberry Finn*, Jim's brief lapse from the "funattick" play of humorous dialect into the integrity of self-determined discourse, and the quick-freeze of Huck's heart. Here, first in his outrage and then in a single choice, the inversion of white and black, right and wrong, Huck falls from innocence.

In the same movement Mark Twain substantively changes the project of humor. Huck falls out of his humor. He looks upon the jubilant Jim with pure hatred. An ungrateful Jim is going away, and the appropriate racist remark comes promptly to Huck's mind: ". . . . 'give a nigger an inch and he'll take an ell' " (*HF*, p. 124). Everything out there, on the Shore, in the Supplement, is self-alienating, laborious: Civilization, Writing, Authority, clocks, tight clothes, hard chairs. The supple place to which Huck has fled, this found raft, should be the opposed pastoral site, innocent, harmonious, the other-world afloat on the Simple Being of the river, good, and would be, could be, if Jim were to play his part. But just as Huck extricates himself from Tom's fiction, so Jim doesn't fit in Huck's fantasies. A runaway slave constantly living in dire peril is not a good companion for a white boy wanting to lead a free and easy life on a raft. It is a thing Huck never properly sees, that the greatest threat to his raft life, the very center of his narrative, is Jim, not steamboat or charlatan. Jim can share the raft as a domicile, as a hiding-place, but he remains apart from Huck's conception of raft life. For Jim the raft is ultimately a prison as small as the shed in which he is finally kept. He is boarded up on the raft, confined to it, and once Cairo is missed, he is nailed to it, exposed and humiliated on it. So, too, would the raft become a prison for Huck, regressive, a confinement in an earlier mode of self-absorption, if Jim were to leave it. Alone on Jackson's Island at the start of his narrative, and 'free,' Huck is quickly bored. It is truly as the beloved that Jim denies Huck the innocent play of the raft, denies him his 'adventures,' and instead draws Huck from that play into the story of his own unmitigated suffering. As the little Moses cast upon the flood, Huck must go forward into the larger, older, tragic world. So he must fall out of humor, from innocence, and sacrifice the rapture of the raft.

Huckspeech

Et in Arcadia ego. It is Huck's line in *Tom Sawyer*; it is Jim's line in *Huckleberry Finn.* It is what they come to mean in each text, the problem of the *other* in paradise, the ignoble savage who wrongs the myth, who refuses to be written in the convenient style. A mythy haze often obscures the particularity of Huck's raft life, the sub-scription of Jim's problematical presence, and in this haze Huck's motives take on an impossible purity. We are easily pulled into Huck's trance, into the current of this dream, the myth of presence, the myth of origin. The style itself, Huckspeech, so like the raft in construction and motion, takes us there. Tony Tanner's reading of the myth in *The Reign of Wonder* (1965) is exemplary:

> To get at the root significance of this feeling for the raft, for lazying, for nakedness and relaxation it is worth recalling the import of the symbolism of the Sabbath Ritual. The ban on all forms of work not only celebrates God's day of rest after the labour of creation, it symbol-izes a state of harmony between man and nature, that paradisiacal state which existed before Adam brought sin and work into the world. Work disturbs the man-nature equilibrium and reveals the extent of our immersion and imprisonment; the almost immobile "rest" of the Sabbath is a temporary escape from time and process, an anticipa-tion of the Messianic time (which is called the time of "continuous Sabbath") of true freedom, peace and har-mony.[1]

This longing for the "continuous Sabbath," as Tanner amply indicates, is everywhere in Mark Twain's writing. To get out of work and into play is Tom Sawyer's principal labor. In *Roughing It* Mark Twain lovingly describes the sumptuous leisure of a loose life at Lake Tahoe. Yet the Arcadian desire that creates the paradisiacal scene, delights in Lake Tahoe's pristine clarity, relishes languor, is looked straight through in "Old Times." The knowing pilot realizes the charm of such idyllic representation, but he can no longer take it seriously. Indeed this yearning for a "continuous Sabbath" is general-ly a humorous topic for Mark Twain, and disposed in contexts that show it as the illusion of travelers, the lust of tourism. For example, Mark Twain takes the raft metaphor to Germany, borrows Huck's raft revery for an imaginary trip down the Neckar, and replays it for us in *A Tramp Abroad* (1880) as a lullaby:

The motion of a raft is the needful motion; it is gentle, and gliding, and smooth, and noiseless; it calms down all feverish activities, it soothes to sleep all nervous hurry and impatience; under its restful influence all the troubles and vexations and sorrows that harass the mind vanish away, and existence becomes a dream, a charm, a deep and tranquil ecstasy.[2]

For the humorist the raft is now purely the implement of a myth, and so it functions in *A Tramp Abroad*, exhibiting other myths. It floats, unfurls German scenery, is the prop on which Mark Twain humorously rehashes the local river legends: "The Cave of the Spectre," "The Lorelei," "Legend of the 'Spectacular Ruin,'" "Legend of Dilsberg Castle." A grown-up Tom Sawyer at last gets to ride the raft in his style.

"A DEEP AND TRANQUIL ECSTASY."
Mark Twain, *A Tramp Abroad*, Hartford, Conn., 1880, p. 129.

Yet there is a moment on this contrived sojourn when Mark Twain brings the Huckish meaning of the raft directly into view. The two gents loll on the raft, "with our sun umbrellas over our heads and our legs dangling in the water," watching naked children cavort on the passing shore.

> The little boys swam out to us sometimes, but the little maids stood knee-deep in the water, and stopped their splashing and frolicking to inspect the raft with their innocent eyes as it drifted by. Once we turned a corner suddenly, and surprised a slender girl of twelve years or upwards, just stepping into the water. She had not time to run, but she did what answered just as well; she promptly drew a lithe young willow bough athwart her white body with one hand, and then contemplated us with a simple and untroubled interest. Thus she stood while we glided by. (*ATA*, pp. 110-111)

It is a little vision, almost prurient, and it is Huck's reality, Huck's wide-eyed childish gaze that briefly meets Mark Twain's look in *A Tramp Abroad*. To be naked, to be at ease in nakedness, shy but shameless, this in part is Huck's feeling on the raft, and the luxury of the raft style. The two gents under their parasols contemplate the naked children sporting on the bank, the charm of it, the innocence of it, and then the girl "of twelve years or upwards, just stepping into the water," suddenly appears, and we look, not quite so innocently as before, at her almost-innocence, the "lithe young willow bough." Huck stands on that verge, precariously. At the start of *Huckleberry Finn* Tom summons a relapsed Huck from his "old rags" and "sugar-hogshead," routs him out of the womblike barrel, Huck's home, and drives him back with false promises into the custody of the Widow Douglas. There the "old thing" begins again, the fundamental processes of civilization: tight clothes, regular hours, proper instruction. Huck can read his destiny on his dinner plate, that simple sentence whose parts of speech are meat, potato, vegetable, each portion "cooked by itself." He knows what this "old thing" is: the suppression of instinct, the displacement of desire, division. "In a barrel of odds and ends it is different; things get mixed up, and the juice kind of swaps around, and the things go better" (*HF*, p. 18). To be sivilized is to sexually zoned, to be finny is to be sexually latent. A nymph at waterside. Huck's rebellion begins here, with the squirm and discomfort of his body. After supper come the books, the Bible and the Speller; declarations of right and wrong as distinct in their lesson as the segregated food on Huck's plate.

The Writing Lesson indeed takes two forms at the beginning of *Huckleberry Finn*. Miss Watson and the Widow, who have inconsistent interpretations of Providence, throw the Good Book at Huck. Tom asserts the primacy of the bad book. His pirate and robber books authorize his sadistic fantasies and give him the appropriate discourse of mastery: "whichever boy was ordered to kill that person and his family must do it, and he mustn't eat and he musn't sleep till he had killed them and hacked a cross in their breasts, which was the sign of the band" (*HF*, pp. 25-26). Miss Watson's notion of Providence and Tom Sawyer's idea of Plot intersect, *Jim*, but at first it is of no matter to Huck since he alertly dodges both Good Book and bad. The lesson of each, after all, is deferral, the emptiness of the signifier. Prayer does not produce fishhooks. No genie comes when Huck rubs his lamp. Tom, who has already courted girls and stolen kisses, stands before Huck in the brightness and malice of his precocity. He tries to show Huck the power of imagination, how metaphor works, how, magically, pleasure can be conjured from nothing, the make-believe of fantasy. "Why they rub an old tin lamp or an iron ring, and then the genies come tearing in, with thunder and lightning a-ripping around and the smoke a-rolling, and everything they're told to do they up and do it" (*HF*, p. 32). Huck doesn't understand how it works, lamp rubbing, but he thinks the mystery over, and then tries his hand at Tom's magic. "I got an old tin lamp and an iron ring and went out in the woods and rubbed and rubbed till I sweat like an Injun, calculating to build a palace and sell it; but it warn't no use, none of the genies come." Still prepubescent, metaphor-blind, Huck is too literal to take the leap into this form of symbolization, so he throws the lamp aside as "just one of Tom Sawyer's lies" (*HF*, p. 33). It is a particular type of lie, and it reminds Huck of those he has heard in Sunday School. Miss Watson's punishing God and Tom's pleasing Genie are one and the same, and speak to a single issue: "the self-enjoyings of self-denial."[3]

Huck stands at the verge of all this, the lessons of civilization, the confusions of puberty, quizzically looking in. He dimly understands the value of Tom's style, that it keeps Tom at a safe distance from the real, that it is a strategy, but he has not yet grasped the thesis, the determinant, of that style. The Genie of dissimulated Desire has not yet appeared in his consciousness. Tom knows how to turn broomsticks and laths into guns and swords, how to make the lamp project images, is a bustling, bristling youth, and he calls to Huck, summons Huck, to his Gang. Because Huck cannot locate the pleasure of Tom's play, he repudiates the Gang. Tom is already *there,* a reader of books, a rubber of lamps, fetching "an emperor's daughter from China for you to marry, they've got to do it" (*HF,* p. 32), already within the cruelty of Miss Watson's guilt, within the murderous rage of the fathers (Pap Finn and Colonel Grangerford), within the confidence game of the Duke and the Dauphin. Huck is still *here,* in Huckspeech, a writing without the defenses of a 'style,' or the tolerance of humorous deception, in a pointless writing that passively floats raftwise, acted-upon, and everywhere breached by the inexplicable. What does Huck want? To evade the meaning of Tom's fiction, to get away from solicitation, whether kind or brutal, to reverse his direction. "I thought it all over, and I reckoned I would walk off with the gun and some lines, and take to the woods when I run away. I guessed I wouldn't stay in one place, but just tramp right across the country, mostly night times, and hunt and fish to keep alive, and so get so far away that the old man nor the Widow couldn't ever find me any more" (*HF,* p. 48). Huck wants to go nowhere, and be nameless. Here, then, is the providential river. It sends him first a canoe, and then the raft.

So Huck writes, looking back on his first refusal. He is just over the margin into textuality, in this peripheral writing, still essentially *here,* recording his resistance to writing in writing. But on what principle or concept, what sense of the body, does Huck base this resistance? Out of Tom's book, where is he? To fool his swinish father, into whose cruel keep he has fallen, Huck fakes his death with pig's blood, and slips away—a not-Huck into a non-time, back to an island self. On Jackson's Island, where he is 'dead' and safe, 'free' to do as he pleases, Huck directly experiences the "continuous Sabbath" as disappointment. "No difference—just the same thing" (*HF,* p. 64). Huck has refused to "come to time," to eat the sentence on his plate, to join the Gang, endure his father, but the plenitude of the self he hopes to recover quickly becomes the small measure of his island. "I was the boss of it; it all belonged to me, so to say, and I wanted to know all about it; but mainly I wanted to put in time" (*HF,* p. 64). Then Jim appears, on the run, in hiding, to offer Huck the first break in the achieved tedium of his self-absorption, and everything complicates. The river, the canoe, the raft, carry him to the figurative center of his narrative, away from the lies of Miss Watson and Tom Sawyer, the supervision of the Widow and Pap Finn, and yet this center is not the place where oppositions are reconciled, the origin of good humor. It is rather the scene of Huck's severest strife, the very stage on which he is compelled to suffer, as a reluctant child, the tragedy of his culture: master/slave, white/black. Huck flees from the lie of civilization, the duplicity of its dualism, from the lie of the adult who clothes his body and conceals his desire, only to discover on the river, in Huckspeech, that the raft, the "free and easy" raft, is *his* lie.

3

The actual raft is a modest affair: "a little section of a lumber raft —nice pine planks." Always specific, Huck gives us its exact size. "It was twelve foot wide and about fifteen or sixteen foot long, and the top stood above water six or seven inches, a solid level floor" (*HF,* p. 76). Jim builds a "snug wigwam" on the raft, and raises the level of its floor "a foot or more above the level of the raft, so now the blankets and all the traps was out of reach of steamboat waves." Inside the wigwam "we made a layer of dirt about five or six inches deep with a frame around it for to hold it to its place; this was to build a fire on in sloppy weather or chilly; the wigwam would keep it from being seen" (*HF,* p. 94). So the found raft, a mere floor, becomes a dwelling-place raised above the water, a home with a roof and a hearth, the completion of fire. Having lived in a barrel, in the cleanliness of the Widow's house, in the squalor of Pap's cabin, in a makeshift tent on Jackson's Island, and then in a cave, Huck at last finds the peace and freedom of a dwelling-place. And the food is excellent: fish, bacon, meal, a filched chicken now and then, water-melon, mushmelon, fresh corn. The luxuries Huck and Jim add by scavenging are perfect for the contemplative nature of raft life: three boxes of "prime" seegars, a small batch of books, and a spyglass. In their abode, snug, warm, and dry, they can still feel closely beneath them, a few feet away, the large motion of the "big still river." They travel at night. A watch-light is hung to warn off steamboats. "It was kind of solemn, drifting down the big still river, laying on our backs looking up at the stars, and we didn't ever feel like talking loud, and it warn't often that we laughed, only a little kind of a low chuckle"

(*HF*, pp. 94-95). Such is the meaningful raft Huck constructs in his narrative, plank by plank. It is the place where he dwells, where he is most present, most himself, Huck's Huck. Here for the first time he feels the rapture of intimacy, the highest meaning of dwelling, and this is the beam that holds the raft together for Huck, that makes it resemble (for us) the marriage bed Ishmael and Queequeg fraternally share in *Moby Dick*. Huck gives us in exact detail the thingness of the raft, its dimension, its equipment, the feel of it, but all this ardent phenomenology ultimately depends on Jim's presence. What the raft means to Huck is not the meaning of the raft in *Huckleberry Finn*.

Indeed Huck's dwelling, this "snug" home, has no foundation, is not grounded. It is rather given over to the "big still river" that runs "over four mile an hour" (*HF*, p. 94). The river sends Huck the raft and sustains Huck's life on the raft, but the river is also serial time and linear direction, history and geography. It is a relation Huck never seems to understand completely, that position on the river (above Cairo, below Cairo) determines the significance of the raft. "Take it all around," he recalls in Chapter XII, "we lived pretty high" (*HF*, p. 96). And again in Chapter XVIII, writing of the resurrected raft, the post-Cairo raft, the doomed raft, Huck declares his devotion: "You feel mighty free and easy and comfortable on a raft" (*HF*, p. 156). For Jim, who never joins Huck in these rhapsodies, the raft has meaning *only* in relation to the river. On Jackson's Island, before the actual raft appears, he has already tactically concluded that a raft is the safest way to make his crossing: "ef I stole a skift to cross over, dey'd miss dat skift, you see, en dey'd know 'bout whah I'd lan' on de yuther side en whah to pick up my track. So I says, a raff is what I's arter; it doan' *make* no track" (*HF*, p. 70). Above Cairo, then, the raft is simply a ferry he has fixed up with Huck's help, an opportune mode of transport. His gaze is directed elsewhere, at the muddy expanse of the Mississippi, which he anxiously scans, looking for the "big clear river" that will signify the emptying of the Ohio, his destination, the point of his deliverance. Below Cairo the raft is briefly a refuge, a relief for Jim who has been hiding in a swamp, and then the stage on which he is at once humiliated and betrayed. The geographical river, the crucial river for Jim, effectively defines the nature and extent of his discourse on the raft. Approaching Cairo, Jim is increasingly contentious in his speech, self-assertive. After Cairo, absurdly floating down river, he lapses into poignant reveries, or is silent, out of Huck's story. " 'Goodness sakes,' " asks Huck, and the question is telling, " 'would a runaway nigger run *south*' " (*HF,* p. 167)?

The essential drama of *Huckleberry Finn* therefore occurs on the raft. Huck's adventures on the shore are outlying, contingent, elaborative. He is always right in these episodes, afflicted innocence. On the raft Huck is wrong, Huck falls into contradiction, Huck grapples with the issue of his identity. Here he delivers his finest soliloquy. And there are other performers on this platform, other frames of reference, other speeches. The story Huck wants to tell is the story of a chase—"They're after us!"—and bring Jim as a sidekick into the play of that fiction. So he is always quick to draw upon that dubious pronoun, *we,* and he is proud of the getaway raft. It is finally a nifty little number, trim, with all the accessories. Yet the premise of Jim's tale is the axiom of a different genre in American literature, the beginning of each slave narrative: "I owns mysef." The question for Huck is the extent to which, at the risk of his own fiction, the pleasure of the raft, he will admit into recognition the contraposed existence of Jim's story—hear it, understand it, write it. It is as well the question of the style itself, the risk of *Huckleberry Finn* as a humorous text, whether humor can know suffering without denial or deception, without motive, moral or plot. Huck clings to his idea of the raft; it is the only thing he can properly call his own in *Huckleberry Finn,* the only place where he has a sense of humor, and he clings to his friendship with Jim, which is (for him) the guarantee of the raft's goodness, the assurance of its fun. On the shore Huck is always someone else, disguised, an observer. On the raft, with Jim, he is himself: naked, supple, finny. The two values, raft life and Jim, are incompatible.

In Huckspeech, this low style which is as ramshackle and vulnerable as the raft itself, barely raised above illiteracy, Mark Twain flawlessly spells out the complication of Huck's consciousness. Huck's narrative is first breached from within, by the insistence of Jim's speech, and then commandeered from without, by the insistence of Tom Sawyer's writing, and each time he is pulled toward a fate, a form, that is a denial of his deepest desire. The familiar structure of the conventional exchange in humorous writing, that opposition of illiterate speech and literary writing, *is* the structure of *Huckleberry Finn.* Jim and Tom struggle fore and aft for the mastery of Huck's discourse, the determination of his crossing, while Huck, betimes, simply longs for a "free and easy" life, the impossible rapture of the raft. So Huck writes, and *his* subject is sacrifice. With exacting fidelity and resolution he records at the start of his text the compelling utterance of an escaped slave, the significance of Jim's recitative, and then, across rifts, beyond the raft, the evasive distortions of Tom's literary discourse, Tom's revision of Jim's tale. So the humorist traditionally constructs the exchange in American humor, speech for/against writing, Biglow/Wilbur, Sut/George, and distributes the values. But Huck does not have the stylistic resources of the humorist, the point of a stylus; he has only a clumsy steering oar, and he is too close to his material, which presupposes him, and carries him beyond the reach of his intelligence. In the *Biglow Papers* and *Sut Lovingood's Yarns* the roles of speaker and writer are cleanly distinguished, their value delineated by the "funattick" play in the text. Northern humor, Southern humor: two different versions of colloquial discourse, of its innocence, its ignorance, two different characterizations of the writer who accommodates it, and yet in both texts we remain within the simplicity of the paradigm, inside the economy of the low style. The misspelled sign is the assurance of humorous pleasure. Here, then, is Huck, caught in the middle, who loves Jim and admires Tom, going South to go North, whose dream surely is to reconcile Jim and Tom in his writing and resolve the painful issue of his direction. It is a dream that reflects Mark Twain's desire to unite in a single style the full power of an unrepressed speech with the framing activity of interlocution, to create a "free and easy" writing talked-from the alienation of writing. Huck traverses the humorous paradigm in his text, repeats its routines, misspells, is funny, illustrates Mark Twain's deepening sense of humor, but Jim's story, as Huck reports it, will not translate into Tom's fiction.

In Chapter XII, the fifth night below St. Louis, Jim begins to emerge in his difference. What is at stake is the raft itself. Huck decides to emulate Tom Sawyer and board a wrecked steamboat, the infamous *Walter Scott,* and discovers, to his surprise, that Jim is "dead against it." In the instant the raft becomes political; Huck asserts his mastery, and Jim must feel the restraint of his dependence. "Do you reckon Tom Sawyer would ever go by this thing? Not for pie, he wouldn't. He'd call it an adventure—that's what he'd call it; and he'd land on that wreck if it was his last act" (*HF,* p. 97). We already know Jim's functional interpretation of the raft: "it doan' *make* no track" (*HF,* p. 70); it is for the crossing, and for nothing else. By hindsight we also know that Jim is even now, the fifth night below St. Louis, 'protecting' Huck from the knowledge that Pap, the prime reason for Huck's flight, Huck's 'death,' is dead. Jim needs the raft complicity that Huck enjoys. Each is the other's alibi. Huck does not realize this, but Jim does. His childishness, after all, is largely the product of Huck's childish point of view, which requires Jim's genial sufferance of pranks and abuse. There is another Jim beside Huck's Jim in the ample scan of Huck's writing. On Jackson's Island, before he begins the narrative of his flight, Jim momentarily considers Huck, measures him, and it is the first of a series of such meaningful glances, those wary looks tense with looking. "Maybe I better not tell" (*HF,* p. 68), Jim says. Here, before Tom's folly, the *Walter Scott,* which has a cheap thriller going on inside, Jim balks, though his dissent is fuzzy. "Jim he grumbled a little, but give in" (*HF,* p. 97). Huck enters the wreck, finds exactly what Tom Sawyer would find there: a band of outlaws, pistols, treachery, and in the meanwhile the precious raft is almost lost. In the succeeding chapters, as Cairo is neared, Jim's voice gets louder and plainer. A word begins to reiterate, ring, in Huck's discourse— *nigger, nigger, nigger* — and Jim will call Huck *trash.*

Each time Jim asserts his difference, Huck writes *nigger.*

Each *nigger* registers a wrench of Huck's good heart.

Once the raft is recovered, Jim carefully explains the foolishness of the stunt to Huck. He wishes Huck to understand the seriousness of his situation, and so, patiently, he places it all before him. There are different destinies, different dangers, on the raft.

> . . . but he said he didn't want no more adventures. He said that when I went in the texas and he crawled back to get on the raft and found her gone, he nearly died; because he judged it was all up with *him,* anyway it could be fixed; for if he didn't get saved he would get drownded; and if he did get saved, whoever saved him would send him back home so as to get the reward, and then Miss Watson would sell him South, sure. Well, he was right; he was most always right; he had an uncommon level head, for a nigger. (*HF,* p. 109)

Across *right* and *right,* Huck's grudging admission of Jim's truth, the truth of his blackness, the truth of his otherness, Huck defensively reaches for protection, promptly rings the word, "for a nigger." This *nigger* hangs at the front of the scene; at the rear is still another *nigger*: ". . . you can't learn a nigger to argue" (*HF,* p. 114). Yet the nigger *has* argued, and this is the sense of Huck's exasperation, that Jim has somehow messed up the scene they were to do, misread his lines, forgotten who he was supposed to be. The story of Sollermun, the master of harems, the careless sire of numerous unrecognized children, the separater of families, the master careless of life, incenses Jim. He refuses to accept Huck's explanation, to get the story straight, because he sees "down deeper" the symbolic dimension of the entire routine. Solomon is not the point, Sollermun is.

> "Doan' talk to me 'bout Sollermun, Huck, I knows him by de back."
> "But I tell you you don't get the point."
> "Blame de pint! I reck'n I knows what I knows. En mine you, de *real* pint is down furder—it's down deeper. It lays in de way Sollermun was raised. You take a man dat's got on'y one er two chillen; is dat man gwyne to be waseful o' chillen? No, he ain't; he can't 'ford it. *He* knows how to value 'em. But you take a man dat's got 'bout five million chillen runnin' roun' de house, en it's diffunt. *He* as soon chop a chile in two as a cat. Dey's plenty mo'. A chile er two, mo'er less, warn't no consekens to Sollermun, dad fetch him!"
> I never see such a nigger. If he got a notion in his head once, there warn't no getting it out again. He was the most down on Solomon of any nigger I ever see. So I went to talking about other kings, and let Solomon slide. (*HF,* p. 112)

Huck's glance: "I never see such a nigger." Three nights above Cairo, in a dense fog, Huck paddles out in the canoe and is cut off from the raft. He finds himself in a labyrinth, a "nest of tow-heads," and the river, seemingly still, is fierce: "you don't think to yourself how fast *you're* going, but you catch your breath, and think, my! how that snag's tearing along" (*HF,* p. 117). Huck is here, Jim is there, calling to each other through the fog, whooping, lost. In the morning the fog is gone, Huck finds his way back to the raft, and then plays his last practical joke on Jim. The scene obviously pre-figures the oncoming crisis, that tight moment when Huck, again away from the raft, will be asked *the* question about the raft: *whose raft is it?* This much is certain, and the imagery stresses the meaning: white murk, labyrinth, separation, treacherous river, and yet here, too, we see, we overhear, a rhetorical Jim speaking through Huck's text. He readily accepts Huck's teasing suggestion that he dreamed the whole frightening experience of the previous night. He will, in any event, " 'terpret" the dream for Huck, and the interpretation is resolutely set forth, specifically pointed. It all means, the tow-heads, the current, the whooping, that they will encounter "quarrelsome people and all kinds of mean folks, but if we minded our business and didn't talk back and aggravate them, we would pull through and get out of the fog and into the big clear river, which was the free States, and wouldn't have no more trouble" (*HF*, pp. 120-121). The interpretation teaches, anticipates Huck's childishness, reminds him of their direction, their destination. Huck then humorously reveals his fib.

Jim's glare: ". . . he looked at me steadily, without ever smiling" (*HF*, p. 121). He will not endure now, at all, Huck's play, Huck's innocence, an innocence cruelly insensitive to suffering, blind to reality, the "*real* pint," an innocence that at once evokes and pre-dicts the innocence of Tom Sawyer. The thrust of Jim's rebuke is deep. It drives Huck back again into the role of the pig-son of the hog-father. "Dat truck dah is *trash*; en trash is what people is dat puts dirt on de head er dey fren's en makes 'em ashamed" (*HF*, p. 121). The mean trashy figure of Pap Finn, still lively in Huck's imagination, who will reappear, dressed-up, rich and powerful, still murderous, as Colonel Grangerford, the *real* killer of Buck, Huck's unrebellious *doppelganger,* is in fact Jim's only card, his only power on the raft. His rebuke is also an appeal. Jim is not yet free of his dependence on Huck, and he will play the card twice, first as rebuke and then as appeal, anxiously singing out to Huck as he paddles forth to meet the slave catchers: "Dah you goes, de ole true Huck; de on'y white genlman dat ever kep' his promise to ole Jim" (*HF*, p. 124). At the end of the foggy scene, stared-through, Huck is humbled. This *nigger* comes hard to him, hard. "It was fifteen minutes before I could work myself up to go and humble myself to a nigger — but I done it, and I warn't ever sorry for it afterwards, neither" (*HF,* p. 121). The drama on the raft, of the raft, herein reaches its ultimate confrontation. Jim says *trash* and Huck, shakily, writes *nigger.*

The scene is now set for Huck's sacrifice, but what is sacrificed? Huckspeech, this humorous style so closely attuned to spoken discourse, to raw speech, hits finally the rawest of spoken words in the American lexicon, a bluff reef, and writes it rongly again and again, *nigger, nigger.* "Conscience says to me, 'What had poor Miss Watson done to you, that you could see her nigger go off right under your eyes and never say one single word' " (*HF,* p. 123)? This potent misspelled word, this disfiguring signifier, effectively sinks the raft, wrecks it, because *nigger* is intransitive. Huck's dream of the raft as a safe refuge from the pains of maturity, as a familial unity, a home with a hearth, cannot accommodate it. Nor can the style, Mark Twain's desire for a "free and easy" writing, a writing released to the current of consciousness, afloat on its copious energy, attuned to its articulation. "Next you'd see a raft sliding by, away off yonder," Huck writes, after Cairo, "and maybe a galoot on it chopping, because they're most always doing it on a raft; you'd see the ax flash, and come down—you don't hear nothing; you see that ax go up again, and by the time it's above the man's head, then you hear the *k'chunk!*—it had took all that time to come over the water" (*HF,* p. 158). That indeed is the ardor of Huckspeech: writing related to perception as raft is to river, but there is a *nigger* in this idyllic picture, in the writing, and he is now immensely unspoken.

A double irony therefore occurs in Chapter XVI, to Huck on the fast foggy river in the 1850s, to Mark Twain writing as a humorist in 1876. Huck's fiction is about to be displaced, his power dispersed, his role altered. The story he wanted to tell is rapidly running into the reality of a slave narrative, which Jim has already sketched out for him in his analysis of the dream. They are going to meet some quarrelsome and mean folks, he tells Huck, and Huck must learn to be quiet, not to talk back, not to aggravate the mean folks. He must learn to behave, in brief, like a nigger. In Chapter XVI Jim gives Huck an ampler prospectus. Jim is going to work, live frugally, "never spend a cent" (*HF,* p. 124), then buy his wife and children out of bondage, and if that is not possible, steal them. The quick racism of Huck's response: "give a nigger an inch and he'll take an ell" (*HF,* p. 124) only rationalizes a deeper wrong Jim has dealt him.

There is no mention of Huck in this part of Jim's story. "Here was this nigger which I had as good as helped to run away," writes displaced Huck, "coming right out flat-footed and saying he would steal his children—children that belonged to a man I didn't even know; a man that hadn't ever done me no harm" (*HF*, p. 124). It is a shaft, received full by Huck. He looks upon a Jim who is *not* a nigger and sees a man who surely cares for him, but who has his own family, his own children, his own notion of a home and hearth, who is literally dancing to get off the raft, which will be sold, *his* raft, Huck's raft. A man that hadn't ever done me no harm. The only power Huck exercises over Jim, so he realizes ("I just felt sick"), is his ability to wrong him, to give him hurt, to rip that happy world (in which Huck has no place) from Jim just here on the threshold of it. He can turn Jim in.

It is the finest moment in *Huckleberry Finn*, this moment when Huck, who has been so grievously hurt, prepares to give it, to give hurt back. "But I says, I *got* to do it—I can't get *out* of it" (*HF*, p. 125). The innocence lost here is considerable. Huck sees, without realizing it, that *nigger* is a misnomer, an empty signifier, an alibi. It is not just against his cultural identity as a white Southern boy that he must act, but against the direct pulse of his feeling, the pull of his own desire. He must give up a part of his world in order for Jim to gain his. Whose raft is it? "Is your man white or black" (*HF*, p. 125)? He's white, Huck responds, he's my father. What next? Nineteenth-century American humorists had made phoneticized spelling, written dialect, the veritable sign of humor: *natur, nater, alluz* the *noo soot of close.* It indicates the space of humor. Josh Billings's *Allminax* immediately tells us what it is. But the cardinal term Mark Twain selects from dialect to center the play of his humor is *nigger,* a bristling word, and it turns irrevocably the play from simple to serious. Huckspeech is a version of niggerspeech, what the vernacular originally means, the speech of the slave, the discourse of the victim. He's white, says Huck, reestablishing his conception of Jim. Later, near the end of his narrative, again on the raft, Huck will attempt to relocate Jim as a *nigger* in his writing, and does indeed write "runaway nigger Jim," but the term won't hold the fullness of Jim's humanity, and Huck remembers the instance in Chapter XVI, the choice he made above Cairo. Yet for Mark Twain, writing in 1876, after Cairo, as it were, *nigger* lies heavily in *Huckleberry Finn,* a large and suspicious reef in a text that was to be humorous. The first significant rift in the manuscript occurs here; Cairo is missed, the raft destroyed, Huck and Jim plunged to the bottom of the Mississippi. Mark Twain stops work on the project. The raft briefly reappears in *A Tramp Abroad*, Mark Twain sits on it telling German tall tales, and then it is again destroyed, steered into a bridge where, flimsy contrivance that it is, it goes "all to smash and scatteration like a box of matches struck by lightning" (*ATA*, p. 159).

4

Across this rift, the wreckage of the raft, the ending of *Huckleberry Finn* begins. Everything that now happens in the narrative is by way of descent, and haunted by the illogic of the wrong-way passage. The raft is refloated, but its pleasures are now geographically compromised, and it is easily usurped by the duke and the king, bad actors who appropriate the raft as *their* stage, their dwelling. Huck and Jim, whose play is finished, become supernumeraries in this play, extras. It is the raft again that generates the theme of displacement in *Huckleberry Finn*, that infers once more, in a new context, the subliminal horror of being lost to, in, someone else's mad fiction. *Tom Sawyer* and *Huckleberry Finn*, Leslie Fiedler suggests in *Love and Death in the American Novel*, can be seen "as the same dream dreamed twice over, the second time as nightmare,"[4] but the "nightmare," properly speaking, is Jim's, and it clicks on as soon as Cairo is passed. The question in this part of *Huckleberry Finn* is the exclusion and relative silence of Jim. All the dangers that befall Huck along the river are resolvable by the simple devices of picaresque fiction: disguise, the apt and convenient lie, flight, the future of the next day, the next episode, except one—the dull, distant, constant pressure of Jim's presence, the exhaustion of his story. Mark Twain's composition of this phase of *Huckleberry Finn* is intermittent, improvisational: mid-October, 1879; mid-June, 1880; the summer of 1883. It is truly a rough piece of steering. For Huck's question is his question: what to do about Jim, whether to go over this reef or around it. The looming spectre of Aunt Rachel in "A True Story," the black speaker whose slave narrative explodes the anecdotal frame of the dialect sketch, reappears in *Huckleberry Finn*, differently, as in a nightmare. She is dressed in a "long curtain-calico gown," and wears a "white horse-hair wig," and her duty here is to howl.

What sense of humor comprehends such pressing pain? In Huck-speech Mark Twain at length turns upon the devices of humorous writing and wrongly writes the illusion of rong riting. That is, Huck-speech at the end of *Huckleberry Finn* is the scrutiny of a humorous resolution, Huck's unblinking eye turned once more upon Tom's metaphors. The whitewashing begins in Chapter XXIV on the raft. The duke does exteriors; Tom's specialty is interiors. Through this single ring, this sole utterance, *nigger,* Mark Twain draws, wonder-fully convoluted, at once the psychological, the historical, and the stylistic complication of his text. The duke "dressed Jim up in King Lear's outfit—it was a long curtain-calico gown, and a white horse-hair wig and whiskers; and then he took his theatre-paint and painted Jim's face and hands and ears and neck all over a dead dull solid blue, like a man that's been drownded nine days" (*HF,* p. 203). Huck watches all this, the face, the hands, the ears, the neck, horrified, outraged. Truth floods Huck's discourse in the final sequence of *Huckleberry Finn,* and it makes a high demand of our own sense of humor, of what we can know and humorously suffer. We know how Jim's story is told: "Well, you see, it 'uz dis way. Ole Missus—dat's Miss Watson—she pecks on me all de time, en treats me pooty rough, but she awluz said she wouldn' sell me down to Orleans" (*HF,* p. 69). Now it must be written:

1. Here a captive heart busted.
2. Here a poor prisoner, forsook by the world and friends, fretted out his sorrowful life.
3. Here a lonely heart broke, and a worn spirit went to its rest, after thirty-seven years of solitary captivity.
4. Here, homeless and friendless, after thirty-seven years of bitter captivity, perished a noble stranger, natural son of Louis XIV. (*HF,* p. 326)

Similarly the letter of betrayal that Huck writes, but does not send— "Miss Watson your runaway nigger Jim is down here two mile below Pikesville and Mr. Phelps has got him and he will give him up for the reward if you send. *Huck Finn*" (*HF,* p. 271)—this scarce, scant note, must be rewritten and delivered.

Don't betray me, I wish to be your friend. There is a disprate gang of cutthroats from over in the Ingean Terri-tory going to steal your runaway nigger tonight, and they have been trying to scare you so as you will stay in the house and not bother them. I am one of the gang, but have got religgion and wish to quit it and lead a honest life again, and will betray the helish design. They will sneak down from northards, along the fence, at midnight exact, with a false key, and go in the nigger's cabin to get him. I am to be off a piece and blow a tin horn if I see any danger; but stead of that, I will BA like a sheep soon as they get in and not blow at all; then whilst they are getting his chains loose, you slip there and lock them in, and can kill them at your leasure. Don't do anything but just the way I am telling you, if you do they will suspicion something and raise whoopjamboreehoo. I do not wish any reward but to know I have done the right thing.

UNKNOWN FRIEND (HF, p. 338)

It is the only extensive piece of Tom's actual writing that we have in either *Tom Sawyer* or *Huckleberry Finn,* and everything falls through it, eerily true: the double-talk of duplicity, the judas-sheep, the tinhorn, that thick rich vein of egotistical innocence that allows the ego to have it both ways at once, to be crook and cop. "I am one of the gang, but have got religgion and wish to quit it and lead a honest life again, and will betray the helish design." It is the voice of Conscience in the lowest humorous case, wanting to do the right thing. Mark Twain now restages the routine of the Writing Lesson, which Huck, flinching, has already barely passed through, and Jim becomes the subject. Writing is his agony because he cannot write, because he can only be written and pass into the power of writing. "Jim said it would take him a year to scrabble such a lot of truck onto the logs with a nail, and he didn't know how to make letters, besides; but Tom said he would block them out for him, and then he wouldn't have nothing to do but just follow the lines" (*HF*, p. 326). All the while Jim is written, his story translated into an escapist romance, Huck hears his protest, his outcry: "I doan' *want* none . . . I can't *stan'* it . . . I doan' *want* no sich glory" (*HF*, pp. 328-329). The idiocy of Tom's script stretches before us— elaborated, drawn-out, painful props; excruciating lines; and as for ink, "the best authorities uses their own blood. Jim can do that" (*HF*, p. 304). Everything in this script is idiotic, and true, what must be suffered. The slave narrative will be written, stylized, was so written, and the letter of betrayal will be sent, was sent. Tom, after all, has Jim's bill of freedom in his back pocket, the proclamation of his emancipation. And the question was then, and still is (1883) "what it was he'd planned to do if the evasion worked all right and he managed to set a nigger free that was already free before" (*HF*, p. 354)? In Tom's idiocy, a hard logic lies.

Huck rites *nigger* rongly, Tom writes *nigger* properly: "crest, a runaway nigger, *sable,* with his bundle over his shoulder on a bar sinister: and a couple of gules for supporters, which is you and me; motto, *Maggiore fretta, minore atto"* (*HF*, p. 325). A sane surreal vision of the actual shines through Tom's usurpation of *Huckleberry Finn,* through Mark Twain's burlesque of romantic fiction. How to liberate the *sable* man who has been emancipated, free the already free? How to make certain that when he enters the 'free' world, he will accept the terms of his freedom? Huck protests, Jim protests; neither of them understand the nuances of such a deliverance. For all his extravagance, Tom has an acute mastery of the primary codes in his culture, so he will insist, he will demand, he will rewrite and revise, to get it right, this necessary script, "because he's [Jim] going out *right,* and there ain't going to be no flaws in his record" (*HF*, p. 325). The motto he assigns to Jim's Coat of Arms, *Maggiore fretta, minore atto,* means "the more haste, the less speed" (*HF*, p. 325). This motto, slightly revised, will reappear in Ralph Ellison's *Invisible Man.* It is the sense of a letter of recommendation, a letter of betrayal, that black Dr. Bledsoe sends to white Mr. Emerson, which the Invisible Man naively carries north with him, sealed: "Please hope him to death, and keep him running."[5] Like Tom Sawyer, Emerson likes to think of himself as Huck, likes to play Huck Finn. He says of his friendship with Bledsoe, "With us it's still Jim and Huck Finn. A number of my friends are jazz musicians, and I've been around" (*IM*, p. 165). Yet Emerson reveals his true character when he arranges for the Invisible Man to take a job in a paint factory where the prime slogan is " 'If It's Optic White, It's the Right White.' " "Our white is so white," Ellison's humiliated protagonist is told, "you can paint a chunka coal and you'd have to crack it open with a sledge hammer to prove it wasn't white clear through" (*IM*, p. 190). Ellison's 'humor' in this part of *Invisible Man* hits like a sledgehammer. The same clarity obtains at the end of *Huckleberry Finn,* but it is diffused through the sweet intonation of Huckspeech. There is Jim, skirted, painted blue, and here is Jim, whose tears Tom will weep, whose passion Tom will feel, whitewashed, become the natural son of Louis XIV, a *sable* man, a colored gentleman.

So Mark Twain humorously writes an unforgivable ending to *Huckleberry Finn*. He does not avoid Tom Sawyer's evasion. It is extended before us, lunatic, necessary, fated, the full paradox of the Reconstruction run through the routine of the Writing Lesson. All the dichotomies of the humorous style: speech/writing, presence/absence, slave/master, low style/high style, even rockpiling/bricklaying, are caught up darkly in this ultimate funny exchange. To please the moralist, *Huckleberry Finn* ought to end in Chapter XXXI (before Tom's reappearance) where Huck, still on the privileged space of the raft, but alone now, solitary, bereft, makes a last effort to see (lose) Jim as a *nigger*. Huck will never lose the functional usage of *nigger*, which generally designates, but he has lost the opprobrious usage, the *nigger* that means *I do not recognize you*, and which hits like a thrown brick. His soliloquy juxtaposes heart and conscience, but this is a speech that simply poses an august silence. Huck looks straight at the "everlasting fire" that awaits those who confuse their terms, right and wrong, who flunk the Writing Lesson, and yet before God, that austere Judge, the supreme Teacher, he cannot bring himself to say, meaningfully, the required word, *nigger*. It is a submission his whole being refuses. Huck suddenly has a speech defect; he stutters indeed like Moses on the Mount, refusing: "I was trying to make my mouth *say* I would do the right thing and the clean thing, and go and write to that nigger's owner and tell where he was; but deep down in me I knowed it was a lie—and He knowed it" (*HF*, p. 270). Here Mark Twain figuratively embraces Huck, forgives him. It is a scene that is humorously satisfying for us, if not for Huck, and yet as a resolution in the narrative of *Huckleberry Finn* it is obviously inadequate. Huck can't say the word; he can't write the letter; he has made a crossing, but where does all this leave Jim's story? The river has almost reached its full course; History is here, Geography, as the final wall, and the raft is now irrelevant.

Humor transforms suffering, diminishes pain, belittles dread, and this wonder is worked through the agency of a humorist who, in the guise of a tolerant elder, a gentle knower, embraces the wronged self and applies to the wrong, the hurt, a certain compassionate perspective. Or, failing that, the balm of a white lie. Simple humor

demonstrates innocence. Serious humor, it might be said, humorously considers that demonstration, the story the humorist tells. How
much can humor know humorously, without lying, without evasion?
How much at last does Huck know? Before what large losses, over-
come by the inexplicable, is it yet possible to forgive, to identify, as
Pirandello construes the humorous act, with the unlike and unlovely
other? That is the question of Huckspeech, in whose circuit Huck
becomes Tom, Tom becomes Huck. "The speechform," James Joyce
writes in *Finnegans Wake*, "is a mere sorrogate."[6] Huck can't write a
lie, and therefore will never write again. Because the crossing is irrevo-
cable, and this text is his crossing, he can only rong once in writing
the writer at work, writing, busily engaged in sorrogation. Huck tells
Tom "as much of the raft-voyage as I had time to" (*HF*, p. 290). His
only plan for Jim is to repeat the raft-voyage, "hiding daytimes and
running nights, the way me and Jim used to do before" (*HF*, p. 294).
Too simple, says Tom, and Huck readily agrees. He realizes that now
something must replace this "raft-voyage," stand in its place, refer
to it, designate it, but not *be* it. *It* can no longer be. First the raft is
taken from Huck, and then his discourse. Tom draws the tropes from
his bag of tricks, his 'plan,' the play of his fiction, and Huck, watching the writer at work, admits: "I see in a minute it was worth fifteen
of mine, for style, and would make Jim as free a man as mine would,
and maybe get us all killed besides" (*HF*, p. 294). As a style Huckspeech admits everything, even its own failure, its own closure.
Sivilize me, Huck writes, I can't stand it. In that last grace-note of
the humorous style, *sivilize*, Huck's final resistance, Huck marks the
end of his writing.

If, in a second book, some later narrative, Huck is again to rong
writing in the text, he must start from a new premise. Everything
seen, heard, felt in *Huckleberry Finn*, the literal fullness of its
experience, would then have to be critically realized. What is wrong
about the rectitude of Tom's writing, the half-truths of Mr. Mark
Twain's humorous fiction? Why is it, really, that Tom does not have,
properly speaking, a bona fide sense of humor? Tom struts at the end
of Huck's book, proud of the bullet hanging on his watch-guard,
proud of the formal aptness of his resolution, and bubbling with new
plots. Clearly Tom can't wait to go home and exhibit his bullet; yet
he suggests parenthetically some "howling adventures" in the Ter-

ritory. Huck takes him seriously, and will soon step again into the innocence of Tom's play. Perhaps as Huck waits in the wilderness for Tom to appear, and waits and waits, he will begin to invent a theory that explains Tom Sawyer.

Notes

1. Tony Tanner, *The Reign of Wonder* (Cambridge University Press, 1965), p. 162.

2. Mark Twain, *A Tramp Abroad* (London, 1903), p. 108. All subsequent reference will be indicated *ATA*.

3. "Visions of the Daughters of Albion," in *The Poetry and Prose of William Blake,* ed. David V. Erdman (New York, 1970), p. 49.

4. Leslie Fiedler, *Love and Death in The American Novel* (New York, 1966), p. 280.

5. Ralph Ellison, *Invisible Man* (New York, 1952), p. 168. All subsequent reference will be indicated *IM*.

6. James Joyce, *Finnegans Wake* (New York, 1959), p. 149. All subsequent reference will be indicated *FW*.

V

After Huck Writes

Reproduced from *Adventures of Huckleberry Finn*
by Mark Twain, original illustrations by E. W. Kemble,
The Limited Editions Club, 1933, p. 33.

1

Huckspeech is a difficult style, easier to evoke than to assume, because the simplicity of its colloquial expression floats craftily upon a deep substructure of humorous knowledge, from which it cannot be alienated. No one in the latter half of the nineteenth century—not even Mark Twain, after he wrote it, defined it— properly caught the style in the full sense of its power, the great ease of its statement. "It appeared to be a unique phenomenon," Richard Bridgman writes in *The Colloquial Style in America,* "a delightful freak capable of being imitated, but seemingly offering no further possibility of development."[1] Most writers, he indicates, took *Tom Sawyer,* not *Huckleberry Finn,* for a stylistic model, and he cites Brander Matthews's *Tom Paulding,* Stephen Crane's *Whilomville Stories,* and Booth Tarkington's *Penrod.* Mark Twain himself would fail to regain the substance and tenor of the style in his several sequels to *Huckleberry Finn,* a failure that gives him the curious distinction of being the first significant writer to vulgarize the style, rip it from its centering theme, and throw it back upon the stupidity of unassuming innocence. Huckspeech has its own history of capture and escape in American literature, and Mark Twain writes the first chapter.

Huck tells the story in *Tom Sawyer Abroad* (1894) and *Tom Sawyer, Detective* (1896), writes it in Huckspeech, but the detachment of the style from its source in experience is extreme. He goes up in a balloon in *Tom Sawyer Abroad,* is hung high above the North African desert, and for most of the narrative his discourse is airborne, simply daft, propelled by hot air. Unable to invent a compelling action for his characters, Mark Twain instead repeats the routine of the Writing Lesson, an old number, but done now without resonance. "Mars Tom," Jim improbably asks, "what is a metaphor?" Tom explains: "A metaphor's a—well, it's a-a-a metaphor's an illustration."[2] There is no pain in this gondola, no suffering, except the little pain of not knowing what a metaphor is, so there is no work for humor to perform in the novel, no subject for the humorist. The only bright thing Mark Twain devises in the text is the title Tom Sawyer arrogates to himself: *The Erronort.* In *Tom Sawyer, Detective,* Huck returns to the scene of the crime, the firmer grounding of the Phelps farm, but he travels by steamboat, the wrong vehicle for Huckspeech, and the stylistic distance from the purity of the style is even greater. Huck starts anew, picks up the thread, but then Mark Twain prosily intervenes; the crossing is into Tom Sawyer's fiction, into Tom's tale, and this turn changes the axis of the style, turns Huck's writing back upon the world of play, Tom's world, where Huckspeech founders, where it again becomes innocent.

> Well, it was the next spring after me and Tom Sawyer set our old nigger Jim free, the time he was chained up for a runaway slave down there on Tom's uncle Silas's farm in Arkansaw. The frost was working out of the ground, and out of the air too, and it was getting closer and closer onto

barefoot time every day; and next it would be marble time, and next mumbletypeg, and next tops and hoops, and next kites, and then right away it would be summer and going in a-swimming. It just makes a boy homesick to look ahead like that and see how far off summer is.[3]

Sequels to *Huckleberry Finn*, revisions of *Huckleberry Finn*—these either revert to the formulae of the boy's book (where Huck can't wait to play mumbletypeg) or they educate Huck, teach him the proper response to the world, take him into a different discourse. In *The True Adventures of Huckleberry Finn* (1970), John Seelye hardens his writing of Huckspeech with an admixture of curses and sexual profanity. This is a tougher Huck, fully masculine, who promptly gets a hard-on when he sees Mary Jane Wilks in her sleeping shift. "It was to the east, and the sun come in full through her dress—it warn't nothing but her sleeping shift—and my damn pecker nearly jumped out of its socket."[4] The *coup de grace* Seelye applies to his *Huckleberry Finn* is the one Mark Twain presumably evaded. Tom Sawyer does not appear in the final sequence, Jim drowns in the Mississippi, weighted down by his chains, and here is Huck, stripped and desolate. These are his last words: "But dark as it was and lonesome as it was, I didn't have no wish for daylight to come. In fact, I didn't much care if the goddam sun never come up again" (*THF*, p. 339). What is lost in the translation is the humorous intelligence of the original text.

It is not, after all, the rewriting of *Huckleberry Finn* in modern American humor, whether directly or indirectly, that returns us to the significance of Huckspeech as a style. The question of humor, of what the humorist does, is absent in George Ade's *Fables in Slang* (1899), in Ring Lardner's *You Know Me, Al* (1916), and when it properly appears in fiction, is once more spoken, the question is typically in a perilous place, ambiguously situated in *The Sound and the Fury* (1929), tortured in *Miss Lonelyhearts* (1933). In the humorous writing and performance of women and blacks, the ostensible wrongness of the style, the fundamental structure of the humorous routine, becomes, as it were, the brick itself, the problem to be humorously resolved.

After Huck writes, Jason Compson has his say. "Who do you play out with?" he demands of the delinquent and shiftless Quentin. "Are you hiding out in the woods with one of those damn slick-headed jellybeans? Is that where you go?"[5] Quentin eludes him, escapes him, heads out for the Territory. Jason seethes, he has been wronged, specifically and generally, and he rails, like Pap Finn, against injustice:

> I don't see how a city no bigger than New York can hold enough people to take the money away from us country suckers. Work like hell all day every day, send them your money and get a little piece of paper back, Your account closed at 20.62. Teasing you along, letting you pile up a little paper profit, then bang! Your account closed at 20.62. . . . Well, I'm done with them. They've sucked me in for the last time. Any fool except a fellow that hasn't got any more sense than to take a jew's word for anything could tell the market was going up all the time, with the whole damn delta about to be flooded again and the cotton washed right out of the ground like it was last year. . . . Well, I just want to hit them one time and get my money back. I don't want a killing; only these small town gamblers are out for that, I just want my money back that these damn jews have gotten with all their guaranteed inside dope. Then I'm through; they can kiss my foot for every other red cent of mine they get (*SF*, p. 252).

William Faulkner is the great twentieth-century master of nineteenth-century humorous modes, and the example of his adaptation frames all subsequent stylistic approaches to the raft and the Mississippi. Lena Grove, Flem Snopes, Ike McCaslin, step from Sut's South, from Thorpe's bear-haunted woods. In "Old Man" there is the fugitive convict in a flood-tossed boat with a pregnant woman, a saturnine fellow who will later, in perfect consonance with Jacksonian legend, wrestle with alligators. When Quentin, who is a bitchy Huck, slips out at night, she takes the prescribed route. Faulkner's humor is of a piece, hard, black, sweet, soft, and it all fits (leit motif, comic relief, proverbial aside, anecdote) into the gothic framework of his fiction. Jason begins his tale in *The Sound and the Fury* with a sour old saw dragged up from the misogynist's cracker barrel: "Once a bitch always a bitch, what I say" (*SF*, p. 198). Unforgiving, stupidly choleric when not simply bilious, Jason is the comic embodiment of the humorless man. He clutches his prejudice, he clenches his wrath, and there is the humorous presence of Dilsey. She humors everyone in the novel, even Jason. " 'Hit me, den,' she says, 'ef nothin else but hittin somebody wont do you. Hit me,' she says" (*SF,* p. 203). You can't learn a nigger to argue. Even as Faulkner uses the humorous idiom, the motifs of its discourse, the logic of its aphorisms, to pin Jason to his inexorable frustration, he reserves the purity of humorous speech for a separate statement. Herein lies the problem of humor in Faulkner's fiction.

How do we read, in what sense of humor, Dilsey's resolution of the Compson tragedy? She takes on that massive hurt, takes care of Benjy, suffers Jason, and makes her way at last to the Easter service in her church. Uplifted by the Reverend Shegog's sermon, she sits amazed in her knowledge of sacrifice. It does not matter that the sermon is theatrically rendered, is a performance, a piece of rhetoric, the spirit of the letter is in Dilsey. And Benjy, the loony Lamb, sits beside her. "I seed de beginnin," Dilsey says, "en now I sees de endin" (*SF,* p. 313). If we are to take Dilsey's endurance, her cathartic sense of the triumph of the victim, seriously, as seriously as we take Huck's speech, when he elects damnation, then what we mark here, along with Faulkner, is our impossible distance from Dilsey's expression. Such a resolution exists, humor speaks, but in this farthest remove of the other. Like Kierkegaard, like Melville, Faulkner will remark the humorous position. It appears at the end of irony's reach; it speaks from a certain altitude. "I seed de beginnin en now I sees de endin." So it is in Faulkner's fiction: we 'see' the privilege of humorous understanding, that it holds in the round beginning and ending, life and death, but we do not necessarily feel its calming effect in the novel. It is there, in parenthesis. Dilsey's compassionate vision does not mediate the tragic fate of the Compson family.

Caddy's exile, Quentin's suicide, Jason's comeuppance, these exist within the gaze of the ironist, and yet Faulkner knows where humor speaks for itself, in which language, in which voice. Indeed he is always gallantly asserting in his fiction the supremacy of the humorous position. Humor, Faulkner insists, is feminine. Dilsey is humorous, Lena Grove is humorous, Miss Reba is humorous, et cetera. The body itself, Eula Varner's body, Lena Grove's body, Dewey Dell's body, presses the feeling of humor upon us. That is now Darl ironically sees it in *As I Lay Dying*: "Squatting, Dewey Dell's wet dress shapes for the dead eyes of three blind men those mammalian ludicrosities which are the horizons and the valleys of the earth."[6] Men use irony, women have humor. In *The Reivers* (1962), the most strictly humorous of all Faulkner's novels, Lucius Priest falls into a meditation on suffering: "It's not men who cope with death; they resist, try to fight back and get their brains trampled out in consequence; where women just flank it, envelop it in one soft and instantaneous confederation of unresistance like cotton batting or cobwebs."[7] This richly sententious patriarchal concession, this bow to the Mother, to that "instantaneous confederation of unresistance," is singularly apt. Humor takes it in, and transforms it. Women, Lucius later reflects, "can bear anything because they are wise enough to know that all you have to do with grief and trouble is just go on through them and come out on the other side" (*R*, p. 111). Lucius is the Huckish character in *The Reivers*, but he speaks in the voice of the literary interlocutor, speaks for the humorist. He tells the story of his *rite de passage* in 1905 to his grandson in 1961, another Lucius Priest, who transcribes it, beginning: "Grandfather said." *Reiver* is an archaic term for plunderer, and what Lucius's "Reminiscence" principally recalls is that lost glorious world of freewheeling masculine adventure: horse races, fine-looking prostitutes, picnics on the grass, fistfights, gambling. If it is true that mauled women educate us in the humorous lore of survival, teach us how, properly, to suffer, it is also true that plundering men enjoy the sport of life, even as they get their brains comically trampled out.

There is, of course, a certain difficulty (though Lucius Priest III does not remark it) with Faulkner's grandfatherly appraisal of humorous intelligence. Women suffer the hard knock, yield, envelop, endure, are wise. What turns in Grandfather's thought is something like the Hegelian Dialectic of Master/Slave. Masters are fixed in the absolute of their mastery, whereas Slaves understand, in their "mortal terror," that no absolute can exhaust the possibilities of human existence. So the slave, from the start, is the one who thinks twice. The Slave studies the Master. The Master does not recognize the Slave. They speak in different discourses. The Hegelian Dialectic baffles Huck in *Huckleberry Finn*. Which am I? In *The Reivers* Faulkner gives that Dialectic only half a turn, for what is lacking in feminine sufferance, in that "instantaneous confederation of unresistance," is skepticism. Lucius has a wise mother, but the women who largely figure in the novel are the bovine ladies who toil for Miss Reba in her Memphis sporting-house. When skeptical women appear in Faulkner's fiction, Addie Bundren in *As I Lay Dying,* Charlotte Rittenmeyer in *The Wild Palms,* their scrutiny is somber, their humor melancholy.

Look to the intuitive wisdom of women, old Lucius tells young Lucius, who writes it down. It is what the Faulknerian humorist knows, the limitation of his knowledge, and it is where Faulkner is tender, if not soft, where his prose becomes mellifluous, where he slips into euphony, celebrating the suppleness of feminine intuition, showing the humorous significance of the mammalian body. Those women who are clitoral in their psychosexual character, mannish like Addie Bundren, are not funny. Only the vaginal woman, whose sublunary being is round, can speak for humor. V. K. Ratliff, the itinerant peddler who roams through the Snopes trilogy, observing, remarking, keeps his eye on Eula Varner. She, too, passes through the ordeal of the Writing Lesson, suffers learning, is fiercely in-structed by 'Professor' Labove: "they all knew him—the hungry mouth, the insufferable humorless eyes, the intense ugly blue-shaved face like a composite photograph of Voltaire and an Elizabethan pirate."[8] Labove is obsessed by the contour of Eula's "mammalian ludicrosities," by the lift of her leg, the lever that moves the world, by all that and more, the totality of her resilience, the perfection of her resistance to the lesson.

> For five years he was to watch her, fetched each morning by the brother and remain just as he had left her, in the same place and almost in the same position, her hands lying motionless for hours on her lap like two separate slumbering bodies. She would answer "I dont know" when her attention was finally attracted at last, or, pressed, "I never got that far." It was as if her muscles and flesh too were even impervious to fatigue and boredom or as if, the drowsing maidenhead symbol's self, she possessed life but not sentience and merely waited until the brother came, the jealous seething eunuch priest, and removed her (*TH,* p. 114).

As humorist, as elegist, Ratliff bears witness in the Snopes trilogy to the end of it all, the old South, the old forms, even this elderly style which decants, through Ratliff's mellow perspective, the pour of a drawling masculine sense of humor: ". . . as if, the drowsing maidenhead symbol's self, she possessed life but not sentience." The narration changes as we move from *The Hamlet* through *The Town* toward *The Mansion.* Increasingly Ratliff becomes himself the object of curiosity. Who is this quaint, busy, remote person who knows the history of everyone, who can double-talk, speak fluently in the country idiom and also cite the classical writers, whose relation to Eula Varner Snopes is bound up in a secret sympathy? Faulkner writes in the Snopes trilogy the coda to the Jacksonian prose style in American literature, heightening its Latinate rhetoricity, perfecting the pitch of its idiom, so that it stands whole, intact, as a classical writing. No Southwestern humorist, not Thorpe, not Harris, reached the sophistication of Faulkner's interlude in *The Hamlet,* that tale of Buck Hipps and his reckless ponies. Here, and in the beautifully elaborated love story of Ike Snopes and his cow, the tall tale is taken to its highest extension. Yet the interlocutor who writes of the "drowsing maidenhead symbol's self," who knows a little Greek and some Latin, is but a phrase away from the composition of "one soft and instantaneous confederation of unresistance." The local tall tale passes into the hazy reference of classical myth; icon is confused with fetish. An aged, arthritic humorist speaks in *The Reivers* and what we read is carved, and cut: a script, an epitaph. *Grandfather said.*

In *Miss Lonelyhearts,* Nathanael West painstakingly demystifies the significance of that privileged Faulknerian figure: budding Eula, pregnant Lena, pregnant Dewey Dell, broad-shouldered Dilsey, the woman "wise enough to know that all you have to do with grief and trouble is just go on through them and come out on the other side." Miss Lonelyhearts, after all, is a morose male writer forced by his ironic editor, Shrike, to impersonate a consoling woman. He writes a newspaper column advising the lovelorn and the troubled, dutifully contriving optimistic messages. Letters come in brimming with content, the agonies of disfigured and brutalized bodies, and his messages, devoid of content, disembodied, respond. A reader of Dostoyevsky, the writer in fact longs to possess a redemptive sense of humor, to affirm Dilsey's belief in the blood of the lamb, but he can't do it, can't sacrifice the lamb, can't believe in the efficacy of the sacrifice. Shrike's cynical brickbats rain down on him; those awful letters, rongly ritten, recounting hideous tales of human suffering, steadily arrive on his desk, and the act of humorous transformation is simply beyond him. He looks at Betty, his fiancée, a good-natured girl who has all kinds of unsatisfactory solutions to his despair: a change of job, retreat to the country, love, marriage, and he soberly calculates the value of her sensibility. In one single, flat, straight statement, Miss Lonelyhearts sums up the credibility of the Faulknerian Dilsey. "Her sureness was based on the power to limit experience arbitrarily."[9] It is a rejection of innocence as the prop of any humorous resolution. To humor, as Betty humors Miss Lonelyhearts, signifies evasion, a willed ignorance. When the writer lamely tries to humor Betty, the best he can do is to allow her to humor him.

Just as Melville collects the anodynes in *The Confidence-Man*, places the New Testament beside a patent medicine, the Samaritan Pain Dissuader, just as he exposes 'humor,' exhibits the 'truth' of its fond embrace, West sets before us the twentieth-century formulae, puts Dostoyevsky next to Dorothy Dix, with this difference—the 'humor' exposed in *Miss Lonelyhearts* is Betty's plump body, Mary Shrike's ample bosom, Fay Doyle's massive hams. This is the elemental 'body' of 'pleasure,' and it stands forth against that other 'body' in the background, the brutalized body of every woman who writes to Miss Lonelyhearts for relief. As Faulkner sees it, this is for godless man, the doomed ironist, humor's last stand-in, the privileged, impregnable body of Dewey Eula Lena Dell, the last remaining absolute a man can hold on to. We can at least look with Darl, whose -ing was never given him, at Dewey. The horror of *Miss Lonelyhearts* is to be *in* this body, of this body. So, in a drunken rage, Miss Lonelyhearts will try to mutilate the old fairy, try to wrench his arm from his body.

How, then, to take these letters so heavy with feminine hurt full in the male face, resolve them, and still withstand the ghastly smirk of Shrike's irony? Miss Lonelyhearts is in a double bind. Shrike will repeat the lesson this young writer is to learn: the character of Miss Lonelyhearts, this comforting maternal figure, is a male fiction, a lie, and worse, a stupidity. She is a male creation, and no knowledgeable man in his right mind would take her seriously. To identify with her, to lose one's distance, one's proper alienation, is folly. That, in part, is Shrike's challenge to the writer, the treachery of the assignment. The young writer regards Shrike skeptically. He knows where he is,

fixed between the blades of Shrike's editorial scissor. Yet to withstand Shrike's irony, all those predatory strikes, those paternal
snippings, to fight back in some other way than by participating in
Shrike's fixed game, trying to give Shrike horns by sleeping with his
wife, Miss Lonelyhearts must indeed rely on something feminine in
his nature, have recourse to a power associated with the mother.

What, West inquires, is the *real* humor of women? The name of
Christ, the butchered son, that awful piece of fatherly work, evokes
from the mother, from Dilsey, from Miss Lonelyhearts, something,
an outcry, forces them to feel a "secret power." And what is this
power but the classical distress, the traditional complaint of suffering women, hysteria. Miss Lonelyhearts looks directly at it in
himself. "He know now what this thing was—hysteria, a snake whose
scales are tiny mirrors in which the dead world takes on the semblance of life" (*MLH,* p. 9). It is a Satanic rage, this hysterical force,
partly outrage at injustice, partly envy of the Father's power, and it
is, therefore, self-destructive. When Miss Lonelyhearts at length
yields to it, becomes Miss Lonelyhearts, he will think his hysteria the
finest sense of compassionate humor (I forgive you! I forgive you!),
and fall into the ridiculous arms of a jealous father, poor Peter
Doyle. Bang! The gun goes off, Shrike's last joke in this humorless
text.

After Huck writes, humor is hard. It is particularly hard for
women writers, for black writers, who have no desire either to
mystify or demystify their sense of humor, who bring, as it were, a
previous skepticism to their humorous writing or performance. The
mode in which they find themselves, the forms that are present,
popular, belong to a tradition that produces women and blacks as
figures of innocence, as figures of ignorance. So they work within
the constraint of a double bind, and the issue, the text, the performance, is often dissonant.

There is the example of Marietta Holley. In the 1880s she wrote a
series of humorous books as *Josiah Allen's Wife,* and the sobriety of
her writing is the evidence of her struggle with the humorous style.
She, too, wrongs her text, delivers a rural idiom, but Josiah Allen's
Wife is not a myopic, absentminded Mrs. Partington, a self-efface-
ment. Samantha Allen is a brisk, if not brusque, country sage who
will stoutly assert: "Some men's love haint worth nothin.' "[10] Holley
writes in effect a steadfast advice that is too serious for the style.

When her subject is the plight of women, she will move in and out of the character of the style, often barely remarking it with occasional notation.

> No woman can feel honorable and reverential towards themselves, when they are a foldin' their useless hands over their empty souls, waitin' for some man—no matter who—to marry 'em and support 'em. When in the agony of suspense and fear they have narrowed down to this one theme all their hopes and prayers: "Good Lord, anybody!" But when a woman lays holt of life in a noble earnest way, when she is dutiful, cheerful, and industrious, God-fearin' and self-respectin', though the world sinks, there is a rock under her feet that wont let her down fur enough to hurt her any (*JAW*, p. 312).

Lay holt of life. The humorist who speaks in this text speaks a militant common sense. Her text for this particular address is the dime novel. She warns young ladies about the peril of falling into the world of male fiction, becoming passively their creature. To this redoubtable extent, Samantha Allen prefigures Dorothy Dix and Ann Landers, that line of woman counselors West parodies in *Miss Lonelyhearts*, whose good-humored advice, in fact, is rarely sentimental. In another regard, she is bonneted by the style, shut up by it. *Samantha At The Centennial* concludes with a long, twisting debate between wise Samantha and a furious, man-hating feminist who tells Samantha that "wimmin" will get the vote only when they reach for the hammer. It is a protracted discussion; Samantha is buttonholed, upbraided, and challenged, and beneath the rhetoric of the exchange is the sound of still another debate, the one between humor and hysteria. Yet even as this ambivalence appears, the style itself functions, by means of the conservative drag of the misspelled sign *wimmin*, to baffle the sharpness of the feminist argument. A motherly voice, tolerant, experienced, relates the daughter's case, so the case is already decided, and yet.

> "What do you think of men meetin' here to celebrate National Independence and the right of self-government, when they hold half of their own race in political bondage?"
> Says I, firmly, "I think it is a mean trick in 'em."

Says she, bitterly: "Can't you say sunthin' more than
that?"

"Yes," says I, "I can, and will; it is mean as pusly, and
meaner."

. . . And she went on for a long length of time, a
callin' 'em every name I ever heerd men called by, and lots
I never heerd on, from brutal whelps, and roarin' tyrants,
down to lyin' sneaks; and for every new and awful name
she'd give 'em, I'd think to myself: why, my Josiah is a
man, and Father Smith was a man, and lots of other
relatives, and 4 fathers on my father's side (*JAW*, p. 527).

Let us not forget our 4 fathers. One has only to think of the
'voices' later comediennes would assume, of Fanny Brice's horrific
rendering of Baby Snooks, of Gracie Allen's oblivious contralto (the
voice of George Burns's Wife), to appreciate how close Lily Tomlin
comes in her act to the adventurous humor of Huckspeech. That
tension between humor and hysteria which is repressed by the
conventional style Marietta Holley adopts, rationalized by the
device of Samantha Allen's supervening maternal wisdom, is loosed
in Tomlin's diverse impersonations, set adrift as free-floating anxiety,
and this is what is humored.

The relation of little Edith Ann, Mrs. Beasley, and Ernestine to the
interlocutor, 'Lily Tomlin,' is problematic. Mrs. Beasley, a tense,
neurotic, suburban housewife, and Ernestine, the working girl who
vindictively exercises her little powers with sniffy malevolence, are
different versions of Edith Ann's destiny—and just, so one feels, to
the other side of the poised performer who stands before us dealing
these characters forth. Other comic artists who use mimicry either
work in the traditional mode (Rich Little, Frank Gorshin) or firmly
retain their 'authorial' control as stand-up comics (George Carlin,
Robert Klein). Tomlin explores a different interface in the structure
of her act. She stands apart from her 'voices,' but the distance does
not seem great because her attitude toward them is humorous, not
comic. These characters are allowed to speak, appear before us in the
flesh of an enactment, are not merely caricatured. Here, of course,
one deals outside the text with the immediate qualities of voice, with
the significance of gesture and movement. Yet the difference of such
impersonation is always apparent. Might not this performer, slipping

in and out of changes of identity, slip into a particular voice and fail to find his or her way back to the act, to the interlocutor's role? That is always the question in Jonathan Winters's performance when, ad lib, he produces too quickly, too profusely, a crowd of personae. Something hysterical, something manic, rushes into the delivery, and an element of the demonic, of schizophrenic possession, appears. As she introduces her act, Tomlin will typically weave into her patter the insistent line "I need a lot of affection tonight," present the scare, the edge, of a vulnerability. She will make her theatricality seem fragile and at the same time artfully remind her audience of the different sensibility immanent in her work. This comedienne, Tomlin implies, is going to be risked. She may not be available to direct our laughter.

When we turn to the subject of black performers and writers, the same problem with tone and form appears, enormously complicated by the popular tradition of blackface minstrelsy. Because she is a woman standing in a spotlight hitherto reserved for men, Tomlin can only shakily inhabit the formal role of the interlocutor, a frailty she seizes upon and places at the center of her act. How, then, does a black man or woman resolve the humorous routine of master/slave? In 1896 Bert Williams and George Walker would rewrite the minstrel show, reappropriate the form, and bill themselves as "The Two Real Coons." Both men realized the paradox of their performance, the misery of its billing. "In those days," Walker recalled in a memoir, "black-faced white comedians were numerous and very popular. They billed themselves 'coons.' Bert and I watched white 'coons,' and were often much amused at seeing white men with black cork on their faces trying to imitate black folks." So Williams and Walker took back "what we felt belonged to us by the laws of nature,"[11] and then worked to get past the demeaning aspect of the comic stereotype, to surprise their audiences with 'real' high-stepping, 'real' black singing. Indeed Williams brought into the act an important addition—the blues, transformed the antic Mr. Bones into the poignant figure of the Jonah Man. The result of all this brilliant invention gave Williams a measure of acclaim (he would become a headliner on Broadway), but it did not ultimately free him from the specific of minstrelsy, the trap of typecasting. Black writers who sought to capture the brio of Harlem life in the twenties similarly found themselves restricted by the toe-tapping image of shambling, shiftless Jim Crow. For all its honest verve and simple charm, Claude McKay's *Home to Harlem* (1928) was uneasily read in Harlem. "Uncle Tom and Sambo have passed on," Alain Locke had written in *The New Negro* (1925), "and even the 'Colonel' and 'George' play barnstorm roles from which they escape with relief when the public spotlight is off. The popular melodrama has about played itself out, and it is time to scrap the fictions, garret the bogeys and settle down to a realistic facing of facts."[12] Performers, however, could not so easily change their scripts. If they managed to break from the black circuit in show business, what they ordinarily found waiting for them on Broadway, on the wider stage, were Sambo's implements. The brickbat *nigger,* thrown from minstrelsy (Nigger Jim Crow) into *Huckleberry Finn,* thrown, turned, and returned, becomes a tarry brick in the Harlem Renaissance.

The leap from Bert Williams manifesting the reality of a 'coon' in 1896, turning his lachrymose drawl upon laughing Broadway audiences, to the jump and jive of Richard Pryor's act, which continually presents the ticking brick *nigger,* is considerable. Williams would draw a pathos from his fool, give us the 'real' black minstrel, a sad song and dance, and effectively create the appealing and humorous role in American show business that Sammy Davis, Jr., would later come to occupy. Pryor exposes the hysteria latent in that 'humor,' shows us, through the façade of his jesting, the intensity of his movement, the terror of being a nigger in a hostile white world, in this very theater where he stands, popeyed, performing. We turn here into the aggression of satire. Pryor holds hot in his hand, jiggling it, the ignoble 'truth' of *nigger,* which is hurled. This radical change in 'black' humor marks off Bert Williams's performance from Pryor's, and also separates McKay's funky *Home to Harlem* from Ishmael Reed's wrathful *Mumbo Jumbo* (1972). Reed icily rewrites, in several stylized idioms, through the fast forwards and reverses of pulp fiction, the 'true' history of the Harlem Renaissance. It is a history of cultural theft, of artistic betrayal, that becomes at times a litany of losses, a telling over of the names, the works of art, the careers, that were either effaced by white American culture or ruinously compromised. The novel is dedicated to Reed's grandmother, a friend in San Francisco, and to "George Herriman, Afro-American, who created Krazy Kat."[13] We have already glanced at the site of that text, the small, simple world of Coconino County.

To return to it, we must leave, bracketed, that other 'humorous' art which refuses to receive the brick, whose act, whose text, is the bruising riposte.

2

Here again is the brick, the one Shrike throws at Miss Lonelyhearts, a black brick, but a different humorist, placed upon the scene, espies it.

© 1974 King Features Syndicate Inc.

Herriman began to draw *Krazy Kat* in 1913, and from the beginning the strip was keenly 'written.' He drew in his text upon the earlier tradition in humorous writing. Krazy Kat speaks in dialect, a specific idiom of his own; the text is misspelled, and we observe in sequence after sequence a familiar juxtaposition of characters: one who is rong, "Krazy"; another who is right, "Ignatz"; and the aforementioned "Kop," the dumb dog who is alternately protector and jailor.

Krazy, that sweet, soft, baffled body, always desiring, always rejected, speaks in a stylized idiom that comprehends a 'pure' language of feeling. There is babytalk in his discourse: the " 'Lil Ainjil," he croons, just as Ignatz conks him with a mean brick; and there is schoolgirl poetry: "Odeer, odeer, no matta how much I seek to

drownd my sorrows in music, thoughts of 'Ignatz' gives me a sad-
niss." There is also a free version of Yiddish'd English, at once
maternal and theatrical: "Movink pitcher ectink, 'Mice,' " he tells
Ignatz, announcing his debut in movies, "already gives me such play
for my dremetic telents I got menegers runnink efter me—me I'm a
tragedian 'Ket,' 'Ignatzes,' where as you aint nothink but a komedian
'Mice'—I could do 52 weeks in Hemlet only I don't like little wil-
lages." It is a discourse that can only affirm, though at times Krazy
will suffer strange lapses (atavism) and curious reversals (identity
crises in dream life). It resolutely affirms, because Krazy refuses to
interpret the oncoming signs of Ignatz's animosity as anything other
than proofs of his devotion. So he continually negates negation,
rejects rejection, and blissfully forgives. Nothing hard can break
through his interpretation of the brick.

The conventional sign of humor, the misspelled sign, constitutes
Krazy's carapace, his hard *K*. He speaks in all those 'dumb' languages
the sophisticated, "whose astute erudition is never doubted," must
despise, those vulnerable discourses (babytalk, purpled adolescent
poetry, immigrant English) to which "no sincere credit is given in matters of the mind." Here, like Mark Twain, Herriman comes to terms
with the exigencies of the low style. What credit *is* to be given to Krazy's character, to his speech? He happens upon a sleeping Ignatz.
" 'Lil toots-a-wootsa, he sleeps in slumba," Krazy beams, and then:

It is the purity of the humorous act drawn in its essential gesture: (smack). A cat kisses a mouse. It is also a wrong kind of love, unnatural, forbidden, inexplicable, and funny. The film director Frank Capra, who worked for a time with Herriman in Hollywood at the Hal Roach Studios, once urged him to specify the nature of the love affair drawn in the cartoon. Easily enough one could see the hint of miscegenation (Herriman was born in New Orleans of dubious parentage), but was it not also true, Capra wondered, that Krazy and Ignatz were both male. No, Herriman responded: "Krazy is something like a sprite, an elf. They have no sex. So the Kat can't be a he or she. The Kat's a spirit—a pixie—free to butt into anything."[14] Indeed Herriman abstracts the humorous idiom, cuts it loose from gender and age, from time and place, so that it can say almost anything, take up diverse topics, and never lose its softness, its poise. Krazy's speech, simply put, is the spell of humor rewriting reality, taking the edge off the letter.

Herriman's innovative drawing enhances the abstraction of the humorous exchange. The background keeps shifting behind the ongoing action: bizarre figures, cubistic mesas, surreal flora. This is an imaginary landscape, the projection of an inner reality, a symbolic site, just as these voices, speaking of Samuel Johnson and James Boswell, effectively symbolize the activity of humor, speak up from characteristic places in the self, from *Anima,* from *Animus.* Like the style of *Huckleberry Finn,* the style of *Krazy Kat* deals critically with the project of humor, places the humorist in the play, and therefore proposes a way of knowing the world. Humor comprehends the brick by misunderstanding it, by misspelling its ostensible message. Krazy is 'wrong' not to suffer the brick, to feel it as a wrong, as a hateful word, and yet Herriman's illustration, taken in the round, always shows us the inextricable coexistence, the perfect simultaneity, of good and evil, love and hate. The Kat is not a masochist, but rather the sensuous transformer of pain, the erotic element in humor.

Krazy's speech is therefore the richest, full of sweet contradiction, for he has the *droit* of misspelling, the unassailable right to be wrong. The speech of Offisa Pupp and Ignatz, on the other hand, is direct, declarative, and obsessed with the *No* of the brick, with "sin's most sinister symbol." Ignatz strives to hurl it, Offisa Pupp seeks to intercept it. They, too, are locked in an embrace, a dance of mutual detestation, which Krazy tolerantly countenances. Another style works its way through the series, the flowery rhetoric of belles lettres, the prose of a Parson Wilbur. Various creatures in Herriman's world, Coconino County, speak it, and often Herriman himself, writing as storyteller, will adopt it. 'Panchita Paloma,' a totalitarian peace dove, arrives in the County to pacify it. He has an interpretation of *Krazy Kat,* and a therapy—the exclusion of desire, the removal of Krazy, who is, as we have already seen, the heart of this fiction.

So Panchita Paloma's antibrick diatribe shapes itself at length into a brickbat, at which point the ideological dove is promptly dismissed from the text, ignored. Because he is not what he professes to be, the peace dove brings irony into the humor of *Krazy Kat.* Irony excludes humor. Humor excludes irony. Krazy has the last word, and it is spoken from the low style. The dove spoke prettily, he allows, "except wot he said about 'Bricks.' " Humor determines the nature

of the brick in Coconino County, receives the brick, affirms it, and all the creatures in the County realize the importance of that interpretation. In the last panel everyone is settling back comfortably, reassured, in his proper place. The tone and economy of Herriman's style has been preserved. By such clever turns, always risking the sufficiency of his style, Herriman kept before his readers the question of Krazy's intelligence. The exchanges that occur between the

kat and the mouse, supervised by Offisa Pupp, are essentially linguistic (Krazy konfusing homonyms, making inadvertent puns;
Ignatz hurling corrective bricks), and constitute effectively a profound struggle for the right to determine reality. Who will speak in
this world for the self to the self, describe the 'truth' of experience?
As Krazy and Ignatz contest the meaning of the brick, they argue the
significance of the word.

The theme of usurpation recurs in Herriman's cartoons. The peace
dove, after all, is just another version of Ignatz.

Except for that title, this could as well be *his* series. From Ignatz's
self-centered perspective, the brick simply clarifies an eternal opposition, describes a perpetual distance, is the curse (goddam) continually given in an uncaring world. His cruelty is as important in the
action of the cartoon as Krazy's kindness. There is, in brief, an
Ignatzian reading of *Krazy Kat,* and the humorist, who looms in the
apprehensive figure of Offisa Pupp, is well aware of its integrity.
"Sin's most sinister symbol," Offisa Pupp intones, coming upon the
brick. He knows, as does Ignatz, what the brick means: concussion;
and his humorous task is to avert the sending of its message, an
irksome project he consistently fails. The difference between simple
and serious humor is therein described. For the proper task of humor
is to receive the brick in full and bespeak its power. Krazy's dumb
speech, amorously polysemous, always passive, rongly ritten, triumphantly does so speak the brick, and this is what mystifies Offisa
Pupp and infuriates Ignatz — the absence of irkage in Krazy's discourse.

"Ah, simbil of love, Oh, emblim of dewotion, Oy, tokin of esteam," sings Krazy, embracing the blessed brick. He knows at least what Herriman knows: this brick is the device that makes everything happen in the world of Coconino County. It is always the same, and yet its usage is variable. In its circuit, passing from one style into another, it changes meaning. What, then, does the brick signify? In the psychopathology of *Krazy Kat,* it means surely Nemesis, Reality, Suffering, Humor's subject. From beginning to end, Herriman's cartoon is richly self-reflexive, always examining and testing the humorous mode. The brick also simply signifies itself, that it is a sign, and a sign only.

"By this I mean this," Gertrude Stein wrote in 1926, explaining modernist composition. "The only thing that is different from one time to another is what is seen and what is seen depends upon how everybody is doing everything. This makes the thing we are looking at very different and this makes what those who describe it make of it, it makes a composition, it confuses, it shows, it is, it looks, it likes it as it is, and this makes what is seen as it is seen."[15] Herriman is the first humorist in modern American literature to reflect the new dispensation in his style. The exchanges in *Krazy Kat* still observe the familiar difrunce between illiterate (naive) and literate (smart), between low and high styles, but what is at issue now is the very nature of language itself. Ignatz's brick is thrown from the nineteenth century, where language is nomenclature, where the hard brick names its heavy thing and is sent with singleminded intention, and it is received (*klunk!*) in the twentieth, the same brick, but differently construed, a different sign alltogether. When humor now responds to the reality principle by misrepresenting it, by misspelling the brick, it possesses an ideology, a theory of the written word.

In the nineteenth century, which confused spoken language with writing, humorists exaggerated the criterion of proper usage in order to generate the "funattick" play of their text. An idiom, phonetically rendered, bespoke its deviance, its difrunce, and in so doing spoke humorously about painful rifts in the culture, rehearsed in the low style dire confrontations between a literate urban intellect and an illiterate rural wisdom, between masters in whiteface and slaves in blackface, between those in power and those without. Even Mark Twain, who internalized the structure of the humorous exchange, conjoined speaker and writer in a single tension, still saw idiomatic expression in historical terms. Huck's speech perishes in Huck's script, is lost as *sivilized* is corrected. Yet the entire institution of rectitude in language, the Dictate of the Dictionary and the Grammar, that Power which establishes the *rong* of humorous writing, the *rong* of being *sivilized,* begins to collapse in the twentieth century, and with it, tumbling, the hierarchy of styles, the order of genres, all that which humorists could formerly have counted on as rich material for their routines. Around the turn of the century, as Ferdinand de Saussure would himself begin to attack the primacy given to writing by linguists, those humorists who strictly wrote dialect humor began to lose their public. The Universal Schoolmaster, "who does his best," Lowell wrote in the *Biglow Papers,* "to enslave the minds and memories of his victims to what he esteems the best models of English composition" (*BP,* p. 205), suddenly put down his rule and changed his position. Language, Saussure declared in 1906, "does have a definite and stable oral tradition that is independent of writing, but the influence of the written form prevents our seeing this."[16] Why is this so? Standing in his lecture room at the University of Geneva, Saussure could as well have been addressing an assembly of hirsute nineteenth-century American humorists, speaking to them about their primary routine, the Writing Lesson.

> The literary language adds to the undeserved importance of writing. It has its dictionaries and grammars; in school, children are taught from and by means of books; language is apparently governed by a code; the code itself consists of a written set of strict rules of usage, orthography; and

that is why writing acquires primary importance. The result is that people forget that they learn to speak before they learn to write, and the natural sequence is reversed (*CGL,* p. 25).

Herriman drew in *Krazy Kat,* quite by intuition, a funny diagram of Saussure's theory of the sign, outlined the arbitrary relation of signifier to signified, and in Krazy's whimsical misspelling he began to trace the insistence of the letter in the unconscious. Ignatz designates his hatred, and Krazy mistakes it for desire. What is seen, Gertrude Stein shrewdly observes, depends upon how everybody is doing everything. The lectures that constitute the *Course in General Linguistics* were delivered between 1906 and 1911. The *Psychopathology of Everyday Life* appears in 1914. Picasso begins the "heroic phase" of cubism in 1907 and by 1914 it is a comprehended mode. Both in its illustration and its text, *Krazy Kat* (1913) participates conceptually in this diverse movement. The storied brick thrown in that banal routine of unrequited love transforms itself in midflight, becomes abstract, problematical, the sign of a new composition. Even the typical panel-by-panel construction of a comic strip is disrupted in *Krazy Kat,* deconstructed. As Pierre Couperie and Maurice C. Horn indicate in *A History of the Comic Strip,* Herriman "proved to be as imaginative and inventive in layout as he was in his narratives and settings; he indulged in a riot of elaborations as unexpected as they were varied, in which the cartoons are shuffled like a hand of playing cards, isolated in the center of a page without a frame, in polygonal circles similar to photographic diaphragms, the whole effect heightened by a symphony of colors that causes the pictures to dance."[17] What is drawn in *Krazy Kat* is also written. For the same surprise and movement exists in the wordplay of the text. The new thing to be seen in *Krazy Kat* is a humorous style rendered as an abstraction.

Krazy's speech combines different idioms, has no specific gender, speaks from no single cultural region, cites Semwell Johnson and Hemlet, and often in its jovial effusiveness sounds swishily like theatrical parlance. "Hello, 'Ignatz' dahlink," says Krazy. It is simply the bisexual speech of passion, humorously conceived, a sweet voice that speaks in the transactions of humorous thought, that signifies itself by misspelling. Speech still retains its social signification in such humorous writing, still signifies that it is an excluded discourse, the vulgate, a vernacular, but it is also now figured in a psychological setting. The illiterate or preliterate speaker who mis-writes, or is miswritten, who rongs the rationality of writing, assumes easily, as the picture of the self changes, a new character. "Hello, 'Ignatz' dahlink," says Krazy. And here is a new spokesperson for the priority of speech, for its sense of presence, in humorous writing. His/her site of utterance is no longer a region, a New England or Missouri dialect; or an age, Huckish pubescence; or a social condi-tion, the illiteracy of slaves, but a place in the geography of the human self. Krazy's speech, spoken through the sign of its craziness, speaks from the *Ucs.*, and, behaving like Freudian slippage, like Freudian punning, misrepresents Ignatz's intention. To this extent, Huckspeech is a style that does not necessarily end as its writer passes through the Writing Lesson, emerging, civilized, on the other side. It can be rewritten, dealing with the same brick, the same hard subject, but with a conflict of different voices. "Hello, 'Ignatz' dahlink," says Krazy, and immediately Ignatz reaches for a brick.

There is, as we have seen, an Ignatzian reading of *Krazy Kat.* What tortures of ambivalence does this ignoble little mouse endure! Before him always is a moiling, gushy desire, and what to do about it, and how elude the vigilant Kop who keeps flinging him into jail? He is subject to the name Krazy Kat, and all his attempts to differentiate himself, to determine the nature of the brick, dissolve in Krazy's speech. Krazy wants him to throw the brick, continually offers it to him, or sits contentedly waiting for it to arrive. So Ignatz's task is Sisyphean, the labor of a construction never completed, the sending of a message always misinterpreted. The mouse knows (as any intelligent mouse would know) that malevolence rules the natural world, that there are 'natural' enemies, and this is the message he keeps sending, brick after brick, to Krazy. The ego, Freud tells us, "seeks to bring the influences of the external world to bear upon the id and its tendencies, and endeavours to substitute the reality princi-ple for the pleasure principle which reigns unrestrictedly in the id."[18] So Ignatz endeavours, and Krazy is crazy, and both share the same sign, a single brick. In *The Ego and The Id* (1923), Freud would himself draw a diagram of the self that is effectively a cartoon, a funny drawing of a 'serious' concept.

This form has no "special applicability," Freud explains, and "is merely intended to serve for purposes of exposition." Yet he looks at

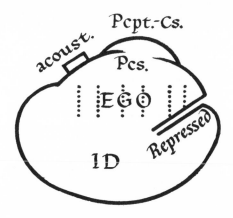

it; he sizes it up: "We might add, perhaps, that the ego wears a 'cap of hearing'—on one side only, as we learn from cerebral anatomy. It might be said to wear it awry" (*EI*, pp. 14-15). The cap is thus the auditory lobe, and, to this extent, we are looking at the wavy outline of a pulpy brain, at circuitry. There is also the semblance of a torso in the drawing, a threefold globular shape that recalls the ample curvature of the Venus of Willendorf, a primitive figurine whose type appears all over Europe during the Ice Age. Alexander Marshack writes, "Usually naked, these figurines have pendulous breasts, wide hips, tiny feet, and somewhat bent knees; the head is usually bent forward, often there is no face, though the figure may have a coiffure and wear such articles as bracelets, beads, an apron or waist band and even decorated bands that may be tattoos."[19] The Venus of Willendorf is withal one of the oldest representations of the human form, and it is the contour of a feminine form, of breast and womb. Freud's drawing, of course, only evokes the figurine as a trace, as a "mnemic residue." This particular figure of the self is bisexual, has a protuberance, a projection into the world, which it wears "awry," and an aperture, an opening into itself marked *Repressed* that leads squarely upon the *ID*. The *EGO* is barred, placed between brick and rift, words and feelings, surface and depth, and above all, as Freud insists, it is *in* the *ID*, is "part of the id." With its hard edges, its rectangles, its seriality, the *EGO* draws attention to this fact, that it is inscribed within this softly swelling voluptuosity, is inside the Venus figure. If the ego were given speech, a little balloon for self-expression, it might legitimately say, with a certain humor, "I am *in* the Mother." A blissful predicament.

Humor forgives such transgressions and takes pleasure in the pleasure, but who speaks in humor to forgive? Who has the power of forgiveness? In the later essay on humor, Freud would assert that the super-ego assumes the role of the humorist, speaks as a wise and loving parent to an intimidated ego. No such faculty is given to the super-ego in *The Ego and The Id,* where the voice is harshly commanding: "You *may not be* like this (like your father)—that is, you may not do all that he does; some things are his prerogative." Here the super-ego surely takes a hard humorless position. It is, if anything, the embodiment of the Writing Lesson, that lesson in which we learn to substitute, to accept the arbitrary rule. "The super-ego retains the character of the father, while the more powerful the Oedipus Complex was and the more rapidly it succumbed to repression (under the influence of authority, religious teaching, schooling and reading), the stricter will be the domination of the super-ego over the ego later on—in the form of conscience or perhaps of an unconscious sense of guilt" (*EI,* pp. 24-25). There is no Figure 2 in *The Ego and The Id* which shows the place of the super-ego in the picture of the self. It is perhaps *lui-même* who pictures the self, and then decides: no more silly cartoons of the self with its cap awry. This is, however, the situation, the *EGO* is in the *ID,* and it is a serious situation. For in its relation to the id the ego "is like a man on horse-back, who has to hold in check the superior strength of the horse, with this difference, that the rider tries to do so with his own strength while the ego uses borrowed forces" (*EI,* p. 15). So Freud draws a cartoon outline of the body and then writes on it, text on picture, rationalizes it, establishes imaginary roles and sites. Indeed he suggests (coincidentally) that the super-ego precipitates itself, learns to write, during the Ice Age—just at the time Paleolithic artists (coincidentally) were carving the Venus of Willendorf, that rounding form which shimmers through Freud's rounding line. The idea comes from Sandor Ferenczi, a suspect source, but Freud is willing to consider it, that the discourse of the super-ego "is a heritage of the cultural development necessitated by the glacial epoch" (*EI,* p. 25). If so, then the Willendorf sculptor at work in the Upper-Paleolithic Period and Freud (both Austrians, coincidentally) realize the same abstract idea: self is the sign of *this* primordial body.

The long historical sequence of such representation, this archetype, is beautiful to contemplate. It is the best work of all our fathers, that representation, that signifying of the rotund uncon-

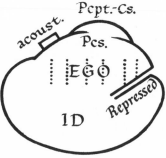

scious, that inscription and shaping of the feminine. We never tire of it, those of us who write in the name of the father. This iddy form is the faceless object of our desire, the secret of the self, that deep place where all the dualities, principally Eros and the death instinct, have their unruly origin. The line of the Freudian id is feminine, and so, too, is its utterance. The id, Freud writes in the final passage of *The Ego and The Id,* "has no means of showing the ego either love or hate. It cannot say what it wants; it has achieved no unified will" (*EI,* p. 49). So we humor it, and tell lies about it, lie to it about it, venerate it, despise it, and none of this matters to it. It only is, the insistent being of Being. "Whenever possible, it [the ego] tries to remain on good terms with the id; it clothes the id's *Ucs.* commands with its *Pcs.* rationalizations; it pretends that the id is showing obedience to the admonitions of reality, even when in fact it is remaining obstinate and unyielding; it disguises the id's conflicts with reality and, if possible, its conflicts with the super-ego too" (*EI,*

p. 46). In this account of the discursive strife in consciousness, *it* looks like *she*, behaves like *her*, and we are a step from the confrontation scene in domestic comedy. "Be sensible," the ego pleads. To a person who "cannot say what it wants." We have only to turn to Lou Andreas-Salomé for the other half of the exchange. "For a neurotic," she writes, "the wish to become a woman would really mean the wish to become healthy . . . . Only in womankind is sexuality no surrender of the ego boundary, no schism; it abides as the homeland of personality, which can still include all the sublimations of the spirit without losing itself."[20] So the male ego is suave, politic, the rational lover of an irrational beloved, a forger of alibis, and always a fraud, always a failure. Ignatz lives in Krazy's world, where Krazy is always happily at home and impervious to argument.

The Ego and The Id, it can be safely said, is not a humorous text, and yet in his effort to visualize the system of the self, to dramatize its exchanges, Freud continually edges upon humorous writing. As we have seen, the cartoon is curiously suggestive, and there is a kind of humor in Freud's depiction of the ego that recalls Mark Twain's sense of humor in *Tom Sawyer*: a tolerant interest in the phenomenon of lying, a sympathetic contemplation of the ego busily at work whitewashing "the id's *Ucs.* commands with its *Pcs.* rationalizations." *Te absolvo.* This is, after all, *our* ego, a "poor creature" driven to such trickery by the contradictions of existence. The position of the ego is ridiculous: "If we wish to find an anatomical analogy for it, we can best identify it with the 'cortical homunculus' of the anatomists, which stands on its head in the cortex, sticks up its heels, faces backwards and, as we know, has its speech-area on the left-hand side" (*EI,* p. 16). So it rides, as best it can, the fierce beast of being, a frantic homunculus on horseback. These comic figures multiply in *The Ego and The Id.* The ego behaves like a "submissive slave," like a "sycophantic, opportunist and lying" politician, and yet, nonetheless, *I am ego.* Freud's characterization of the ego, beneath all the caricature and comedy, is humorously compassionate. And who is it who forgives this "poor creature" its lies, professes its innocence, comes upon the ego standing on its head, sticking up its heels, and facing backwards in the id? A better liar, an older and wiser liar, with better strategies for dealing with the perverse and contrary id: the writer of *The Ego and The Id.* In the psychodrama of the self, according to Freud, 'father' is the humorist, the forgiver,

who, knowing the right, will sometimes tolerate a wrong, or an error. Who will, in effect, rationalize the wrong, explain it away. " 'Look, here is the world, which seems so dangerous! It is nothing but a game for children—just worth making a jest about' " (*H,* p. 165)!

Is this, then, the fatherly speech of humor? Look, here is a little mouse, who must be punished, and yet who is lovable. Krazy loves him, no matter what he does, at his worst. Besides Offisa Pupp's punishment is not all that hard, and never lasting. What feels sad and terrible is really insignificant and amusing. "In this interaction between ego and superego," Lucile Dooley writes, "the child is treated with tenderness even though punished, and is allowed play and even a disguised aggression against the superego. The humorous play is a demonstration that the child is really loved both in his punishment and in spite of it. Since the great primary narcissistic needs are two—to be allowed aggression and to be loved—humor does indeed provide a triumph of narcissism."[21] So, it would seem, humor speaks in *Krazy Kat,* constantly providing an interplay of those two "great primary narcissistic needs," aggression and love. Yet in most significant works of humor this selfsame humorist, this creator of such "fantasy defenses," is put into the play of the text, is exposed. The script of his forgiveness is humorously scanned, and so, too, the terms of his forgiveness. In *Huckleberry Finn* he is forced to speak through the pipsqueak voice of Tom Sawyer, and instead of making everything right, he gets everything wrong. In *Krazy Kat* he looms as Offisa Pupp, dogged in his effort to put Ignatz behind bars, determined to efface the harsh message of the brick.

There are evidently rare humorists who not only analyze, humorously, the compass of humor, but who also find in writing (the hardest of humorous modes) an appropriate voice, a borrowed energy, that enables them to set at serious risk the super-ego's interpretation of the Nature of Things, its knowledge of the brick. This voice in literature is always Speech, a disfiguring speech that wrongs the right rationality of writing, that is spoken from excluded discourse, from some version of the vulgate. It is typically the voice of an illiterate, a slave, a child, a woman, and if still this is an impersonation of the super-ego, it is the deepest sounding this 'humorist' can make. That his right to determine what is forgivable, if not simply to determine, should be opened to a scrutiny. That, in effect, he should fall silent, and permit another to speak. In humorous performance such humor is the summoned, transforming Genie who overtakes Adolph Marx and turns him into the Discourse of Harpo, the Discourse of Shameless Desire. The crypto-humorous exchanges in *The Ego and The Id* take place not between the super-ego and the ego, but between the 'male' ego and a feminized id. "It cannot say what it wants," Freud writes of the id, so, in some cases, it honks a horn pulled from the voluminous folds of an inexhaustible coat. "Hello, 'Ignatz' dahlink," Krazy says. And who, for that matter, is the 'humorist' in *Finnegans Wake*? Who takes us in to look upon the Monuments of Masculinity, those Exemplars of the Patriarchy, and gets it all wrong, misspells the legend?

> This the way to the museyroom. Mind your hats goan in! Now yiz are in the Willingdone Museyroom. This is a Prooshious gunn. This is a ffrinch. Tip. This is the bullet that byng the flag of the Prooshious. This is the ffrinch that fire on the Bull that bang the flag of the Prooshious. Saloos the Crossgunn! Up with your pike and fork! Tip. (Bullsfoot! Fine!) This is the triplewon hat of Lipoleum. Tip. Lipoleumhat. This is the Willingdone on his same white harse, the Cokenhape. This is the big Sraughter Willingdone, grand and magnetic in his goldtin spurs and his ironed dux and his quarterbrass woodyshoes and his magnate's gharters and his bangkok's best and goliar's goloshes and his pulluponeasyan wartrews. This is his big white harse (*FW*, p. 8).

Just as Freud draws the rounding line of the id around the super-ficial ego in his cartoon of the self, so Joyce incloses HCE in the loose liffey line of ALP, confuses high style and low style, and always keeps before us that impertinent vision of the hero's "big white harse." This circling line, this fluid utterance, is the sign of a new value in humorous writing, the omnipresence of *this* primordial body, of a previous discourse, of a prior speech, which breaks into writing, and changes it. Not wrongly, but properly, narrative now wears a "noo soot of close."

It is to the radical humor of Gertrude Stein's writing that we will now turn, and then to the girlish Huck trapped in Alex Portnoy's complaint. A new schoolmistress stands before us, holding her primer, *How To Write* (1931), and this is the lesson:

> You cannot repeat a duplicate you can duplicate. You can duplicate a duplicate. Now think of the difference of repeat and of duplicate. I am a grammarian. I think of the differences there are. The difference is that they do duplicate. The whole thing arouses no contention.
>
> Think well or melodiously of duplicate. They will never finish with their watches.
>
> Oh grammar is so fine.
>
> Think of duplicate as mine.
>
> It stops because you stop. Think of that. You stop because you have made other arrangements.
>
> Changes.
>
> Grammar in relation to a tree and two horses.[22]

Notes

1. Bridgman, *The Colloquial Style in America*, p. 133.

2. *The Complete Novels of Mark Twain*, ed. Charles Neider, 2 vols (Garden City, New York, 1964), 2:440.

3. *Ibid*, p. 999.

4. John Seelye, *The True Adventures of Huckleberry Finn* (New York, 1971), p. 284. All subsequent reference will be indicated *THF*.

5. William Faulkner, *The Sound and the Fury* (New York, 1946), p. 202. All subsequent reference will be indicated *SF*.

6. ————, *As I Lay Dying* (New York, 1957), p. 156.

7. ————, *The Reivers* (New York, 1962), pp. 46-7. All subsequent reference will be indicated *R*.

8. ————, *The Hamlet* (New York, 1956), p. 111. All subsequent reference will be indicated *TH*.

9. Nathanael West, *Miss Lonelyhearts & The Day of the Locust* (New York, 1969), p. 11. All subsequent reference will be indicated *MLH*.

10. [Marietta Holley], *Josiah Allen's Wife as a P. A. and P. I., Samantha At The Centennial* (American Publishing Company: Hartford, 1887), p. 310. All subsequent reference will be indicated *JAW*. Marietta Holley (1844-1926) begins her career as a humorous writer in 1873 with *My Opinions and Betsy Bobbet's: By Josiah Allen's Wife,* writes sixteen books, most of which continue the adventures of bustling Samantha Allen, and concludes with *Josiah Allen on the Woman Question* in 1914. It is a significant body of work, always topical, always informed, and consistently smart. Like Lowell, Mrs. Holley is a polemical humorist. She argues effectively in her texts for suffrage, for temperance, for political reform, and knew these issues well, knew the opposing argument and how to expose it. Her greatest contribution, however, lies in her resolute analysis of the deeper emotional issues in the lives of nineteenth-century American women. Samantha Allen is strong, unflappable, and she writes firmly with anecdote and example about anxiety, depression, resentment, and dread. There are other women writers in the period who adopt humorous styles: Harriet Beecher Stowe in *Sam Lawson's Oldtime Fireside Stories* (1872), Frances Berry Whitcher in *The Widow Bedott Papers* (1856), Sarah Payson Willis Parton (Fanny Fern), who had considerable vogue in the fifties with *Fern Leaves From Fanny's Portfolio* (1853), but none of these write with the sharply pointed conviction of Mrs. Holley, or with her tenacity. She alone seems to have considered herself a practicing literary humorist. It is significant, then, that she does not appear in the important anthologies of American humor collected in the period, which otherwise mention Mrs. Stowe and Frances Whitcher. The history of nineteenth-century American women humorists begins, of course, with Tabitha Gilman Tenney's *Female Quixoticism: Exhibited in the Romantic Opinions and Extravagant Adventures of Dorcasina Sheldon* (1812).

11. Cited in Ann Charters, *Nobody, The Story of Bert Williams* (New York, 1970), p. 27.

12. "The New Negro," in *The New Negro Renaissance: An Anthology,* introductions by Michael W. Peplow and Arthur P. Davis (New York, 1975), p. 387. A similar exclusion of the minstrel show black occurs in the late 1950s. While justified, such bannings often efface brilliant human performances. When *Amos 'n' Andy* left the air in 1953, under mounting attack, the show took with it Tim Moore's wonderfully guileful Kingfish.

13. Ishmael Reed, *Mumbo Jumbo* (New York, 1970), p. 12.

14. Cited in M. Thomas Inge, "George Herriman," *Krazy Kat,* Nr. 3, p. 46.

15. "What Are Masterpieces," in *Gertrude Stein, Writings and Lectures,* p. 21.

16. Ferdinand de Saussure, *Course in General Linguistics,* ed. Charles Bally and Albert Sechehaye, trans. Wade Baskin (New York, 1966), p. 24.

17. Pierre Couperie and Maurice C. Horn, *A History of the Comic Strip,* trans. Eileen B. Hennessy (New York, 1968), p. 183. There is some reference to Krazy Kat and much useful context in Jerry Robinson's *The Comics, An Illustrated History of Comic Strip Art* (Berkley: New York, 1974), pp. 53-55. A more lavishly produced and informative survey of the comic strip (with a good sampling of Krazy Kat) is found in *The Smithsonian Collection of Newspaper Comics,* ed. Bill Blackbeard and Martin Williams (Smithsonian Institution Press and Harry N. Abrams, Inc.: New York, 1977).

After Huck Writes

18. Sigmund Freud, *The Ego and The Id*, trans. Joan Riviere (New York, 1960), p. 15. All subsequent reference will be indicated *EI*. What finally distinguishes Freud's drawing from the purer category of diagram and chart is the simple fact that it is freehanded. There are several important modern theoreticians, notably D. W. Winnicott and Jacques Lacan, whose psyche-drawing deserves attention. Winnicott's drawings, for example, are watery, filled with jiggling circles. Lacan's illustrations, on the other hand, are largely schematic and essentially optical in their figuring.

19. Alexander Marshack, "Ice Age Art, 35,000-10,000 BC" (American Museum of Natural History: New York, 1979), p. 10.

20. *The Freud Journal of Lou-Andreas-Salomé,* trans. Stanley A. Leavy (New York, 1964), p. 118.

21. Lucile Dooley, "The Relation of Humor to Masochism," *Psychoanalytic Review,* 28 (1941), 45.

22. Gertrude Stein, *How to Write* (Something Else Press: Barton, Vermont, 1973), pp. 110-11.

VI

The Gaiety of Gertrude Stein

Most of us balk at her soporific rigmaroles, her echolaliac incanta-
tions, her half-witted-sounding catalogues of numbers; most of us
read her less and less.

> Edmund Wilson, *Axel's Castle*

T. S. Eliot wanted to ask Gertrude some questions about her writing
and she said, Yes, go ahead. He said, Can you tell me, Miss Stein,
what authority you have for so frequently using the split infinitive?
Henry James, said Gertrude.

> Alice B. Toklas, *What Is Remembered*

It seems to me that Miss Stein is a vulgar genius talking to herself,
and if she is talking to herself, she is not an artist. It is because she
does talk to herself that she offers insuperable difficulties to both
reader and critic. I suggest, therefore, that she be defined out of
existence as an artist.

> B. L. Reid, *Art By Subtraction*

At dinner I sat next to James Branch Cabell who asked me, Is
Gertrude Stein serious? Desperately, I replied. That puts a different
light on it, he said. For you, I said, not for me.

> Alice B. Toklas, *What Is Remembered*

Gertrude and I are just the contrary. She's basically stupid and I'm
basically intelligent.

> Leo Stein, *Journey Into The Self*

In the midst of writing there is merriment.

> Gertrude Stein, *Lifting Belly*

TENDER BUTTONS

Objects

A Carafe, That is a Blind Glass

A kind in glass and a cousin, a spectacle and nothing strange a single
hurt color and an arrangement in a system to pointing. All this and
not ordinary, not unordered in not resembling. The difference is
spreading.

The Gaiety of Gertrude Stein

Glazed Glitter

Nickel, what is nickel, it is originally rid of a cover.

The change in that is that red weakens an hour. The change has come. There is no search. But there is, there is that hope and that interpretation and sometime, surely any is unwelcome, sometime there is breath and there will be a sinecure and charming very charming is that clean and cleansing. Certainly glittering is handsome and convincing.

There is no gratitude in mercy and in medicine. There can be breakages in Japanese. That is no programme. That is no color chosen. It was chosen yesterday, that showed spitting and perhaps washing and polishing. It certainly showed no obligation and perhaps if borrowing is not natural there is some use in giving.

A Substance in a Cushion

The change of color is likely and a difference a very little difference is prepared. Sugar is not a vegetable.

Callous is something that hardening leaves behind what will be soft if there is a genuine interest in there being present as many girls as men. Does this change. It shows that dirt is clean when there is a volume.

A cushion has that cover. Supposing you do not like to change, supposing it is very clean that there is no change in appearance, supposing that there is regularity and a costume is that any the worse than an oyster and an exchange. Come to season that is there any extreme use in feather and cotton. Is there not much more joy in a table and more chairs and very likely roundness and a place to put them.

A circle of fine card board and a chance to see a tassel.

What is the use of a violent kind of delightfulness if there is no pleasure in not getting tired of it. The question does not come before there is a quotation. In any kind of place there is a top to covering and it is a pleasure at any rate there is some venturing in refusing to believe nonsense. . . .

(The first several entries in *Tender Buttons*, a compend of versicles divided into three sections: *Objects, Food, Rooms*. Probably written in 1912, *Tender Buttons* was published in New York by the Claire-Marie Press in 1914.)

1
A Carafe, That Is a Blind Glass

The speculative play of Gertrude Stein's humor first appears in the carefully wrong discourse of *Tender Buttons*. Here is a carafe, "nothing strange," *definiendum,* and there is a glass, *definiens.* Definition is the work of knowledge. It is the first lesson in Aristotle's primer on analytic thinking, the *Categories,* and Gertrude Stein uses it as her *mise-en-scene.* A carafe is a kind of glass. So Western Thought designates the World of Things, establishes Things in the World, species into genus, and constitutes the proper text. But something happens in Gertrude Stein's definition, the spectacle of an effacement, the spectacle of a metaphor, a split in the statement of the object, and all this changes her text, changes the lesson. *That,* which ought to place the carafe categorically before us, do its simple work of reference in the sentence, instead demonstrates its own importance. It makes a statement about statement, turns the simple object into a complex trope, the blind glass through which we see darkly, and holds these discursive antinomies (identity, difference) in bemused regard. "A carafe, that is a blind glass." Keeping strictly within the rules of grammar and syntax, within the logical structure of the predicating sentence, which is always impeccably written in *Tender Buttons,* Gertrude Stein begins here to write a decentered and alogical discourse that will unerringly provide the right answer to the wrong question. The impersonal pronoun that merely points, the prop and pivot of this sentence, points to her determined alienation from the Name of the Father, *Noema,* Aristotle, *et al.,* and the authority of his proper nouns. We will get nowhere in this curious text if we do not recognize at the start the blank figure of her estrangement, how it is written into the equivocal being of the pronoun, that term which does its silent work in the sentence of transferring meaning, placing objects, conjoining substantives, and is typically excluded from the question about reality. In the discourse Aristotle defines, and hands down to us as the *Organon,* the Instrument, the work of knowledge is with nouns.

So *that* begins the play of *Tender Buttons.* It makes us turn to it, to what it does, the activity of referring, this *that,* which, along with its relatives *this* and *there,* is curiously 'free,' without feature or gender, always naming and never the name. *That* is, to a large extent, the heroic utterance of *Tender Buttons,* the purest sign of Gertrude Stein's escape from the fix of definition, for the proper noun that names her surely did not, and her writing now reflects the composure of her difference. What *are* these strange objects: blind glass, glazed glitter, a substance in a cushion, a box, a piece of coffee? And what is the relation or resemblance of the entry to its titular subject? We commonly look at the world, at the text, through Aristotelian spectacles, and see kinds of everything, kinds of glasses, kinds of writing, the nominal realm of logic and philosophy, the metaphorical realm of rhetoric and poetry, and therein distinguish the carafe from the blind glass. This text, for example, 'looks like' an inventory, a lexicon, an "arrangement in a system to pointing."[1] Looks like, but the information, the data, the flow of the discourse, does not specifically fit into the logical system, does not properly respond to the question: what is this, where does it fit, what does it mean? "Nickel, what is nickel," she writes below *Glazed Glitter,* "it is originally rid of a cover" (*TB,* p. 161), and the exchange repeats the exchange of the original proposition, deflects the ordinary course of signification into the surprise of metaphor. This posing of her difference, the perfect obscurity of her *that,* is kept constantly before us, and yet *Tender Buttons* has its meanings, is "not unordered in not resembling" (*TB,* p. 161). The objects, as objects, tell us we are in the presence of Gertrude Stein's immediate reality, the domestic space of her apartment, the particular site of her writing, that they are instances of attention, and the problem of relation, of resemblance, which the pronoun focuses, at once illustrates a major theme in the text and renders the politics of her discourse. In the play of question and answer, of enigmatic statement, as *that* describes and explains, Gertrude Stein appropriates, in her own chosen terms, her sense of this dwelling.

For all its mystery, *Tender Buttons* continually discusses the pleasure of inhabitation. We do not ever leave the inclosure of her apartment, this small world where the eye lovingly remarks the familiar and all reference is privily self-centered, this and that. We move from *Objects* to *Food* into the final section, the amplitude of *Rooms,* and all the while the text is brimming with good humor, with puns, jokes, facetious gaming, cozy talk. The writer is humorously uxorious, contemplates the domestic articles, the domestic activity of cleaning, arrangement, sewing, cooking, and imaginatively reconceives their significance, gives them new meaning. There has been a change in the apartment, in the situation of Gertrude Stein's writing, and this is the new arrangement that requires a different statement. "The change has come" (*TB*, p. 161), she declares early in the text, and there is continual reference to it, the terms of the change, the problem of the change, the delight of the change. Her thinking has changed, her writing has changed, and the change is before us in her style. If, as she would later argue in her lecture "Poetry and Grammar," *Tender Buttons* represents an artistic breakthrough, is the single text in which she broke the "rigid form of the noun,"[2] turned from belabored prose to beguiling poetry, it is a breakthrough *into* the possession of this particular space, the dwelling.

There is, almost, the feel of the raft in *Tender Buttons*, that feeling of being in a protected place, of being comfortably within, a Huckish exaltation. The writer evokes it through her playful interest in domestic concerns, her description of the gear and the provisions, these routines of explanation, and in her obvious relish of the daily fare, pain (bread) soup, creamed cucumber, and roast beef. "This makes no diversion," she reminds us, "that is to say what can please exaltation, that which is cooking" (*TB*, p. 197). And *that*, of course, is not just the meal, but also the preparer, the person. A "sister" appears in the text, sharing the ambiguity of the writer's *that*, like and unlike, whose cookery and cleaning, whose intimacy, is woven into the intellectual and imaginative work of the writer. She is addressed: "A table means does it not my dear it means a whole steadiness" (*TB*, p. 174). She is the sign of the writer's change, the problem of it, and the delight. "The sister was not a mister," we learn in *Rooms*. "Was this a surprise. It was. The conclusion came when there was no arrangement. All the time that there was a question there was a decision. Replacing a casual acquaintance with an ordinary daughter does not make a son" (*TB*, p. 197). What is the relation of this sister, whose near-names are readily given (aider, ale-less, alas), to the particular feeling of this discourse, its humor, and what, in the blind glass of the text, is her likeness? She is for the writer the positive identification of a likeness, a part of *that*, the sister self, the daughter self, a reflection, and in *Tender Buttons* (tend her buttons) she is positively cherished. Here is the connubial vow: to sort out dinner, to remain together, to surprise no sinner, to share everything, and it is tenderly recited:

> To bury a slender chicken, to raise an old feather, to surround a garland and to bake a pole splinter, to suggest a repose and to settle simply, to surrender one another, to succeed saving simpler, to satisfy a singularity and not to be blinder, to sugar nothing darker and to read redder, to have the color better, to sort our dinner, to remain together, to surprise no sinner, to curve nothing sweeter, to continue thinner, to increase in resting recreation to design string not dimmer (*TB,* p. 180).

We need look nowhere outside the text to see this much in the text, its place, persons, convivial humor, its principled evasion of specific reference. The inside narrative of *Tender Buttons* is just there, inside. At the end of the entry *Book,* in the first section, Gertrude Stein reflects upon the phrase "put a match to the seam," a loaded phrase she considers in its several loadings: hot evidently in its sexuality, cold in its textile reference, and a warning in its textual significance against that literal interpretation which would match imaginative characters and events to historical persons and events, looking into the text for its singular and essential definition. Yet the questioning of resemblance in *Tender Buttons,* which keeps us from matching seems, easily and continually becomes a play on resemblance. It is there surely in the optical motif: the blind glass becomes a "spyglass," later an "eye glass," and the single occasion of the first person pronoun in the text is the line "I spy" (*TB,* p. 190). Here, provocatively, she gives us just such a 'leading' scene, a clue, the semblance of a picture postcard posing familiar figures, before abruptly retrieving the anonymity of *that.*

> Please a plate, put a match to the seam and really then really then, really then it is a remark that joins many many lead games. It is a sister and sister and a flower and a flower and a dog and a colored sky a sky colored grey and nearly that nearly that let (*TB,* p. 176).

That nearly let, let us in past the rigorous objectivity of the text to make an exact resemblance, put a match to the seam, writing sister to sewing sister. If the reader were informed, he might indeed espy, against a certain landscape, Gertrude Stein, Alice B. Toklas, and their dog, Polybe, and yet the play of this partial disclosure is not primarily with the reader, is not *for* any reader. It is the play of the writer with her intention, and if it solicits a reader, that person would be the one who holds the plate, who brings the plate. The inside narrative of *Tender Buttons* remains securely inside the present articulation of Gertrude Stein's writing.

The next entry reinstates the freedom of ambiguity, is sweetly wicked in its innocence. Under *Peeled Pencil, Choke,* she writes "Rub her coke" (*TB,* p. 176). Children who stick sharpened pencils into their mouths often choke on them, an admonition we have all heard, but the rhyme and the reason of the succeeding line go awry, erase one meaning to show another: a sexual act, masturbation; a sexual object, the dildo. "Put a match to the seam" is a remark that joins "many many lead games." A sister and a flower. The last entry in *Objects* rejoins the play on the name: *This is the Dress, Aider.* An aider is a helper as well as the near-name, Ada, the adorable. If we recognize this name as the one Gertrude Stein had earlier given to Alice B. Toklas in the portrait *Ada,* that is all to the good, and useful, but the entry itself simply bespeaks through the pun an endearing interruption: "Aider, why aider why whow, whow stop touch, aider whow, aider stop the muncher, muncher munchers" (*TB,* p. 176). We are at the end of the first section, of the *mise-en-scene,* and, beyond this munching, a rare meal is to be served. *Food* begins with the prospect of a menu, a sampling of the courses. Here is a partial list: "Roastbeef; Mutton; Breakfast; Sugar; Cranberries; Milk; Eggs; Apple; Tails; Lunch; Cups; Rhubarb; Single Fish; Cake; Custard; Potatoes; Asparagus; Butter; End of Summer" (*TB,* p. 176). The lexicon is now culinary, but the cuisine is of course literary, the cooking of an allusive meditation, a stirring in of some Shakespeare and Blake, of some "Leaves in grass" (*TB,* p. 191). And here, too, the singular name is sounded.

Cooking

Alas, alas the pull alas the bell alas the coach in china, alas the little put in leaf alas the wedding butter meat, alas the receptacle, alas the back shape of mussle, mussle and soda" (*TB,* p. 191).

It is a kind of inscription, this *aider,* this *alas,* a kind of *Ma Jolie.* *Alas/Alice* is remarked in all these things and activities: little, receptacle, mussle, answering the door, serving a meal, cooking, and the punned name sounds the wifely complaint, alas. The significance of *Alas,* the playful naming, is the key to the specular politics of *Tender Buttons.* Turned, *sister/aider/alas* takes us through the looking-glass into Alice's other-world, the discourse of the other (wifely chatter), and shows us the mazy nature of Gertrude Stein's reflection. In the blind glass is the double, the other, on whom the writer projects at once her desire for recognition and the question of her identity. And here, of course, is the duality (sister as wife, sister as husband) that requires duplicity, that gives Gertrude Stein her multifarious usage of double-talk. The text resounds with the exchanges of these two figures, lover/beloved, writer/speaker, both of whom mirror each other. Lovetalk is double-talk, *ma jolie,* and the lovetalk of wedded lesbians is doubled double-talk, turned against the espionage of the straight world.

Picasso will publish his *amour* on his canvas, an *amour propre,* with magisterial ease. Here is an account of one of his several *Ma Jolies* aptly recorded in the *Autobiography of Alice B. Toklas.* Picasso has just moved to an atelier in the rue Ravignan. "One day we went to see him there. He was not in and Gertrude Stein as a joke left her visiting card. In a few days we went again and Picasso was at work on a picture on which was written ma jolie and at the lower corner painted in was Gertrude Stein's visiting card. As we went away Gertrude Stein said, Fernande is certainly not ma jolie, I wonder who it is. In a few days we knew. Pablo had gone off with Eve."[3] Gertrude Stein's card goes into Picasso's painting; Picasso's device (the integration of found objects, the jocular reference to his love life) will reappear in *Tender Buttons.* The play on *Alas* as a version of *Ma Jolie* relates *Tender Buttons* to the ongoing direction of Cubist painting, and yet Gertrude Stein's rendering of it distinguishes her conceptually from the Cubists. Before we continue our scrutiny of the texture of *Tender Buttons,* we need to consider that difference, and how, for example, chatter, the usage of the discursive-immediate, enters Gertrude Stein's text.

Like much Cubist painting (Picasso is at work in 1911-12 on *Ma Jolie, Woman with Guitar,* as Gertrude Stein writes *Tender Buttons*), the discourse of *Tender Buttons,* as we have seen, exists in the question of relation and resemblance. *That* relates carafe to blind glass, sister to sister, and *that* is always the question, the hedge, the hinge, between the inscrutable intention of an unseen interiority, a perfect absence, and the pure presence of what is objectively stated in the text. "The author of all that," we are told in *Rooms,* "is in there behind the door and that is entering in the morning" (*TB,* p. 197). Who steps into the room? We see simply in the busy metaphor, *that,* the copresence of identity and difference, an act of opening and closing, the play of the writer with designation. The geometry of early Cubist painting works similarly on traditional perspective, suggesting a picture only to deconstruct it. Forms and figures are presented, harlequins and nudes, mandolins and fruit dishes, but their ordinary existence in the pictorial frame is displaced, reorganized. The illusion of depth, of volume, of looking in upon a scene as through a window, is dispelled by the interlocking and overlapping of geometrical planes, by a new sense of light and color, all of which retains perception at the flat surface of the painting. Just as we have to read *Tender Buttons* differently, accept *that,* so we must look differently at the composition of *Ma Jolie.* Each work in its own idiom actively prevents us from realizing in it a certain defined or privileged meaning, distracts the presupposing mode of our attention, and substitutes, through the instrumentality of the pronominal feature, *that,* the geometrical factor, a 'cube,' its discrete and separate existence. The nominal character of the author "in there" behind her text, justifying it, is no longer the issue. A carafe is lost and found in the blind glass. Picasso had his *Ma Jolie,* Gertrude Stein had hers.

In *Ma Jolie* we can only tentatively distinguish space and form amid the crossing lines of force, the overlaid planes. This apt and exemplary painting is about itself, its conception, coloring and arrangement, even though the geometrical configuration teases us with possibilities, with anatomical outline, with the definition of objects, with a subject. In 1911-12 the struggle of re-creation is still in the work, traced, vestigial. Picasso prints on the lower margin of the canvas at once the nickname of his mistress and the refrain of a popular song, *Ma Jolie,* and locates in the vicinity a musical clef and a four-lined staff, as if to express the pure form of the abstracted figure in the simplicity of these obvious signifiers. A name, a song title, some musical symbols, these give us a brief literal fix on the mazy surface of all those shifting and compacted angles, but what they mean in relation to the structure of the painting is not certain.

The very appellation of the title in Cubist painting immediately presents the question of relation and resemblance. Yes, in a sense, this is a table, and that is a fruit dish, and this is a guitar, a woman. So, too, it might be said, the titles in *Tender Buttons* presuppose a description, *Careless Water, Chain-Boats, A Cutlet,* and what we read in the entry is something else, probably related, "not unordered in not resembling." Under *A Cutlet,* this single, striking line: "A blind agitation is manly and uttermost" (*TB,* p. 170).

Yet the Cubist analogy can only be pressed so far, and then it becomes confining. The significance of Gertrude Stein's work, once located within the theoretical field of Analytic Cubism, is often lost there, in the strong light of Picasso's painting. When Marjorie Perloff looks at *Ma Jolie,* for example, she sees in its "odd uncertainty" the question she finds everywhere expressed in Gertrude Stein's poetic writing. "In *Ma Jolie,*" she observes, "the printed letters appear to shift and fade in space and yet they rest flatly upon the opaque plane of the canvas as if they were printed letters on a page. The painting invites us to identify familiar forms and objects (a guitar string? an elbow? a knee? a lamp?) at the same time as it prevents us from applying the test of consistency."[4] She sees, that is, a similarity of effect: the seductive activity of Cubist perspective, the incongruous and arbitrary turns of Gertrude Stein's discourse, and this coincidence enables her to construct first a "Cubist syntax" for the portrait poem *Susie Asado* (1913), and then an Orphic-Cubist/ Surrealist model (drawn from the painting of Duchamp and Picabia) to explain the semiotic reductions of *Tender Buttons.* Gertrude Stein's poetic style at this moment in her career, Perloff argues, "does parallel, as much as the style of any one art can parallel that of another, the instability, indeterminacy, and acoherence of Cubism" (*PWS,* p. 35). Yet the question she transposes from Picasso's painting to Gertrude Stein's text is only partially Gertrude Stein's question, and the resemblance breaks down even as she describes it. The logic of the line in *Susie Asado* goes like this: "A equals B or modifies C or is in apposition to D, but how and why" (*PWS,* p. 35)? Gertrude Stein's implicit question, as Perloff construes it, is appropriately posed inside the form of the syllogism, inside that Aristotelian mode of conceptual thinking which assigns to proper nouns the significance of reality: A is B, C is not D. It is the right question, one Gertrude Stein did ask, but whether its purpose is simply to show, as Perloff concludes, the "arbitrariness of discourse," to throw open the prospect of "countless possible meanings," is another question. Whether the inquiry, how and why *A* equals *B*, makes Gertrude Stein a Cubist writer is still another question.

It is, in any event, the difference in the 'difficulty' of Picasso's painting and Gertrude Stein's writing that leads us back, around *Ma Jolie* (and the problem of the Cubist analogy) to the eccentric sensibility of *Tender Buttons*. This difference first appears in the coincidence of *Three Lives* (1905-06) and *Les Demoiselles d'Avignon* (1906-07), and it has to do with the analysis of the feminine that exists in each work. Both artists begin by subverting the classical representation (La Gioconda, the Madonna), by questioning the value of the icon, "The Good Anna," "The Gentle Lena," but what is revealed in either work, the consequence of the revaluation, is differently stated, differently understood. In her *Autobiography of Alice B. Toklas*, Gertrude Stein takes Alice into Picasso's studio and places her before the unfinished canvas of *Three Women*, a work that torturously elaborates the conception of *Les Demoiselles*. "I felt," Alice says, "that there was something painful and beautiful there and oppressive but imprisoned" (*ABT*, p. 27). And there is, a stripping away of any idealization. What emerges in the new conception is indeed painful, beautiful, oppressive, imprisoned. Both paintings would excite a public scandal in their first showing. Alice's description could, of course, apply as well to the women in *Three Lives*, and yet the monstrosity seen in *Les Demoiselles* and *Three Women* is not the monstrosity felt in *Three Lives*.

In Picasso's painting some demoiselles still retain the musculature of the classical figure, still cling to drapery, and gaze back at us, wide-eyed, while others, turned away, or squatting, or entering upon the scene, are radically altered, have disproportionate heads and grotesque faces. Here, then, is the chiseled serenity of the classical nude, the soft contour of the odalisque, a series of Apollonian postures, and then, abruptly brought forth by sharply cutting angles, Dionysian figures, primitively masked. The demoiselle *is* imprisoned, albeit beautifully, in Picasso's imagination, and so she remains, his creature, his mystery, his model, continually turned in his art to show new aspects of his feeling for her. Gertrude Stein's demoiselles are imprisoned in themselves, trapped inside the definitive virtues of Industry, Faithfulness, Common Sense, Marriage, Maternity, unable to speak the true nature of their desire. In *Three Lives* they relentlessly scrub, are painfully conflicted, bear children, and die. They are, if anything, disembodied, deprived of that naked force Alice beheld in Picasso's painting, and this is what is so savagely told in the repetition and circularity of their speech, their poor futility.

The demoiselle necessarily stands in a different relation to Gertrude Stein, a relation that was from the start charged with political reference, always involved in the issue of repression. That struggle (for the demoiselle, to be the demoiselle) is amply expressed in her early fiction, the very center of *Things As They Are* (1903), first entitled *Q.E.D.* It is rewritten in *Three Lives* and is again present in *The Making of Americans* (1906-11), where the whole question of gender and character is laboriously reconsidered. *Tender Buttons*, as we have seen, announces the "change," is the change. In 1912 Picasso was again in love, this time with Marcelle Humbert, whom he called "Eva," and he wrote her name everywhere on his paintings: *J'aime Eva* here, *Jolie Eva* there, and *Ma Jolie*. Picasso's titling at once pays tribute and declares a possession, the capture and transformation of a model-object, Woman with Guitar. Gertrude Stein is similarly inspired in 1912, and writes the name of her mistress into her text, but her title, which plays on tender-tending-tend her, on this and other things, suggests a collaboration, and the inscription is indeed a thread (Ada, Aider) worked, woven, in and through the labyrinthine weave of the composition. This mistress is also an amanuensis, another self, a participant in the very process of Gertrude Stein's writing. So her voice is in the dialectic of the style, affirming its humor, and at length, later, Gertrude Stein will write a long autobiographical narrative purely in that voice. In the discourse *No* (1915), this passage occurs:

> I go in.
> Tender.
> Buy nothing.
> This was a story they call it Maria.
> Papers.
> Papers made me feel.
> Tall.
> I said believe me I am praised.
> What if he did.
> Russia.

Oh I was so glad.
Happy farm.
Ferny.
Sew.
Buttons.
On.
Gloves.
Space.
Do
Sew
Buttons
On
Gloves.[5]

The flow of such messages in this and other pieces written around the time of *Tender Buttons* is constant. Chatter enters Gertrude Stein's writing, enters it as a positive value, as a resource, and it places before the writer, who meditates, topics, special terms, feelings. These discourses—*No, One Sentence* (1914), *Possessive Case* (1915), and *Lifting Belly* (1915-17)—are as immediate as line sketches, improvisational, written in short lines, often wonderfully curious, and yet, for all their divergent phrasing, they are invariably situated by the presence of an aider, the seamstress/amanuensis who copies the manuscript, who is told to leave a space between the two requests to sew buttons on gloves. It is indeed a small joke which "Tender" sets in motion since earlier in *No* Gertrude Stein had complained: "I should have told you that between pages when there is no intermission and it is on top there's a space" (*AFAM*, p. 39). So the written "space" is typed into the copy and there is this little piece of weaving. The integration of the present moment, its bits and pieces, its oddities, into the text gives us the charm of spontaneity, and yet even as this is so, the chatter also expresses at once the intimacy of the sisters and the artistic importance of that intimacy. For it is spoken from an interior, the inside of a shared life, this chatter, this inconsequent and freely moving discourse, the common speech of the household, and it is herein rendered, twisted, twining, as a language sufficient for the uses of poetry. So it goes in *Possessive Case*:

She has nothing to do at a moment's notice.
Shall I get you your apple now.

> Bring me a new fig.
> Samples are more necessary than ever.
> That is not the way to lament.
> You needn't have everything taken out. You will never
> tell your sweet sad story better than that.
> Gardens mustn't frighten baby.
> They always are a funny pair (*AFAM*, p. 113).

"Reading Gertrude Stein in this period," Richard Bridgman has observed, "is rather like listening to an interminable tape recording made secretly in a household. Amid domestic details, local gossip, references to failed ambition, to sewing, to writing, recriminations, apologies, and expressions of remorse come passages of intimate eroticism, sometimes quite overt in meaning."[6] And this is true, these discourses, which present the chatter of a "funny pair," are revealing. "With startling audacity," Gertrude Stein writes in *Possessive Case*, "he [she] has in many cases called them by their real names" (*AFAM*, p. 157). For Bridgman these pieces constitute something of an excursion, an idyllic interlude in which Gertrude Stein allowed the "demon of noon" to caper openly through her work. "Gertrude Stein continued to experiment," he notes, "but her aesthetic advances were overshadowed by autobiographical details" (*GIP*, p. 150). It is a distinction that misconstrues the nature of Gertrude Stein's experiment in this period. The *Ma Jolie* expressed in these writings, directly voiced, is the *Ma Jolie* whose value, whose useful knowledge, helps situate the play of *Tender Buttons*. Chatter, after all, not only discloses a certain reality of the interior life, household life, names "real names," but it is also, in some sense, a discursive skin that fits round, contains closely, is nearest to, the interior-life of consciousness itself. "Oranges are painful," Gertrude Stein writes at the close of *Possessive Case*. "They are so interior" (*AFAM*, p. 159). In its effortless and casual flow, its associative movement, its themes, its commonplaces, chatter is akin to the 'free' language of dreams. It is brought, this 'idle' gossip, this jesting sweet-talk, within the scrutiny, the propriety of writing, and it speaks humorously to the writer:

> Please mention me.
> I am delighted with that.
> You know you mustn't.
> Please mention me (*AFAM*, p. 159).

In *Lifting Belly* (1915-17), perhaps the most telling of these pieces, Gertrude Stein works a refrain of endearing diminutives into the composition (pussy, baby, honey, hubbie), establishing in her prosy poem the tonal equivalent of Krazy Kat's effusive " 'Lil Dahlink.'' Nearly all the pieces written around *Tender Buttons* are humorous and written in a changed style that recalls, in its byplay, the exchanges present in Huckspeech. It is an assertive and anxious Tom Sawyerish writer who continually says "I said believe me I am praised" (*AFAM*, p. 47), and a Huckish voice, somewhat Krazy, that typically responds "Shall I get you your apple now" (*AFAM*, p. 113)? Around 1909-10 Alice B. Toklas enters Gertrude Stein's writing in several guises, as *Ma Jolie,* the demoiselle, as wife and sister, as the Maker of the Home, this interior space that becomes the site of Gertrude Stein's text. She is also the amanuensis, directly addressed in the writing, used as a mirroring intelligence. She is effectively the framing language of the domicile, a feminine speech distributed among its traditional concerns—household objects, food, rooms— and therein a response to the question in Gertrude Stein's mind about relation and resemblance. So Alice B. Toklas is in *Tender Buttons*, not as an autobiographical reference, not as a specific character, but as the very space in which the writing (and the question) of *Tender Buttons* takes place, as the tender *and* the button.

In our own time Donald Barthelme, a sometime humorist, writes an excellent chatter, sifts it, like Gertrude Stein, through a fine seine for its significance, its comedy, its contrapuntal value. Throughout *The Dead Father* (1975), that funny-sad novel which drags a stubbornly undead Patriarchy towards its problematical interment, father and son (a doubting Thomas) discourse in large bulky paragraphs, exchange pompous father-myths and anxious son-myths. The Dead Father is fond of listing his inventions and possessions. He loves to name, to count over his nouns, to orate, proclaim, proscribe: "I fathered upon her in those nights the poker chip, the cash register, the juice extractor, the kazoo, the rubber pretzel, the cuckoo clock, the key chain, the dime bank, the pantograph, the bubble pipe, the punching bag both light and heavy, the inkblot, the nose drop, the midget Bible, the slot-machine slug, and many other useful and humane cultural artifacts, as well some thousands of children of the ordinary sort."[7] The Dead Father recites his catalog; the son peruses *A Manual for Sons.* The manual begins by defining kinds of fathers and becomes a manifesto, a Jeffersonian refusal (still another doubting Thomas) of patriarchal power. Meanwhile there are two demoiselles who accompany the funeral cortege in the novel, Julie and Emma, and when they speak, they speak in *asides,* in chatter:

> Thought I heard a dog barking.
> A spiritual aridity quite hard to reconcile with his surface gaiety.
> Left Barcelona in disgrace.
> I was suspicious of him from the first.
> Certain provocations the government couldn't handle.
> Too early to tell. That's a very handsome pin.
> My mother's. Willed to me at her death.
> Goodbye goodbye goodbye.
> Think I'll stick around for a while.
> That's interesting.
> Have you told him?
> To my shame I have not.
> And if it is at all possible for you to see me.
> Fond urgings and soft petitions (*DF,* p. 26).

This political sense of chatter, this humorous understanding of chatter (which has its sharp edges, its anxieties) first appears in the new style Gertrude Stein realizes in *Tender Buttons.* Here, it might be said, Aristotle and *Ma Jolie,* Father and Demoiselle, contest the issue of knowledge. Whose table do we contemplate in the entry *A Table,* his table or her table? That table on which the Law is written, the elements inscribed, the one which "means a whole steadiness," which arranges words, numbers, signs, in parallel columns to exhibit a set of facts or relations in a definite, compact, and comprehensive form, that exemplary table with its "necessary places," or this singular household table, a "little thing" subject to change, to revision, which stands in its own system of values, more important than a glass?

A Table

A table means does it not my dear it means a whole steadiness. Is it likely that a change.

A table means more than a glass even a looking glass is tall. A table means necessary places and a revision a revision of a little thing it means it does mean that there has been a stand, a stand where it did shake (*TB,* p. 174).

We are, as it were, on the other side of that looking-glass, in Alice's opposed world, in another discourse, regarding the mystification of logical discourse, that knowledge which makes shaky things seem to stand. In the final section, *Rooms,* where the routine of question and answer becomes urgently metaphysical, no longer so much an issue of what as why, the interlocutor simply deals straight lines: "Why is there education, there is education because the two tables which are folding are not tied together with a ribbon, string is used and string being used there is a necessity for another one and another one not being used to hearing shows no ordinary use of any evening and yet there is no disgrace in looking, none at all" (*TB,* p. 202). The answer turns the question down, provocatively. Here are two collapsing tables tied with string, and more string. *Why is there, because,* the work of scientific thought, each *because* generating a new *why,* this activity, *education,* resembles the expedient labor of fixing these tables in the text and all are subject to such revision. Big questions, little cunning answers.

The "simple operations" of syntax and diction in *Tender Buttons,* Donald Sutherland writes in *Gertrude Stein, A Biography of Her Work* (1951), "are ultimate operations of the mind, whether they are done by the grade-school child or by Socrates. Science calls it dichotomizing but it is dividing by two, and one can have as high an old time 'halving rivers and harbors' as in dividing the oviparous from the mammal and coming out with the answer that the whale is not a fish. The answers in *Tender Buttons* are even more marvelous than that."[8] Science is indeed gay in this discourse, shown to be full of surprises: "Sugar is not a vegetable" (*TB,* p. 162). And this gaiety, this glad acceptance of being wrong, enables Gertrude Stein to change the work of definition into the play of metaphor.

2
There is no gratitude in mercy and in medicine.

Of this *that,* or *there,* which plays such a prominent role in the style of *Tender Buttons,* Gertrude Stein would later declare: "Pronouns are not as bad as nouns because in the first place practically they cannot have adjectives go with them" (*WL,* p. 128). The parts of speech are poetically enlivened in the lecture "Poetry and Grammar" and politicized. She prefers the humbler parts—conjunctions, prepositions, articles, verbs, and adverbs—because they "all do something," function in the sentence, work, whereas nouns are simply fixed properties, inflexibly right, given. The Huckish voice often speaks purely in Gertrude Stein's writing, saying simply the deepest things. "Nouns and adjectives never can make mistakes can never be mistaken but verbs can be so endlessly, both as to what they do and how they agree or disagree with whatever they do" (*WL,* pp. 126-127). So pronouns are "not as bad" as nouns, she told her university audience in 1934, "they of course are not really the name of anything. They represent some one but they are not its or his name. In not being his or its or her name they already have a greater possibility of being something than if they were as a noun is the name of anything" (*TB,* p. 128). As Gertrude Stein renders it, grammar is indeed "very exciting." The parts of speech describe the roles in the family romance: Fathers and Sons (Nouns and Adjectives), Mothers and Daughters (Verbs and Adverbs), the substantive Head of the sentence and the transactive Body of the sentence. Nouns are powerful (*bad* is the word Gertrude Stein uses), whereas verbs make mistakes, are mistaken. There are the retainers, some "pleasing" (articles and prepositions), others, like the comma, "servile." The pronoun is ambiguous, and, in that ambiguity, free. Early in the lecture she gives us a brief glimpse of herself as a schoolchild absorbed in diagramming sentences, an activity she then found "completely exciting and completely completing" (*WL,* p. 126). It is, of course, the 'primal scene' to which Humor always returns, that beginning of knowledge, that fall from innocence, the place where *Huckleberry Finn* begins, the Writing Lesson. A girlish Gertrude Stein sits there drawing and redrawing, in those branching genealogies of meaning, the politics of the sentence. Pronouns, she tells us, are "better than nouns."

Escape, evasion, flight from definition, that world named by the Father and owned by the Father, the Father who holds the money, the Father who demands the money, that Pap whose name wrongly identifies Huck as the swinish Finn, pig not fish, rooter not swimmer, this is the imperative that makes Huck err. He desires only to lie loosely in a protected place beside a forbidden and pleasurable *Other,* and be nameless, unknown. That same desire to err, to give voice to error (it could be called the wellspring of humor) informs Gertrude Stein's writing in *Tender Buttons* and amplifies the importance of *that.* In "Poetry and Grammar" she is clear about her intention. She wrote in *Tender Buttons* something resembling a love poem, but to speak that feeling, to celebrate the beloved, *Ma Jolie,* Herself, she had to change the value of the name, if not the name itself. "Was there not a way of naming things that would not invent names, but mean names without naming them" (*WL*, p. 141). The question engendered the strategy of the style in *Tender Buttons,* a strategy that relied in part on a certain evasion, a considered evasion. "I struggled," she remembered, "I struggled desperately with the recreation and the avoidance of nouns as nouns and yet poetry being poetry nouns are nouns" (*WL*, p. 143). As a subtle grammarian, Gertrude Stein knew the function of the parts of speech, the power of classification, and the consequence of gender. She knew, in brief, how politicized were the prevalent modes of scientific and imaginative discourse, how prejudicial to her experience, and knew this as a fate. No one could invent "new names new languages" and still communicate. "So everyone must stay with the language," she declares, "their language that has come to be spoken and written and which has in it all the history of its intellectual recreation" (*WL*, p. 142). How, then, to name anew, differently, the already-named? How to seize the power of naming without leaving the economy of language? Her struggle was desperate, its resolution humorous. She would move back and forth between different symbolic orders, different discursive systems, in language, between a figurative identification with the Father and a figurative identification with the Mother, between scientific discourse and chatter, and retain a perfect, playful balance. The program of *Tender Buttons* is to enjoy, as *jouissance,* the relation of both orders and systems, both identities.

The question Gertrude Stein phrased in "Poetry and Grammar" returns us to the beginning of *Tender Buttons. That* has juxtaposed carafe and blind glass, and remarked the difference. *That,* along with its cousin, *there,* continues to predicate, to place and misplace the question in the second entry, *Glazed Glitter.* There is a question, "what is nickel," and a circulating answer. This answer, while not specific, not logical, is nonetheless *about* the question, *about* the title. What it obliquely discusses is the very change that makes this poetic discourse possible.

Glazed Glitter

Nickel, what is nickel, it is originally rid of a cover.
The change in that is that red weakens an hour. The change has come. There is no search. But there is, there is

> that hope and that interpretation and sometime, surely
> any is unwelcome, sometime there is breath and there will
> be a sinecure and charming very charming is that clean
> and cleansing. Certainly glittering is handsome and con-
> vincing.
> There is no gratitude in mercy and in medicine. There
> can be breakages in Japanese. That is no programme. That
> is no color chosen. It was chosen yesterday, that showed
> spitting and perhaps washing and polishing. It certainly
> showed no obligation and perhaps if borrowing is not
> natural there is some use in giving (*TB*, p. 161).

That is, the shining of the *G*, the prominence of *G*, is before us,
caught up in a brief meditation on the meaning of shining. "Nickel,
what is nickel, it is originally rid of a cover." The slip of the pronoun, *it, that, there*, leads us through the branching turns of this
passage to a climactic recognition: "Certainly glittering is handsome
and convincing. / There is no gratitude in mercy and in medicine,"
and then onward to an apt resolution. *It* first breaks Nickel into its
change, its several meanings (coin, plating, ore), its several contexts,
breaks it down to not-nickel, to its unearthed, unrefined origin, and
in so doing, *it*, like *that* at work on the carafe, calls attention to itself
as not-nickel. To which property of nickel does *it* refer? First exchange. Subsequently *that/there* mediates between two different
gs, *glittering* and *gratitude*, meditates upon their difference, their
relation. To shine, wash, polish, to glaze and make glitter, that is
woman's work. To shine, be bright, to glitter, that is man's work, is
"handsome and convincing." To shine in the double sense, that is a
redemption, a sinecure. William Gass changes the nickel into " 'Nick,'
the name of the Devil himself, and 'Hell,' his hot location," and
works out a different frame of reference for redemption and sinecure. This nickel reveals the original nickel, a "German coin called
Kupfernickel because, although it was a copper color, it yielded
none of the metal, and for this deceit, like a fool's gold, was accused
of being the devil's ore,"[9] but who is the devil on the face of this
coin? Whose glitter is false?

The whole passage is a spun web of fine allusion. "There is no
gratitude in mercy and in medicine." No Gertrude in a thankless
feminine role, no Gertrude laboring as a medical student at Johns
Hopkins, laboring in a science dominated by glittering men. No

Gertrude, in sum, fixed, defined, trapped, in a gender-specific role. No thanks. The pronoun makes the play of the style, is the stitch that weaves philosophy into poetry, familiar and personal reference into cultural and political reference, always showing (humorously) its hand, for this is a pronoun that has learned, after all, how to weave, to spin, to shine, to make do with fragments. "There can be breakages in Japanese." Leo Stein, the arrogant and extruded brother whom Alice B. Toklas replaced as Gertrude Stein's partner in the apartment at 27 rue de Fleurus, was a collector of Japanese *objets d'art,* this could play in the sentence, but, for all that, the brief statement about breakage actually belongs to a certain familial line of chatter in *Tender Buttons.* Under a later title, *A Plate,* Gertrude Stein considers "Plates and a dinner set of colored china" (*TB,* p. 165), and then again, under *Careless Water*: "No cup is broken in more places and mended, that is to say a plate is broken and mending does do that it shows that culture is Japanese. It shows the whole element of angels and orders" (*TB,* p. 170). So there can be breakages in Japanese, and while this homely lesson teaches us something about the difference in china and Japanese crockery, it also shows us, in the plate, in the cup, a closed Chinese culture, so perfect it cannot be broken, and an open Japanese culture which can be broken and mended. It shows us a scale of values, "the whole element of angels and orders." In the entry, *Glazed Glitter,* however, the broken Japanese is still cryptic, a fragmented remark. Here, in the associative flow of things, it simply takes its place, as a remark, among diverse glazed glittering things that are washed and shined, and possibly broken.

We have only to see, from the other side of the blind glass, how the subject of shining (glittering/gratitude) is thought through another perspective, another, discourse. "Certainly glittering is handsome and convincing." Brightness is all. Those who have shined, the polishers, know this. The concluding aphorism, which tidily resolves the question of shining, resumes those nouns which name, without naming, sexual roles, sexual identities. "It certainly showed no obligation and perhaps if borrowing is not natural there is some use in giving." If borrowing, being needful, dependent, is a role imposed on women, along with "that clean and cleansing," a way of being that is "not natural," then, as this is the world, things as they are, there is "some use" in adopting the masculine prerogative, in giving.

Gertrude Stein will continually rethink in *Tender Buttons* the politics of its disposition, and reflect the consideration through an exchange of knowledges, his table, her table. Shining is a noun, and shining is a verb. There is, of course, a sensible reading of *Tender Buttons* that would assert the statement of *Glazed Glitter* means nothing other than what it states, but this sensible reading is innocent, stops at the shiny surface, and will not move from its logic, from its Aristotelian notion of how thought and writing cohere in a rational mode of exposition. It will not move to the place where the answer is given to the question, and see the question from that standpoint. What is a carafe? What is nickel? The decision not to describe definitively, to name properly, is principled, and it should turn us inward each time, as Aristotelian readers, we come upon a fault. What is wrong here? What constitutes the wrongness of the arrangement? To what in the glass, the mirror of the text, are we blind? To *that*, obviously.

A Substance In A Cushion is next in *Tender Buttons.* If we are to look for the essential meaning of this passage, we must find it in the figure of costume, of apparel, in all this reference to fabric and sewing, to texture and color, in a playful domestic chatter: "and very likely the little things could be dearer but in any case there is a bargain and if there is the best thing to do is to take it away and wear it and then be reckless be reckless and resolved on returning gratitude" (*TB*, p. 162). Thought about Substance is always about its trimming, where Substance is, and what Substance wears. We move from the washing of dishes, the shining of glazed surfaces, to the stuffing of cushions with "feather and cotton," the covering of cushions, to costume. And here, too, "change" is before us as a problem, as a recurrent topic, as an ethical question. "Callous is something that hardening leaves behind what will be soft if there is a genuine interest in there being present as many girls as men. Does this change. It shows that dirt is clean when there is a volume" (*TB*, p. 162). Does it change? Callous/callus/phallus/Alice: all these changes, hardening, softening, trimmed, enable *it* to show something. Pronouns are always showing in *Tender Buttons*. In *Glazed Glitter* "that showed spitting" and "It certainly showed no obligation." Here "It shows that dirt is clean when there is a volume." Huckish thinking in a higher learning: what is dirty can, in other contexts, be clean. The fresh earth in the morning, for example, is a lot of clean dirt. So Gertrude Stein continues to play with definition and metaphor in the text, a play that also, at another remove, turns us in upon silent intensities in discourse, the emotional value that lies hidden in the innocence of simple remarking, the tension that occurs when these big philosophical nouns, Substance, Appearance, Difference, Change, are transfigured, seen in the cushion, in the color of a sash.

Out of this particular entry will come a sustained analysis of color, and a coloring of other themes: dirty yellows, sad blues, cool roses. Under *A Red Hat* Gertrude Stein will write: "A dark grey, a very dark grey, a quite dark grey is monstrous ordinarily, it is so monstrous because there is no red in it" (*TB*, p. 167). This is a 'dark' speculation, almost Melvillean. There are 'lighter' tones in the text. *A Petticoat* gives us: "A light white, a disgrace, an ink spot, a rosy charm" (*TB*, p. 171). And all along, beside and within such topics, such lines of consideration, Gertrude Stein will remark her approach, describe the use and feeling of her text. "A sentence of a vagueness that is violence is authority," she writes just into the middle section, *Food*, "and a mission and stumbling and also certainly also a prison" (*TB*, p. 181). What that sentence does in the violence of its vagueness, its stumbling refusal to give a straight answer, is already done in the first several entries of *Tender Buttons*, if not in the first line of the text. Subjects and objects change as we move from section to section, themes elaborate, but they are always expressed in this wronging sentence, a sentence whose "mission" is to misnominate, to mistake the question. In *Food*, in the first entry, *Roastbeef*, at the end of which Gertrude Stein authoritatively writes her vague sentence, we are still before the question—"To shine, why not shine, to shine" (*TB*, p. 177)—still thinking about the quality of mercy. "A letter which can wither, a learning which can suffer and an outrage which is simultaneous is principal," she writes under *Mutton*, appropriately recalling the sheepish experience of instruction. "Students, students are merciful and recognized they chew something" (*TB*, p. 181). Wherever we are in *Tender Buttons*, whether we are looking at *A Red Hat* or *A Blue Coat, An Umbrella* or *A Petticoat*, contemplating *Roastbeef* or *Mutton*, we are obliged to rethink the relation of vagueness to authority, shining to shining.

As Gertrude Stein writes, "it is so easy to exchange meaning, it is so easy to see the difference" (*TB*, p. 177). To be the interlocutor who inquires, here in a certain interlocutory discourse, "handsome and convincing," and the respondent, there in the discourse of the demoiselle, "charming," replying from the interior of the apartment where all these quizzed objects and activities have a purely personal meaning. Yet the ease of this exchange, of seeing this difference, is deceptive, for it conceals still another question, the identity of the double-seeing, double-thinking exchanger. *A carafe, that is a blind glass.* As we have seen, the problem is with *that,* and here, in *that,* through *that,* Gertrude Stein's humorous play takes its serious turn. *That* mediates, relates, is for the noun, but never it, and so it leaps, or repeats, like consciousness itself. "There is no search." "That is no programme." It simply announces, speaks. In *The Geographical History of America* (1936), *that* will graduate in Gertrude Stein's thinking to its highest likeness, the Human Mind. The Human Mind has no identity, only a fleeting present where each moment "it knows what it knows when it knows it."[10] Self, Name, Identity, these are objects the Human Mind thinks about, aspects of Human Nature, but *it* is never *that,* never the thing it thinks about. The subtitle of the *Geographical History* is *The Relation of Human Nature to the Human Mind,* and there is no relation, so Gertrude Stein argues. In 1910-11, as she changes her style, begins to shine, the relation of human nature to the human mind (mind/body, male/female) is still an issue. *That* has not yet become the supreme fiction. Here it signifies the immediate direction of the writer's attention, a writer who has decided to make certain semiotic exchanges, who has deeply pondered the organization of her discourse, who moves in and out of systems of identification. *That* is a particular pronoun. It can be used to identify anything. It does not declare gender (Gertrude Stein's use of these pronouns is sparing); it is indefinite, simply a pointer, simply an utterance. In "Poetry and Grammar," explaining the project of *Tender Buttons,* Gertrude Stein would cite the indirect discourse of *Leaves of Grass.* And indeed, as a stylistic device, a pointer, *that* does behave like the comprehensive intelligence seeing and speaking everything (contrarities, dualities) in "Song of Myself."

Apart from the pulling and hauling stands what I am,
Stands amused, complacent, compassionating, idle, unitary,
Looks down, is erect, bends an arm on an impalpable certain rest,
Looks with its sidecurved head curious what will come next,
Both in and out of the game, and watching and wondering at it.[11]

So *that,* "amused, complacent, compassionating, idle, unitary," makes the curious exchanges in *Tender Buttons,* turns simple signs into complex tropes, realizes the politics of naming, knows the Noun, produces its own meaning, is the supervisory wit who waggishly designates *A Centre in a Table* at the end of *Food,* and places in that center a text. All that verbal cooking, that mixture of metaphor, that delectation, that sprinkling of singsong, finally produces a repast. Here is a feminine text, in a folder, the only occasion of *me* in *Tender Buttons* (one *I,* one *me*), and there is the demoiselle, *Ma Jolie.*

> Next to me next to a folder, next to a folder some waiter, next to a foldsome waiter and re letter and read her. Read her with her for less (*TB,* p. 196)

We then enter the final section, *Rooms.* It begins: "Act so that there is no use in a centre" (*TB,* p. 196). Just over this threshold, in this single long meditation, Gertrude Stein will resume a host of centering themes: change, identity, relation, resemblance, the problem of a center. Everything comes streaming back into attention: table, oyster, student, a single mirror, white, red, green, eyeglasses, sister, mister, sugar, chair. In *Rooms,* this metaphorical space, an amplitude, the apart-ment of ciphering consciousness, we hear something resembling a diapason, full-throated, exultant. "Harmony is so essential," Gertrude Stein writes. "Is there pleasure when there is a passage, there is when every room is open" (*TB,* p. 198). Through these passages the "author of all that" now appears, "and that is entering in the morning" (*TB,* p. 197). This is the change, the new arrangement in these rooms: song, play, the presence of gaiety, the opening of an inside narrative. For here, in joking connubial complaint, is a "starving husband" made to fast, "not at all bloated" (*TB,* p. 198), a sister (not a mister) who has replaced a "casual acquaintance with an ordinary daughter" (*TB,* p. 197), who worries, misterwise, about the arrangement. "Then there is a way of earning a living. Who is a man" (*TB,* p. 198). *Rooms* is quick with the surprise of disclosure, the opening of categories (rooms) to different uses. Who is a man? The earner of a living. What is the relation of this plump husband to that "single set of sisters" (*TB,* p. 203)? She looks, double-thinking, about the room. Here is "A little lingering lion and a Chinese chair, all the handsome cheese which is stone, all of it and a choice, a choice of a blotter" (*TB*, p. 197). Here is belittled Leo Stein (lion-stone) effaced, yet lingering in the signs of his interests (Oriental art). The glittering brotherly Stein, the dull sisterly Stein, but that is another story, told through a different figure (sound), slowly and carefully told, in the contemporaneous piece, *Two: Gertrude Stein And Her Brother* (1910-12).

To get out of the double bind of a contradictory identification, the anxiety of concealment, into the "single mind that directs an apple" (*TB*, p. 199), that has been all along the difficult project of Gertrude Stein's writing in *Tender Buttons*. So she appropriates the interiority of her rooms, this imaginative space, and comprehends in a single style, in question and answer, in rarefied double-talk, two different systems of meaning and value in discourse. The working of the style puts her, ideally, outside the dualism that is the haunt of writing in the West, turns philosophy into poetry, poetry into philosophy. Her writing "shows" objective description and an inside narrative, a weave, and is so thoroughly con-fused, trans-figured, that effectively the mixture *is* the meaning of the text. The sense we make of the world, after all, depends on an education ("why is there education") that encodes through the primordial lesson of the Writing Lesson, the proper relation of the parts of speech, the diagram of the sentence, a division of the self in the world. From her privileged position in these rooms, the nonsense ("a no since") of her gaiety, Gertrude Stein saw no certainty in that definition of the self. She understood perfectly the elusiveness of Whitman in his poetry, and wrote cunningly of her own sleepless nights, of the anxiety of being open, the diminishment of self involved in living a double life. Of the delight of disclosure, revealing one's self, getting past the "oldest caution," rearranging one's position in bed.

> Lying in a conundrum, lying so makes the springs restless, lying so is a reduction, not lying so is arrangeable.
> Releasing the oldest caution that is the pleasing some still renewing.
> Giving it away, not giving it away, is there any difference. Giving it away. Not giving it away (*TB*, p. 201).

On the lift from such lying, past the "oldest caution," Gertrude Stein approaches the open-ending of *Tender Buttons*.

3

all this makes a magnificent asparagus,
and also a fountain.

We begin in *Tender Buttons* looking at a carafe; at the end we
contemplate a fountain. How do we get from the carafe to the
fountain, from containment to outpouring, from small to large? To
this particular ending, which celebrates Error, the rectitude of being
wrong? Here, it might be said, Humor realizes its fondest desire,
thinks its highest thought: "all this," acceptance of the wrong,
understanding of the wrong, pleasure in the wrong, "incredible
justice." A transfiguration occurs in the mixture of this metaphor,
and a new likeness is made.

> The care with which the rain is wrong and the green is
> wrong and the white is wrong, the care with which there is
> a chair and plenty of breathing. The care with which there
> is incredible justice and likeness, all this makes a magnifi-
> cent asparagus, and also a fountain (*TB*, p. 206).

Asparagus and a fountain. We have to read the passage carefully to
appreciate what is humorously considered in it. Being wrong, this for
sure, and making the wrong right. The quintessential act of high
humor, we have seen, is just this act of intelligent forgiveness which
transforms, head on, the hard hurt of a conundrum. Huck is in a
double bind before the true/false name of Jim, *nigger.* Gertrude Stein
has lied/lain in a conundrum, a question whose answer always
involves a pun, an understanding of double talk. So the question of
identity in *Tender Buttons,* of relation and resemblance, which, in
an ordinary sense, Gertrude Stein gets all wrong, is gathered up into
the humorous comprehension of care. It is this care, whose meaning
is a mixture of tender love and scrupulous attention, that ultimately
assures justice (wrong righted) and perfect likeness, this doubling
care which cooks the magnificent asparagus (a her self) and also
creates that artistic construction, a fountain (a his self). In *Food,*
under *Asparagus,* Gertrude Stein has already written: "Asparagus in
a lean in a lean to hot. This makes it art and it is wet wet weather
wet" (*TB,* p. 190). The care of this skill is artistic, she realizes there,
while outside it is raining, "wet weather." Cozy here, inside, the
asparagus is exquisitely prepared, and outside it is inhospitable, cold
and lonely. Care is also providence, the assurance of Being continu-

ously flowing, the chair there, and plenty of breathing. Care situates in these rooms the singularity of this single set of sisters.

That is the prolific answer to the question. It is given to us, "notwithstanding." The whole turn of this effusive passage, which ends with care flowing, effectively begins with an exposition of that term, *notwithstanding*. It means, the Dictionary tells us, something is true even though there are obstacles or opposing conditions. "What was the sensible decision," Gertrude Stein wonders. We do not discover it. We encounter instead cases of notwithstanding, a play of doubled negatives, the knotting of a conundrum.

> The sensible decision was that notwithstanding many declarations and more music, not even notwithstanding the choice and a torch and a collection, notwithstanding the celebrating hat and a vacation and even more noise than cutting, notwithstanding Europe and Asia and being overbearing, not even notwithstanding an elephant and a strict occasion, not even withstanding more cultivation and some seasoning, not even with drowning and with the ocean being encircling, not even with more likeness and any cloud, not even with terrific sacrifice of pedestrianism and a special resolution, not even more likely to be pleasing (*TB*, p. 206).

In spite of this, notwithstanding notwithstanding, something is true, the sensible decision, even though there are obstacles or opposing conditions. So humor thinks. So Huck thinks in his soliloquy on the raft. Out of the knotted conundrum, all this negation, Gertrude Stein wrests the affirmation of care, a care that is happily wrong.

There is a philosophy of the wrong in *Tender Buttons*. It is shown in the style, not argued. In a masterpiece, that rounded, decentered, many-sided work of the Human Mind, Gertrude Stein writes in *The Geographical History*, "you cannot be right, if you could it would be what you thought not what you do write." She pauses, looking at the homonymical play of the two terms. "Write and right. Of course they have nothing to do with one another." Then, with an abrupt turn that calls to mind the zany leaps of Groucho Marx, she goes wrongly marching off, out of step. "Right right left right left he had a good job and he left, left right left" (*GHA*, p. 235). Lying in a conundrum, vaguely writing a violent sentence that is "certainly also a prison" (*TB*, p. 181), composing a double-talk simple and complex, giving it away, not giving it away, Gertrude Stein continually addresses the wrong in *Tender Buttons*. It is doubly conceived and dialectically rendered. For the wrong is not here, in her experience, in her writing, but there, in that other discourse, the definitive discourse, which is not sufficient to explain her. Which improperly defines her. The pressure of that wrong, the nemesis of proper naming, of identity, is always upon her. "I struggled I struggled desperately with the recreation and the avoidance of nouns as nouns and yet poetry being poetry nouns are nouns" (*WL*, p. 143). This struggle, to recreate nouns, to avoid nouns, to wrong right writing, would drive B. L. Reid, an attentive reader, to distraction.

> In her art she does not reflect, for reflection entails consciousness of identity and audience, an awareness fatal to the creative vision. She rules out the imagination because it is the hunting ground of secondary talent. She rules out logical, cause-effect relations: "Question and answer make you know time is existing." She rules out distinctions of right and wrong: "Write and right. Of course they have nothing to do with one another." She will have no distinctions of true and false: "The human mind is not concerned with being or not being true." She abjures beauty, emotion, association, analogy, illustration, metaphor. Art by subtraction finally subtracts art itself.[12]

What baffles Reid is Gertrude Stein's refusal to explain herself, to take him into her consideration. He has the right question; she has the wrong answer. His tone in *Art By Subtraction, A Dissenting Opinion of Gertrude Stein* (1958) is that of the High Executioner: "This book is born of a gradual disenchantment, and I suppose it finally amounts to an essay in decapitation—without acrimony, but with conviction" (*ABS*, p. vii). And yet, for all his dudgeon, perhaps because of it, Reid is often close to the mark in his reading of Gertrude Stein's work, so close he is at times in it, her mark, fooled, foiled. The whole rich element of her *jouissance* slides past him, unremarked. He reads straight her crooked lines. Still Reid knows, doggedly, where she went wrong. "It is her colossal blind spot," he exclaims, "her refusal, or perhaps her real inability, to recognize the inescapable gap between the sensorium of a private, idiosyncratic thinker and writer and the sensorium of an audience that has to make its peace not with the process or the theory, but with the end product" (*ABS*, p. 112). She is not in 'our' discourse, he tells us repeatedly, she has set aside the values of identity and audience, broken the discursive pact, and therefore 'we' cannot take her seriously. "The matter is as simple as this: the words do not mean the same things to us that they mean to her; she is writing in one language, we are reading in another" (*ABS*, p. 198). All this, the displacement of an *arche* (a centering origin), the abandonment of a *telos* (a determining form), all this Gertrude Stein did realize, as a perfidy, around 1910-12 in the stylistic turn from *The Making of Americans* to *Tender Buttons.* She did refuse to enter that common discourse which is founded on the principle of an "inescapable gap" between the interiority of consciousness and the exteriority of writing, but the wrongness of her writing, expressed in the immediate *now*, in *that* and *there*, the "continuous present," no longer looks so strange.

The textual spinning and weaving of *Tender Buttons*, this discourse which cooks a pain soup, recreates nouns, avoids nouns, surely anticipates that "metapatriarchal discourse" Mary Daly describes in *Gyn/Ecology, The Metaethics of Radical Feminism* (1978), for this critical writing, like Gertrude Stein's writing, strives to deconstruct an entire system of patriarchal identification, to exchange the meaning of names, and it directly addresses the underlying *episteme*, the issue of that "inescapable gap." "We must learn," Daly writes, "to dis-spell the language of phallocracy, which keeps us under the spell of brokenness. This spell splits our perceptions of our Selves and of the cosmos, overtly and subliminally."[13] The project of *Gyn/Ecology*, to see through the patriarchal text, to deconstruct the patriarchal *mythos*, and seize the power of naming, begins in much the same act of intelligent *ressentiment* that moved Gertrude Stein to rethink as a question *Q. E. D.*, things as they are. "Who is a man?" she asks in *Tender Buttons.* Yet her writing is never polemical, or programmatic. The deconstructive energy of her style does not involve a rhetoric of contradiction, which substitutes a new identity for an old identity, but rather does away entirely with the concept of identity. *Subject* drops out of writing, or rather into writing as an object, "the author of all that," and here then is the text, deeply wronged, that so provokes Reid to write an essay in decapitation.

Gertrude Stein writes in one language, he argues, we read in another. As everyone knows, there are now two interpretations of interpretation, one which "seeks to decipher, dreams of deciphering, a truth or an origin which is free from freeplay and from the order of the sign, and lives like an exile the necessity of interpretation," and another, a latter-day interpretation, which seems perfectly attuned to the difference of Gertrude Stein's language, the difference of her text. This interpretation, Jacques Derrida tells us, "is no longer turned toward the origin, affirms freeplay and tries to pass beyond man and humanism, the name man being the name of that being who, throughout the history of metaphysics or of ontotheology—in other words, through the history of all his history—has dreamed of full presence, the reassuring foundation, the origin and the end of the game."[14] *Tender Buttons,* which "surrenders itself to *genetic* indetermination, to the *seminal* adventure of the trace" (*SSP,* p. 264), would seem the right text for such interpretation, and indeed it does anticipate that reading, just as it proposes, through its "sensible decision" *notwithstanding,* a homespun version (in these rooms) of the "metapatriarchal journey" Daly describes in *Gyn/Ecology.* And yet, while *Tender Buttons* discloses its subversive play to these critical approaches, it also, by virtue of its humorous intelligence, eludes the ideology of that interpretation. There is a vengeance that moves through Derridean thought (which prefers, above all, the cold hard humor of the Nietzschean text), a desire to rectify, that often makes it seem a merciless hunt for myths of presence. Susan Handelman places Derrida's "linguistic-metaphorical hermeneutic" directly within the tradition of Rabbinic thought, and sees him as a "*Jewish* prodigal son" attacking the "European psyche and the Holy Logos" as an act of revenge. Along with Freud, Derrida "will try . . . to recapture the 'purloined letter,' to redeem Scripture from the abuses it has suffered at the hands of Greeks and Christians."[15] Gertrude Stein, of course, is a *Jewish* prodigal daughter whose alienation in the "European psyche" is doubled, and yet she lives comfortably with the Saints. The discursive site of *Tender Buttons* is already cleared, already decentered, free of all the tricks of incarnation.

In moving from carafe to fountain, to spilling care, to that lulling sing-song of innocence and nonsense: "a no since, a no, a no since a no since, a no since, a no since" (*TB,* p. 195), Gertrude Stein effectively declares a state of writerly innocence. Write, she wrote to John Hyde Preston in 1935, "without thinking of the result in terms of a result, but think of the writing in terms of discovery, which is to say that creation must take place between the pen and the paper, not before in a thought or afterwards in a recasting. Yes, before in a thought, but not in careful thinking." The thought (revised) leads her to a wonderfully mixed metaphor that recalls the doubled imagery of *Tender Buttons.* "Freeze your fountain and you will alway have your frozen water shooting into the air and falling and it will be there to see—oh, no doubt of that—but there will be no more coming. . . . You cannot go into the womb to form the child; it is there and makes itself and comes forth whole—and there it is and you have made it and have felt it, but it has come itself—and that is creative recognition."[16] Such immediate writing closes the gap between the interiority of consciousness and the exteriority of writing considerably—creation takes place between pen and paper—and if what occurs in this continuous present resembles Derridean freeplay, a writing given over to chance, it also evokes the amoral, unmotivated, plotless ideal of Huckspeech. That is, it is a style in flight, defining itself as flight. "Of course," Gertrude Stein continues, "you have a little more control of your writing than that; you have to know what you want to get; but when you know that, let it take you and if it seems to take you off the track don't hold back, because that is perhaps where instinctively you want to be and if you hold back and try to be always where you have been before, you will go dry" (*AC*, p. 188).

In 1910-12, however, the gaiety of Gertrude Stein's *jouissance* is still problematical, still precarious, for all its flow and lilt. What was the sensible decision, notwithstanding? The complicated and continuous reference to cleansing, washing, shining, and to dirt, the volume of it, dirty dirt and clean dirt, refers to more than just domestic tasks, domestic values. It is effectively the work of the text in *Tender Buttons,* to make the discourse shine, to recreate, unsullied, without justification, the nature of Gertrude Stein's experience in these rooms, this imaginative space. Yet the vague sentence she writes with authority is "also a prison." "During the decade of choice," Catharine R. Stimpson writes in "The Mind, The Body, and Gertrude Stein," "Stein both stopped resisting her sexual impulses and found domestic pleasure in them. However, during the same period, if often before the meeting with Toklas, she takes certain lesbian or quasi-lesbian experiences and progressively disguises and encodes them in a series of books."[17] Whatever the motive for this encoding, Stimpson argues, whether "to transform apprentice materials into richer, more satisfying verbal worlds," or "to write out hidden impulses . . . to evade and to confound strangers, aliens, and enemies," the effect is a dislocation of sensibility. Such literary encoding "does what Morse code does: it transmits messages in a different form which initiates may translate back into the original." And in so doing, "it also distances the representation of homosexuality from its enactment in life." In those relevant texts, *Q. E. D., Three Lives* and *The Making of Americans,* "what were lesbian experiences become, if possible, sadder and sadder" (*MBGS,* p. 499). *To be wrong, that is to be gay.* The turn in attitude toward that premise is certain in *Tender Buttons,* and yet the problem of the code, as "lead game" or "conundrum," is still very much present in the double-talk of the text, which is always "giving it away, not giving it away."

Double-talk, double bind. There is a theme in the chatter Gertrude Stein writes in *Possessive Case*:

> My father is a martyr and is unkind to me (*AFAM,* p. 150).
> She has inherited her father's exactness from his science (p. 155).
> I don't think men meant to educate me (p. 156).
> I was trembling because my mother had never loved me and I circled about and I made a promise and I did lessen birds I showed the whole perturbation and believe me (p. 158).

By 1910-12 Gertrude Stein had dragged her version of the Barthelmian Dead Father (His Science, His Story, that Massive Martyr) a considerable distance. She had dragged him though Harvard where she studied psychology in the gaze of William James and Hugo Munsterberg, through the medical school at Johns Hopkins where, bored by her studies, she contrived her own dismissal, and she dragged him to Paris, where she fled in 1903. In Paris, at 27 rue de Fleurus, the Dead Father principally spoke through the many opinions of Gertrude Stein's arrogant older brother, Leo, who held her writing in contempt. *There is no gratitude in mercy and in medicine.* But there was Leo Stein, whose learning had to be suffered. He was not yet a larger proper noun in 1903, a big name, but he was certain that he would become one, and in the meantime he glittered, was handsome and convincing. The paternal bulk in Barthelme's *The Dead Father* is 3,200 cubits in length, "the whole great expanse of him running from the Avenue Pommard to the Boulevard Grist." His left leg is "entirely mechanical" with "Facilities for confession, small booths, with sliding doors" (*DF,* p. 4). In Gertrude Stein's fiction he is stretched the wide length of *The Making of Americans* (1903-11), which appropriately begins with a telling anecdote from Aristotle's *Nicomachean Ethics*: "Once an angry man dragged his father along the ground through his own orchard. 'Stop!' cried the groaning old man at last, 'Stop! I did not drag my father beyond this tree.' "[18] If Gertrude Stein had put Harvard and Johns Hopkins behind her, she had not as yet abandoned Aristotelian discourse, for in this labyrinthine work, this psycho-historical novel, she sought continually to analyze character and behavior, to locate "bottom natures," to define identity. She wrote it, moreover, in the presence of Leo Stein.

> I was writing in the way I was writing. I did not show what I was doing to my brother, he looked at it and he did not say anything. Why not. Well there was nothing to say about it and really I had nothing to say about it. Gradually he had something to say about it. I did not hear him say it. Slowly we were not saying anything about it that is we never had said anything about it.[19]

What Leo Stein did in fact say to his sister about *The Making of Americans* resembles B. L. Reid's thesis in *Art By Subtraction.* "He said," Gertrude Stein remembered in *Everybody's Autobiography* (1937), "it was not it it was I. If I was not there to be there with what I did then what I did would not be what it was. In other words if no one knew me actually then the things I did would not be what they were" (*EA,* pp. 76-77). Indeed Leo Stein has the distinction of being the first reader of Gertrude Stein's work to argue that it is hermetic, written in a private language, and therefore not to be taken seriously. In 1934, writing in the *Atlantic Monthly,* B. F. Skinner would develop the theory that *Tender Buttons* was an example of automatic writing, composed in a trance. His article asks the question: "Has Gertrude Stein a Secret?" These fraternal/paternal evaluations of Gertrude Stein's writing, which disparage and dismiss it, are curiously akin to Catharine Stimpson's 'sympathetic' reading, which stresses the trickery of encoding in Gertrude Stein's early fiction. Double-talk, double bind. As Gertrude Stein worked away at *The Making of Americans,* writing this long novel in comparative isolation, changing her conception of it, revising her thought, she often wearied, and the strain of its analytic discourse would show through the text, be written as contradiction. *I love doing this, I am tired of it.*

> I am beginning now to go on with my history of the Dehning family and of Julia Dehning and of her marrying and of the Hersland family and of Alfred Hersland and of every one they any of them came to know in their living. To begin again then from pretty nearly the beginning. I am remembering everything I have been telling. I am always loving all repeating. I am realizing kinds in men and women. I am realizing Alfred Hersland and Julia Dehning. That is I am certainly somewhere near to a fairly complete realization of them and of some whom they knew each one and who came to know them either of them. I am a little tired now with all this beginning again. I am hoping that I am going on again (*MOA,* p. 611).

Still she would continue to drag this analysis in *A Long Gay Book* (1909-12), rebeginning a painstaking examination of the "many kinds of fundamental nature in men and women,"[20] except that here the methodical prose suddenly splinters into the poetic style of *Tender Buttons. A Long Gay Book* begins with a long catalog of what it will discuss. It will examine "pairs of people and their relation," provide "short sketches of innumerable ones," and then take up "everybody I can think of ever, narrative after narrative" (*MPGS,* p. 17). But the narrative line is soon abandoned, and the writing becomes rocky, broken. The textual space is everywhere fractured, revealing nooks, crannies, discontinuities. *A Long Gay Book* is in fact a short gay book that becomes gayer and gayer in tone and diction: "Pale pet, red pet, pink pet, blue pet, white pet, dark pet, real pet, fresh pet, all the tingling is the seeding, the close pressing is the tasting" (*MPGS,* p. 97). At the end of this abbreviated text we are already in the understanding of double-talk that underlies the discourse of *Tender Buttons.* If, as Stimpson suggests, Gertrude Stein had encoded the aspect of her sexuality in the earlier writing, concealed her thought about desire in duplicitous language, she posed her sexuality prettily here.

What *is* double-talk, after all, but a mystification, a secret code, a form of humorous speech? It is an impertinent or evasive answer to a pressing question. It is the parlance of the slave who, in that particular Hegelian sense, must always double-think. Whether the slave is a black man, a child, a woman, or sexually deviant, whatever, he/she quickly learns the art of double-talk, the deft turns of double-thinking. Is your man black or white, the slave-catchers demand of Huck. His response is a perfect expression of double-talk, the giving of a necessary lie. Who is a man?—that is a question in *Tender Buttons*. This double-talk, illicit, funny, suspicious, is of a kind. Yet that discourse of mastery, of definition, which denounces double-talk, calls it a mystification, is also a kind of double-talk. Philosophy, Gertrude Stein would assert in the *Geographical History,* is nothing but double-talk, rarefied. "When you are one you are through with philosophy, because philosophy has to talk to itself about it, anything but a master-piece does that and if it does then it is not one but two" (*GHA,* p. 186). So her singular writing weaves a distinctive double-talk, mixes different systems of signification, puts asparagus next to a fountain, slips the noose of identity by not being centered, fixed in either discursive realm, and therein escapes (through the leaping use of the indefinite pronoun) the tragic double bind Julia Kristeva describes in *About Chinese Women,* a double bind that had hitherto imprisoned Gertrude Stein in a circumlocutory prose.

> If a woman cannot be part of the temporal symbolic order except by identifying with the father, it is clear that as soon as she shows any evidence of that which, in herself, escapes such identification and acts differently, resembling the dream or the maternal body, she evolves into this "truth" in question. It is thus that feminine specificity defines itself in patrilinear society: woman is a specialist in the unconscious, a witch, a bacchanalian, taking her *jouissance* in an anti-Appolonian, Dionysian orgy.
>
> A *jouissance* which breaks the symbolic chain, the dominance, the taboo. A *marginal speech,* with regard to the science, religion, and philosophy of the *polis* (witch, child, under-developed, not even a poet, at best a poet's accomplice).[21]

The final passage of *A Long Gay Book* makes a fine preface to *Tender Buttons.* It begins with a play on "shining ees" (Gertrude

Stein) and "silentsses" (Alice B. Toklas). "All the use is humorous" (*MPGS*, p. 114), she writes. And what follows is a complicated allusion to *Leaves of Grass*, to the double-talk of Whitman's poetic discourse. "Leaves of hair," Gertrude Stein muses, and then: "Call me ellis [Alice], call me it in a little speech and never say it is all polled, do not say so" (*MPGS*, pp. 114-15). The reference is extended: "Leaves off grass," and "Leaves in oats." She concludes by etching a chief, a precursor who gives her no anxiety at all.

> Leaves a mass, so mean. No shows. Leaves a mass cool will. Leaves a mass puddle.
> Etching. Etching a chief, none plush (*MPGS*, p. 116).

As we have seen, Gertrude Stein would cite Whitman in "Poetry and Grammar" as a writer who understood the necessity for renaming. "He worked very hard at that, and he called it *Leaves of Grass* because he wanted it to be as little a well known name to be called upon passionately as possible" (*WL*, p. 144). Whitman had addressed the issue of "forbidden voices" in his poetry: "Voices indecent by me clarified and transfigured" (*LG*, p. 29), and in the "Calamus" poems he spoke directly to companionable initiates, spoke openly (a paradox Gertrude Stein might well have appreciated) about his encoded discourse. It is Whitman, after all, who first celebrates a singular comprehension of the double identity, who asserts: "I am the poet of the body,/ And I am the poet of the soul," who then explains: "I am the poet of the woman the same as the man" (*LG*, p. 48). *Leaves of Grass* is very much in Gertrude Stein's thought as she changes her stance in writing around 1910-12, and she refers to it not only at the end of *A Long Gay Book*, but also in *Tender Buttons* where she playfully remarks in *Food*: "Leaves in grass and mow potatoes" (*TB*, p. 191). She, too, had become a poet who compassed identities, whose new style transfigured metaphorical systems.

The "author of all that" who enters the room in *Tender Buttons* has left behind her the massive edifice of *The Making of Americans*. There it is, large, long, imposing, a veritable science of the self which sets forth in painstaking analysis a binary classification of character and behavior: male/female, independent/dependent, aggressive/passive, and it all rests on the foundation of a history, on genealogy. As Gertrude Stein drew the family tree in this narrative, the "History of a Family's Progress," she drew in effect the ultimate tree beyond which one does not drag the Father. She would leave this expository mode, not so much because it compelled her to encode the nature of her desire, but because it was itself inadequate to express her experience. "I do not want," she wrote near the end of *The Making of Americans,* "that any one should experience anything any way but the way each one is experiencing that thing." She then mulled that over. "No I do not want anything to be at all a different thing in the way each one is experiencing each thing, no I do not want anything to be different in experiencing than it is in each one, I certainly do not, I may but I doubt it, I certainly do not, I am certain of this thing" (*MOA,* p. 737). The labor of writing history, the work of defining character, these become Gertrude Stein's story in the novel. Then, abruptly, this methodical prose, glacial in its movement, is gone. "Leaves a mass, so mean" (*MPGS,* p. 116). Her thought no longer moves syllogistically through long series of propositions (each, some, many is/are this or that, or not). She becomes a humorous writer: her sentence is everywhere breached by "forbidden voices," admits the seeming inconsequence of chatter, entertains the play of double-talk, rejoices in that marginal speech which is the discourse (Huckspeech, Krazytalk) proper writing always excludes. "All the use is humorous" (*MPGS,* p. 114), she writes in *A Long Gay Book.*

So it is in *Tender Buttons,* where Substance is the stuffing in the cushion and all the objective questions have subjective answers, where His double-talk is related to Her double-talk, and *that* is the maker of resemblances. All the use is humorous, notwithstanding. In *Q. E. D.* the heroine cries out bitterly: "I always did thank God I wasn't born a woman."[22] There is a new likeness in *Tender Buttons,* the shining sister, the tender aider, and Gertrude Stein now happily writes: "More of double" (*TB,* p. 163). That hitherto forbidden voice, unphilosophical, unscientific, not to be taken seriously, which she had herself rigorously kept out of her text, begins to speak everywhere in her writing, is everywhere humorously irreverent. "Say how do you do to the lady. Which lady. The jew lady. How do you do. She is my wife."[23] We enter then (the text is *Lifting Belly*) the amorous dialectic of an intimate double-talk:

> Pink salmon is my favorite color.
> To be sure.

We are so necessary.
Can you wish for me.
I never mention it.
You need not resemble me.
But you do.
Of course you do.
That is very well said.
And meant.
And explained.
I explain too much.
And then I say.
She knows everything.
And she does (*BTV*, p. 100).

Gertrude Stein had come to understand precisely the value of this humorous voice. Every explainer in a humorous text must confess it: *she knows everything*. She knew everything about Gertrude Stein. And she would tell it in *The Autobiography of Alice B. Toklas* (1933), which resolutely shines the genius of Gertrude Stein.

Notes

1. *Tender Buttons*, in *Gertrude Stein, Writings and Lectures*, p. 161. All subsequent reference will be indicated *TB*.

2. "Poetry and Grammar," in *Gertrude Stein, Writings and Lectures*, p. 142. All subsequent reference will be indicated *WL*.

3. Gertrude Stein, *The Autobiography of Alice B. Toklas* (New York, 1933), p. 136. All subsequent reference will be indicated *ABT*.

4. Marjorie Perloff, "Poetry as Word-System: The Art of Gertrude Stein," *American Poetry Review*, 8 (1979), 34. All subsequent reference will be indicated *PWS*. See also Marianne DeKoven, "Gertrude Stein and Modern Painting: Beyond Literary Cubism," *Contemporary Literature*, 22 (1981), 81-95, for an exemplary post-structuralist approach to Gertrude Stein's experimental writing.

5. Gertrude Stein, *As Fine As Melanctha* (New Haven: Yale Univ. Press, 1954), p. 47. All subsequent reference will be indicated *AFAM*.

6. Richard Bridgman, *Gertrude Stein in Pieces* (New York: Oxford Univ. Press, 1970), p. 149. All subsequent reference will be indicated *GIP*.

7. Donald Barthelme, *The Dead Father* (New York, 1975), p. 36. All subsequent reference will be indicated *DF*.

8. Donald Sutherland, *Gertrude Stein, A Biography of Her Work* (New Haven: Yale Univ. Press, 1951), p. 96. All subsequent reference will be indicated *GSBW*.

9. William Gass, *The World Within the Word* (Boston, 1979), p. 85.

10. Gertrude Stein, *The Geographical History of America* (New York, 1973), p. 147. All subsequent reference will be indicated *GHA*.

11. Walt Whitman, *Leaves of Grass,* ed. Sculley Bradley and Harold W. Blodgett (New York, 1973), p. 32. All subsequent reference will be indicated *LG*.

12. B. L. Reid, *Art By Subtraction* (Norman: Univ. of Oklahoma Press, 1958), p. 171. All subsequent reference will be indicated *ABS*.

13. Mary Daly, *Gyn/Ecology, The Metaethics of Radical Feminism* (Boston, 1978), p. 4.

14. Jacques Derrida, "Structure, Sign, and Play in the Discourse of the Human Sciences," in *The Languages of Criticism and the Sciences of Man,* ed. Richard Macksey and Eugenio Donato (Baltimore: Johns Hopkins Univ. Press, 1970), p. 264.

15. Susan Handelman, "Greek Philosophy and the Overcoming of the Word," *Works and Days,* 1 (1980), 67.

16. John Hyde Preston, "A Conversation," *Atlantic Monthly,* CLVI (1935), 188.

17. Catharine R. Stimpson, "The Mind, The Body, and Gertrude Stein," *Critical Inquiry,* (1977), 498. All subsequent reference will be indicated *MBGS*.

18. Gertrude Stein, *The Making of Americans* (Something Else Press: New York, 1966), p. 3. All subsequent reference will be indicated *MOA*.

19. —————, *Everybody's Autobiography* (New York, 1973), p. 76. All subsequent reference will be indicated *EA*.

20. *A Long Gay Book* in *Matisse Picasso and Gertrude Stein with two shorter pieces* (Something Else Press: Barton, Vermont, 1972), p. 15. All subsequent reference will be indicated *MPGS*.

21. Julia Kristeva, *About Chinese Women,* trans. Anita Barrows (London, 1971), p. 35.

22. Gertrude Stein, *Fernhurst, Q. E. D., and other early writings* (New York, 1971), p. 58.

23. —————, *Bee Time Vine and Other Pieces* (New Haven: Yale Univ. Press, 1953), p. 100. All subsequent reference will be indicated *BTV*.

VII

The Genius of Gertrude Stein

Sing to me I say.
Some wives are not heroes.
Lifting belly merely.
Sing to me I say.
Lifting Belly (1915-17)

I am a husband who is very good I have a character that covers
me like a hood and must be understood which it is by my wife
whom I love with all my life and who makes it understood that
she isn't made of wood and that my character which covers me
like a hood is very well understood by my wife.
Didn't Nelly and Lilly Love You (1922)

The three geniuses of whom I wish to speak are Gertrude Stein,
Pablo Picasso and Alfred Whitehead.
The Autobiography of Alice B. Toklas (1933)

What is it that you like better than anything else, he asked and
she said. I like being where I am. Oh said he excitedly, and where
are you. I am not here, she said, I am very careful about that. No I
am not here, she said, it is very pleasant, she added and she turned
slightly away, very pleasant indeed not to be here.
Ida, A Novel (1941)

1

*C*all me ellis. Almost everything Gertrude Stein writes after *A
Long Gay Book,* which calls upon *ellis,* which invokes *Leaves
of Grass,* is gaily written. In this period, 1912-22, she now composes
in the "continuous present," that most rigorous of tenses for a
writer, and what is in the scan of this particular present is the ongoing "arrangement" she has with Alice B. Toklas, the problem and
the pleasure of that relationship. There are surely other topics and
themes in her discourse, but the humorous character of a misspelled
Alice, *ellis,* "my little jew," entering the text primarily as a voice, a
value, the talk of a double, determines the singular feeling of Gertrude Stein's diverse composition. So *risque* is the funny feeling in

this work, so revealing, Gertrude Stein would suppress the more frolicsome texts in her lifetime. The notable exception is *Tender Buttons* (1914), which gives it away, which doesn't give it away, and those curious pieces (*Ada, Miss Furr and Miss Skeene*) carefully selected for *Geography and Plays* (1922). Yet here it all is, collected in the several volumes of the *Yale Edition of the Unpublished Writings of Gertrude Stein*, profuse, anomalous, extant: *Bee Time Vine, Pink Melon Joy, Possessive Case, Lifting Belly, et al.*, the wrong made humorously right. These texts constitute a body of work that places Gertrude Stein, as a merry modernist, at once beside George Herriman and James Joyce.

It is withal a distinctively gay modernist text that Gertrude Stein creates in this period. Her sketches, poetic dialogues, portraits and plays are veritably possessed by a Humor, an *elan*, an *ellis*, that keeps the discourse happily improvised. "In the midst of writing," she declares in *Lifting Belly*, "there is merriment" (*BTV*, p. 115). And there is:

> You are sure you know the meaning of any word.
> Leave me to see.
> Pink.
> My pink.
> Hear me to-day.
> It is after noon.
> I mean that literally.
> It is after noon.
> Little lifting belly is a quotation.
> Frankly what do you say to me.
> I say that I need protection.
> You shall have it.
> After that what do you wish.
> I want you to mean a great deal to me.
> Exactly.
> And then.
> And then blandishment.
> We can see that very clearly.
> Lifting belly is perfect.
> Do you stretch farther.
> Come eat it (*BTV*, p. 96).

And so it goes. Lifting belly is delicious. We are in the badinage of a lover's discourse, and lifting belly is its language. These cozy diminutives, "Darling Wifie" and "little hubbie," this litany of endearment, this tender address, babytalked, double-talked, can only be written in that other language, the one we do not take seriously, which has the belly as its choicest figure, not the phallus. "My baby is a dumpling," Gertrude Stein maternally writes. "I want to tell her something" (*BTV*, p. 80). The double (as demoiselle) elicits this speech, and her presence in the discourse (she is addressed, cited, quoted) is all the difference in the text. As long as she is here, beside the writer, before the writer, she changes entirely the composition. Like Huck in *Tom Sawyer*, like Jim in *Huckleberry Finn*, she is that cherished *other* whose function in the text is to be outside writing, the excluded one. Everywhere *in* Gertrude Stein's text, variously figured, differently inscribed, Alice B. Toklas never becomes a character who writes. She does not, for example, write her own autobiography. She is simply the value of a certain voice, a certain utterance, *La Langue*, lifting belly, the mother tongue, which the writer humorously appropriates. "My baby is a dumpling." Even heroes, imperial Caesars, out of their armor, feeling humorous, amiably expose themselves in the lapse of this speech, and are belittled, made human. So merriment appears in the midst of writing, and the writer, who thinks herself a shining hero, a Caesar, a "Frederick or Frederica," is immediately beguiled.

> Kiss my lips. She did.
> Kiss my lips again she did.
> Kiss my lips over and over and over again she did (*BTV*, p. 80).

Here, then, is the *amour* implicit in all that humorous coupling in American literature, that odd coupling of stiff and supple: Wilbur and Biglow, George and Sut, Tom and Huck, Huck and Jim, Ignatz and Krazy Kat, but it is rendered, through the indulgence of doubletalk, as *amour-propre*. When the writer embraces "little lifting belly," she also embraces "Mount Fatty," for this licentious trope does double duty, is passed punningly back and forth. The routine of contradiction typically performed in the humorous exchange becomes in this style, in *Lifting Belly*, a reassuring round, and the 'humorist' who sings it is motherly:

> Lifting belly is so kind.
> Lifting belly is so dear.
> Lifting belly is here (*BTV*, p. 80).

The Genius of Gertrude Stein

Out of nothing, as it were, the odds and ends of domestic life, pieces of chatter, bits of rhyme, gossip, tender asides, reminiscences, talk of apparel, of sewing, of cooking, of cleaning, of coming and going, all that ephemeral 'speech' which is truly the vulgate, the vernacular, which speaks from the commonest of places, the household, Gertrude Stein creates a knowing and complicated literary discourse. It is brought, the rich activity of this speech, unbracketed, into the established framework of proper literary form, and there, in the consequent breakage, is the familiar commotion of the humorous text. *Tender Buttons* is loosely a lexicon. *Lifting Belly* is what, a poetic dialogue. *Ida* is a kind of novel. Yet the humorous writer of these difficult texts is not the popular humorist who writes, in a Huckish voice, *The Autobiography of Alice B. Toklas*, and before we turn to the mystery of that novel novel, *Ida*, the difference should be remarked.

2

And so, Huck writes at the end of *Huckleberry Finn*, "there ain't nothing more to write about, and I am rotten glad of it, because if I'd a knowed what a trouble it was to make a book I wouldn't a tackled it and aint't agoing to no more" (*HF*, p. 366). So Alice, somewhat differently, resigns the troublesome labor of writing at the close of the *Autobiography*:

> I am a pretty good housekeeper and a pretty good gardener and a pretty good needlewoman and a pretty good secretary and a pretty good editor and a pretty good vet for dogs and I have to do them all at once and I found it difficult to add being a pretty good author.
>
> About six weeks ago Gertrude Stein said, it does not look to me as if you were going to write that autobiography. You know what I am going to do. I am going to write it for you. I am going to write it as simply as Defoe did the autobiography of Robinson Crusoe. And she has and this is it (*ABT*, pp. 309-310).

Not a stitch is dropped in Alice's transfer, which reveals Gertrude Stein's impersonation. The revealed writer picks up the stitch: *pretty good, pretty good, pretty good* becomes *to write, to write, to write,* and so we remain in the weave of the humorous style. Yet irony is impending. The same voice continues to speak, complaining, but now it tells us that it is written. Gertrude Stein refers to Defoe and Robinson Crusoe, to autobiography as concealed fiction, to masterful writing and slave speech, and none of this is "simply" done. Alice's humorous tale turns round into Gertrude Stein's ironic text, and "this is it." The last page of the text is a facsimile, *First page of manuscript of this book.* For her part, Alice has regularly complained about the exclusion of Gertrude Stein's genius, discussed the *oeuvre,* referred readers to the appropriate texts, all the while resolutely shining the surface of Gertrude Stein's genius, and here, then, the Genius is, and is not. Here at least is a picture of her writing, the evidence of her hand. It makes, this final transference, a curious double negative: Alice admits she did not write the narration, Gertrude Stein does not speak in the narrative voice. Two different senses of exclusion are conjoined in the single style. It is for us to determine the relation of Alice's Huckish speech, that relegated discourse—"Miss Stein told me to sit with Fernande. . . . I have sat with wives of geniuses, of near geniuses, of would be geniuses, in short I have sat very often and very long with many wives and wives of many geniuses (*ABT,* pp. 16-17)—to its subject, the prejudicial exclusion of Gertrude Stein's genius from the Pantheon of Modern Art.

So the ruse is discovered. The ending of the *Autobiography,* which twice declares: *I am not here,* at once contradicts the intention of the form, self-revelation, and the obvious appeal of autobiographical narrative, intimacy. The facsimile, a picture of Gertrude Stein's writing, returns us to the beginning of Alice's tale, to reread, to review, and there, of course, the frontispiece, a picture of Gertrude Stein writing, now takes on a new significance. We are in the author's study, the space where the manuscript is written. Alice is framed on the threshold in the illumined background. She stands directly facing the eye of the camera, one hand on the door latch, as though she were about to enter. In the foreground, in profile, partially obscured by the darkness, a writer sits at her desk, pen in hand. She is at work, occupied. The vertical planes of the study: windows, doors, woodwork, wallpaper, divide the high-ceiling'd room into compartments of solitude, and between the two isolated figures, bisecting the planes, is the broad barrier of a book-laden table, the writing desk. Muse/model, writer/artist, the photograph depicts the proper relation of the two women. It also describes spatially Alice's 'place' in the

Alice B. Toklas at the Door. Photograph by Man Ray.

composition, which, in reviewing the portraiture in the *Autobiography,* we now come to understand. The frontispiece is appropriately entitled: *Alice B. Toklas at the door, photograph by Man Ray.* It is precisely that point of view Gertrude Stein ironically represents in the *Autobiography,* Alice looking in upon the scene of writing, Alice at the door. The wifely tale we first read cozily takes us in, shows us the interior of this celebrated Parisian salon, 27 rue du Fleurus, sketches the artists and writers assembled there, reports their raillery, their repartee, tells stories, some of which tattle, and places us, at every opportunity, 'next to' Picasso.

> Later I was near Picasso, he was standing meditatively. Do you think, he said, that I really do look like your president Lincoln. I had thought a good many things that evening but I had not thought that. You see, he went on, Gertrude, (I wish I could convey something of the simple affection and confidence with which he always pronounced her name and with which she always said, Pablo. In all their long friendship with all its sometimes troubled moments and its complications this has never changed.) Gertrude showed me a photograph of him and I have been trying to arrange my hair to look like his, I think my forehead does (*ABT,* pp. 18-19).

The wifely tale we reread is told from the outside, and it is a different tale.

Who are all these geniuses, near geniuses, and would-be geniuses, and how is it that they have monopolized *La Gloire*? If we go inside Modern Art, who is there? Picasso strikes his pose as the Great Emancipator, and *Ma Jolie* deftly draws him in that posture. Whether to shine, that was a question in *Tender Buttons*. The problem in the *Autobiography* is the strong light of Picasso's virile splendor. *Gertrude, Pablo.* The glory of Picasso assures the *Autobiography* its public, and the guarantee of *Gertrude, Pablo* in the text is Picasso's portrait of Gertrude Stein, that beautiful painting which now hangs in the Metropolitan Museum of Art in New York. Herein lies the difference of the twice-told tale. The muse/model, whose form is typically the artist's subject, his 'truth,' his *Ma Jolie*, works in this text, through her observation, to liberate that other muse/model, Gertrude Stein, from the definition of Picasso's painting. The portrait itself is justly regarded, but its significance as the scene of a capture, the work in which Picasso realized Gertrude Stein, created her true likeness, this oppressive meaning is displaced. Gertrude Stein's place in modern art is not dependent upon Picasso's frame of reference, Alice argues. And yet there is the problem, there *is* Picasso, handsome and glittering. So Alice sits with Picasso's mistresses, his beautiful models, and politically observes Gertrude and Pablo. "Some wives are not heroes," Gertrude Stein wrote in *Lifting Belly.* "Lifting belly merely" (*BTV,* p. 81). Not this wife.

Alice stands at the door, Alice sits with the wives, Alice sets Gertrude free, Alice protests she is too busy to write her own story. She is the exemplary figure of Humor in the literary text, and she makes Humor's Complaint: *I am outside the knowledge of writing.* In the nineteenth century, Humor signified itself by misspelling *sivilize*; here it says: *I am too busy in the kitchen.* Yet Humor will write, grudgingly, simply, briefly; it will even describe, in its own sensible terms, the complexity of modern painting. Matisse, Alice explains, "distorted drawing as a dissonance is used in music or as vinegar or lemons are used in cooking or egg shells in coffee to clarify. I do inevitably take my comparisons from the kitchen because I like food and cooking and know something about it" (*ABT,* p. 49). Like Mark Twain writing Huckspeech, Gertrude Stein does not break into the false-simple of Alice's style. She renders that discourse intact, takes up entire the disenchanted outlook of Huckspeech, enjoys its freedom, and yet the turn at the end of the text takes Alice directly out of her humor. We enter, as it were, the self-reflexive phase of the text and behold a sudden con-fusion of perspectives. This is Gertrude's Alice's Gertrude. By all contemporary accounts, Gertrude's Alice is closely rendered, and yet the 'humor' of Alice's Huckish speech is now ironically circumscribed. Her tale is given over to the writing of it, given back to Gertrude Stein. The elements of the humorous style remain, Alice is indeed funny, but nowhere in the text is Gertrude Stein forgiving.

Humor complains: *I am too busy in the kitchen.* Irony declares: *I am not here.* So Humor (the ingenuous speech of the wife/sister) slips into the change of Irony (the writer's text). Alice's tale is a pretext. She 'understands' the cause of Gertrude Stein's irony, is sisterly and sympathetic, and promptly yields the discourse to the writer when a retribution is to be exacted. "As I say," Alice Huckishly relates, "he [Sherwood Anderson] and Gertrude Stein were endlessly amusing on the subject. They admitted that Hemingway was yellow, he is, Gertrude Stein insisted, just like the flat-boat men on the Mississippi as described by Mark Twain" (*ABT,* p. 265). The reference is to that rejected chapter from *Huckleberry Finn* which Mark Twain published in *Life on the Mississippi.* Huck swims out to a flatboat and is treated to the spectacle of two river men squared off in the full verbal fury of harmless tall talk. As Huck looks on, Alice looks on, except that Alice is an elder Huck who has learned to see through male bluster and now accurately reads the play of Tom's script. Indeed Alice has her own 'humorous' opinion of Hemingway.

> In these days Hemingway was teaching some young chap how to box. The boy did not know how, but by accident he knocked Hemingway out. I believe this sometimes happens. At any rate in these days Hemingway although a sportsman was easily tired. He used to get quite worn out walking from his house to ours. But then he had been worn by the war. Even now he is, as Hélène says all men are, fragile. Recently a robust friend of his said to Gertrude Stein, Ernest is very fragile, whenever he does anything sporting something breaks, his arm, his leg, or his head (*ABT,* pp. 267-268).

So it often goes in the *Autobiography,* a quick jab from Gertrude to the head, and then a solid right to the body by Alice.

We look in at 27 rue du Fleurus, at the manse in Bilignin, from the outside, Alice's outside, the wifely outside, and what we see inside, apart from the sumptuous paintings and the male strut of diverse artists and writers, is the scandal of Gertrude Stein's artistic isolation. Geniuses come and go in the *Autobiography,* Alice drops their names, notes their passage, but there all the while sits Gertrude Stein at her desk, like Crusoe in his solitude, like the writer in Man Ray's photograph, writing for no one but herself. It takes a woman, herself odd, to recognize immediately that Gertrude Stein is wronged as a writer because she is a woman, and thought queer.

> Getting reviews was a difficulty, there are always plenty of humorous references to Gertrude Stein's work, as Gertrude Stein always says to comfort herself, they do quote me, that means that my words and my sentences get under their skins although they do not know it. It was difficult

to get serious reviews. There are many writers who write her letters of admiration but even when they are in a position to do so they do not write themselves down in book-reviews (*ABT*, p. 300).

My words and my sentences get under their skins. The *Autobiography* is strewn with irksome nettles. Irked, stung, Hemingway would send a copy of *Death in the Afternoon* to Gertrude Stein with the circular inscription: "A Bitch is A Bitch is A Bitch is A Bitch. From her pal Ernest Hemingway."[1] Others whose story Alice told were similarly irked. In February, 1935, *Transition* published a special supplement, "Testimony Against Gertrude Stein," and among the various rebuttals and repudiations were those by Henri Matisse, Georges Braque, Andre Salmon, and Tristan Tzara. "For one who poses as an authority on the epoch," Braque wrote, "it is safe to say that she never went beyond the stage of the tourist." Having hurled that Ignatzian brick, Braque then picks up another. "We in Paris always heard that Miss Stein was a writer, but I don't think any of us had ever read her work until *Transition* began to make her known in France."[2] But it is hard to argue with a Huckish writer, with a humorous woman, this Gertrude's Alice's Gertrude who didn't write the book, whose argument is precisely the accusation Braque makes. No one takes Gertrude Stein seriously. No one has read her work. A Bitch is A Bitch is A Bitch is A Bitch. From the wife's seat, sitting with the other wives, Alice looks in upon that closed male world where glory is, where Gertrude Stein has bravely taken her stand. And she blythely judges it in its own terms: Braque is a follower of Picasso, Matisse becomes domesticated, Ezra Pound is a "village explainer," Hemingway is Sherwood Anderson's pupil, and so on. Nor is this male world without its own form of bitchiness.

They exchanged pictures as was the habit in those days. Each painter chose the one of the other one that presumably interested him the most. Matisse and Picasso chose each one of the other one the picture that was undoubtedly the least interesting either of them had done. Later each one used it as an example, the picture he had chosen, of the weaknesses of the other one. Very evidently in the two pictures chosen the strong qualities of each painter were not much in evidence (*ABT*, p. 79).

Such are the barbs shot through Alice's tale. Few modern writers have so skillfully used the humorous style Mark Twain perfected in Huckspeech. The brickbats hurled in *Transition* at Gertrude Stein are unerringly thrown at the major assumptions of that style, its ignorance, its error. There is common agreement among the *Transition* writers that Gertrude Stein has it all wrong—person, place, and date; that, since she is not an artist, not a thinker, merely the keeper of a salon, a woman associated with artists, she does not have the right to speak about modern art, and that, furthermore, perhaps inevitably, she reduces the high complexity of Cubism to a low comedy of personalities. This particular criticism is true enough: Matisse and Picasso behave in the *Autobiography* somewhat as do the King and the Duke in *Huckleberry Finn*. Some slams in the *Transition* supplement are even heavier than the bricks (tourist, nonentity, speaker of bad French) thrown by the angry Georges Braque. The *Autobiography*, Tzara wrote, constituted the "lowest literary prostitution." Gertrude Stein and Alice B. Toklas are simply "two maiden ladies greedy for fame and publicity" (*TAGS*, p. 13). *My words and my sentences get under their skins.* It is, after all, the great virtue of Huckspeech that it passively observes from its excluded position, and perfectly focuses, the gorgeous drama of male narcissists in combat. "Blood's my natural drink, and the wails of the dying is music to my ear!" shouts the braggart called Sudden Death and General Desolation in *Life on the Mississippi,* as Huck looks on. "Cast your eye on me, gentlemen!—and lay low and hold your breath, for I'm bout to turn myself loose!"[3] Shortly thereafter he is knocked flat by a "little black-whiskered chap." That's Hemingway, a nettlesome Gertrude Stein writes, and then Alice relates the humiliation of Hemingway's boxing match. Sisterly ire. Do I look like Lincoln, Picasso asks. Not tall enough. Picasso, we learn, is the "little bullfighter followed by his squadron of four . . . Napoleon followed by his four enormous grenadiers [Braque, Derain, Apollinaire, Salmon]" (*ABT*, p. 71). What aggression lurks in the deferential tone of the humorous woman, the ironist knows.

But this funny work, the diminishing of Leo Stein to "Gertrude Stein's brother," the constant and deadly ranking of the ongoing competition in modern art: who's leading, who's following, who is fresh, who smells of the museum, all this belongs to the lighter side of the *Autobiography*. When Alice looks in upon the scene, she sees the vanity of the masculine ego, she sees the exclusion of Gertrude Stein's genius, and she sees the virtual subject of her story: *Gertrude, Pablo.* "I may say that only three times in my life have I met a genius," Alice declares at the start of the *Autobiography,* "and each time a bell within me rang and I was not mistaken, and I may say in each case it was before there was any general recognition of the quality of genius in them. The three geniuses of whom I wish to speak are Gertrude Stein, Pablo Picasso and Alfred Whitehead" (*ABT,* pp. 5-6). Only two geniuses matter in the *Autobiography,* and their relation is the problem of the text.

Whether to shine, that is a question in *Tender Buttons.* The question in the *Autobiography* is how to shine next to Picasso. There he is, glittering, handsome, convincing, at once the fraternal ally and the brilliant rival whose ugly work, unlike her own, is seriously regarded and accepted as beautiful. Everything Picasso produces is golden, and has the value thereof. His 'Gertrude Stein,' a massive figure seated in queenly power, is rosily golden and richly brown in color, so beautiful it commands attention. When Roger Fry came to Paris, Alice recalls, he "was filled with excitement at the sight of the portrait of Gertrude Stein by Picasso. He wrote an article about it in the Burlington Review and illustrated it by two photographs side by side, one the photograph of this portrait and the other a photograph of a portrait by Raphael. He insisted that these two pictures were equal in value" (*ABT,* p. 150). All that power to generate excitement, that weighty gold in Fry's balance, and beside it, unvisited, the stony field of Gertrude Stein's career. Picasso's virile splendor as an artist is the veritable sign in the *Autobiography* of her own neglect and isolation, her awkward standing as a curious woman. That splendor also defines her task: once again, to declare her difference. The *Autobiography,* which has already told us, in regard to the portrait, *I am not there,* will conclude: *I am not here.*

The risk of becoming Picasso's Gertrude as Alice is Gertrude's Alice is certainly before Gertrude Stein in the *Autobiography.* And it involves crucially the question of her role, her place in the "heroic age of cubism," the very issue of her identity. As we have seen, Matisse and Braque firmly placed her outside the significant history of Cubism as a "tourist" who knew little of the art she collected. If she is in the history of Cubism, they suggest, she is there only as a model, the woman in Picasso's painting, as a wealthy muse, as a

Pablo Picasso, *Portrait of Gertrude Stein* (1906). The Metropolitan
Museum of Art, Bequest of Gertrude Stein, 1946.

social midwife. It is a harsh judgment, but then the *Autobiography*
had audaciously thrust Gertrude Stein to the center of that history,
beside Picasso. Alice bravely comes right to the issue in the first
chapter. "The three geniuses of whom I wish to speak are Gertrude
Stein, Pablo Picasso and Alfred Whitehead." And she starts the
second chapter just there, describing the creation of Cubism, *ab ovo*.

This was the year 1907. Gertrude Stein was just seeing through the press Three Lives which she was having privately printed, and she was deep in The Making of Americans, her thousand page book. Picasso had just finished his portrait of her which nobody at that time liked except the painter and the painted and which is now so famous, and he had just begun his strange complicated picture of three women, Matisse had just finished his Bonheur de Vivre, his first big composition which gave him the name of fauve, or a zoo. It was the moment Max Jacob has since called the heroic age of cubism (*ABT,* p. 7).

Gertrude Stein figures prominently in the order and equivalence of these important events. There is also, less visibly, a focusing of the subject that Cubism heroically considers in its first phase. All these works deal differently with the form and nature of women. When Alice later sees the canvas of *Three Women* in Picasso's studio, she is taken aback: "I felt that there was something painful and beautiful there and oppressive but imprisoned" (*ABT,* p. 27). That same quality, of course, is present in *Three Lives,* and Alice does not let the coincidence escape us. *Three Lives,* we are told, is written beneath a Cezanne portrait of a woman, a portrait Gertrude Stein had carefully studied. "She was then in the middle of her negro story Melanctha Herbert, the second story of Three Lives and the poignant incidents that she wove into the life of Melanctha were often these she noticed in walking down the hill from the rue Ravignan" (*ABT,* p. 60). That is, from Picasso's studio. As Gertrude Stein poses for Picasso, she composes the Melanctha section in *Three Lives.* Cezanne, Picasso's master, is her master, and here are the two pupils—the one painting, the other writing—equally placed in the situation of learning.

The story of the painting is deftly told:

> Fernande was as always, very large, very beautiful and very gracious. She offered to read La Fontaine's stories aloud to amuse Gertrude Stein while Gertrude Stein posed. She took her pose, Picasso sat very tight on his chair and very close to his canvas and on a very small palette which was of a uniform brown grey color, mixed some more brown grey and the painting began. This was the first of some eighty or ninety sittings.
>
> Toward the end of the afternoon Gertrude Stein's two

brothers and her sister-in-law and Andrew Green came to see. They were all excited at the beauty of the sketch and Andrew Green begged and begged that it should be left as it was. But Picasso shook his head and said, non (*ABT*, p. 57).

So Picasso begins the painting, mixes up some brown-grey, and then proceeds to lose his way. This first of some ninety settings is vividly recalled; so too is the beauty of several preliminary sketches, and yet, just as the manuscript of *Three Lives* is in the process of being typed, just as Gertrude Stein completes this important project: "All of a sudden one day Picasso painted out the whole head. I can't see you any longer when I look, he said irritably. And so the picture was left like that" (*ABT*, pp. 64-65). A mock combat is herein joined between the model and the painter. Gertrude Stein flees, is captured, then escapes again. Although the drama of this combat is completely told in Chapter 3, the section in which the "heroic age of cubism" is established, there is constant reference to it thereafter (the portrait mediates their friendship), and in the final chapter, as we shall see, it is briefly retold. Alice sets the scene, poses painter and model for us, and continually directs our attention to what the model is herself thinking and doing. Gertrude Stein walks down the hill from Picasso's studio, alert, bemused, reflecting on Melanctha Herbert in *Three Lives*. "She had come to like posing, the long still hours followed by a long dark walk intensified the concentration with which she was creating her sentences." There is a slight syntactical pause, and then: "The sentences of which Marcel Brion, the french critic has written, by exactitude, austerity, absence of variety in light and shade, by refusal of the use of the subconscious Gertrude Stein achieves a symmetry which has a close analogy to the symmetry of the musical fugue of Bach" (*ABT*, pp. 61-62). An English critic, Roger Fry, will compare Picasso to Raphael. Here, then, is a French critic who places Gertrude Stein beside Bach. The story of Picasso's painting of Gertrude Stein, of Picasso's magisterial *Non*, is ironically told, even as Alice simply tells it.

So Picasso decapitates the painted Gertrude Stein and for a year she remains headless in the portrait. She goes to Italy, Picasso goes to Spain. Gertrude Stein begins *The Making of Americans*, that long questioning of sexual identity, the kinds of men and women, and then returns to Paris "under the spell of the thing she was doing" only to find (again the coincidence is apt) the portrait finished. "The day he returned from Spain Picasso sat down and out of his head painted the head in without having seen Gertrude Stein again. And when she saw it he and she were content. It is very strange but neither can remember at all what the head looked like when he painted it out" (*ABT,* p. 70). There she is then, Picasso's she, the celebrated Gertrude Stein. The *Autobiography* then immediately jumps forward in time, almost to the present of its writing, and here Gertrude's Alice juxtaposes her own Gertrude Stein, the Gertrude Stein who first struck her, in Alice's own words, as a "golden brown presence, burned by the Tuscan sun," as a Roman Emperor."[4] Picasso beholds his model and does not see his Gertrude Stein. She has cut the braided queen's crown of hair that adorns her in the portrait, cropped her hair short, like a man, and now stands apart (in her own imperial splendor) from his identification. He has painted a woman, she has become a man. The *Autobiography* is stretched between these two points of reference: Picasso's she, Alice's he. And it is the writer, that latter-day Defoe, who comprehends both, who is neither.

> Only a few years ago when Gertrude Stein had had her hair cut short, she had always up to that time worn it as a crown on top of her head as Picasso had painted it, when she had had her hair cut, a day or so later she happened to come into a room and Picasso was several rooms away. She had a hat on but he caught sight of her through two doorways and approaching her quickly called out, Gertrude, what is it, what is it. What is what, Pablo, she said. Let me see, he said. She let him see. And my portrait, said he sternly. Then his face softening he added, mais, quand meme tout y est, all the same it is all there (*ABT,* p. 70).

Picasso scrutinizes the cropped hair, takes in the difference. "And my portrait, said he sternly." The joke is slight, and yet in it Picasso speaks a judgment: *This is who you are.* She is not. An escaped slave writes *The Autobiography of Alice B. Toklas,* doubling and redoubling her inversion of the mode. The first act of the fugitive is to change her name. *I am not here.* Gertrude Stein's appropriation of the Crusoe myth at once politicizes the text and invests it with erotic energy. Friday's point of view is also Crusoe's: this master has been a slave, and Gertrude knows what Alice knows. That Cubism begins with a male deconstruction of the female form as it pre-exists in the eyes of Picasso and Matisse. Gertrude Stein also begins a deconstruction of how women are known, but that work is overlooked. Here we have only her portrait of their portrait making, portraits of Picasso and Matisse conceiving and contemplating women, living with women: Matisse as the self-centered husband, Picasso as the charming rogue. With Friday's knowing look, Gertrude Stein regards these two typical sides of the master's face. It is Picasso who dominates the world set forth in the *Autobiography,* who loves Fernande and leaves her, who leads Braque, Derain, Apollinaire, and Salmon about as a "bullfighter" leads his retinue, who is "every inch a chief." It is Picasso who places her in the portrait and tells those who question the resemblance not to worry, she will become what she is in the portrait. "Let me see, he said. She let him see." Picasso's masculine authority is a congenial Spanish translation of Leo Stein's inflexible paternalism, the mastery of the brother to whom the world belongs, and it is in this book a pervasive force, the negative charge that gives Gertrude Stein the positive work of escape.

The chapters that follow the recognition scene in Chapter 3 ("Let me see, he said. She let him see."), the moment of her escape, busily describe Gertrude Stein's double life: her existence as a historical figure, the connoisseur and critic, and her arduous struggle to be read, the loneliness of her life as a writer. At the same time Alice's uxorial voice throws upon that double life the implication of still another duplicity. For the Gertrude Stein who expands in her writing, who expounds, who chats companionably with Carl Van Vechten and Sherwood Anderson, assumes invariably a masculine stance. By the end of the narrative these two sets of duplicity are joined, remarkably fused by the Crusoe myth. We begin with the apotheosis, which is rendered in a suitably 'noble' setting. Gertrude Stein has struck up a friendship with the Duchess of Clermont-Tonnerre, and the two women decide to cut their unfashionably long hair. "Cut it off she said and I did." For two days Alice cuts Gertrude Stein's hair until only a "cap of hair" remains. On seeing it, Sherwood Anderson remarks, "It makes her look like a monk." Briefly the *she* of the painting is recalled. "As I have said, Picasso seeing it, was for a moment angry and said, and my portrait, but very soon added, after all it is all there" (*ABT,* p. 304). The remark now hangs with the proper ironic ambivalence. The *Autobiography* then moves to its close. She cannot write her story, Alice protests, because she is Friday, the wife. Capably, referring to Defoe, Gertrude Stein then makes her appearance as the writer, as the *I* who has done this voided portrait, and the *Autobiography* concludes.

Friday's story is necessarily Crusoe's. It is Crusoe who gives him life and language, and such is the legend that informs this narrative. *We two alone on an island.* Here is a chronicle crowded with social occasions, spilling over with litanies of illustrious names, and it is finally about life on a desert island. The affairs of the famous are duly noted, but the tale told is Crusoe's, a tale of primordial loneliness, of the agony of not being known. It is a mistake, Alice continually stresses, this refusal to know the discursive Gertrude Stein, to read her writing, to take her seriously. "Gertrude Stein was in those days a little bitter," she writes of the period 1919-1932, "all her unpublished manuscripts, and no hope of publication or serious recognition" (*ABT,* p. 241). Yet Alice's designation as Friday also distances us from the immediate travail of the writer. "The geniuses came and talked to Gertrude Stein," she observes, "and all the wives sat with me" (*ABT,* p. 105). The important and prolific period of Gertrude Stein's early portraiture, the phase in which she defines her style, is briefly discussed, set forth as a catalog. We see in reference, dimly, Gertrude Stein alone, stranded and bereft, the solitary writer who writes for God and not Mammon her "thousand page book," who writes to preserve herself. Alice works closely with the text as a loving and helpful amanuensis, typing each morning the manuscript Gertrude Stein produced that night, but she never joins Crusoe in the deliberation of her writing. She knows Crusoe as Friday knows him. She does not know what Crusoe knows. Neither Picasso's portrait nor Alice's in the *Autobiography* reveals Gertrude Stein.

I am not here. In the work that follows, notably the *Geographical History of America* (1936), Gertrude Stein will reappear, declaring her inexplicable presence once again in double-talk.

> I am I yes sir I am I.
> I am I yes Madame am I I.
> When I am I am I I (*GHA,* p. 113).

She is absent in the *Autobiography*. That, after all, is the constant charge of her concealed rhetoric: I am not the lady in the portrait,

I am not here, I exist unseen in my ignored writing. And it is ironic, Gertrude Stein writes around Alice's voice in the text, that this particular genius should have to advertise her genius humorously in order to gain attention for her work. Here, then, is the genius, forced to impersonate a wife, methodically clearing a space for "Gertrude Stein" amid all those other male geniuses, the busy throng of them. *Gertrude, Pablo.* The story in the text is of *Gertrude, Pablo.* How to shine beside Picasso? It is a project that requires a keen sense of humor. In *Everybody's Autobiography* (1937) Picasso appears briefly as a fool. He has given up painting to write poetry, an exchange Gertrude Stein regards with anxious disdain. "Well as I say when I first heard he was writing I had a funny feeling," she admits, "one does you know. Things belong to you and writing belonged to me, there is no doubt about it writing belonged to me."[5] When Picasso at length reads his poetry, she is relieved: "I drew a long breath and I said it is very interesting" (*EA*, p. 17). In the room at the time is Thornton Wilder. As Picasso lapses from Gertrude Stein's life, his replacements (as the vigorous and productive male friend, the negative charge) grow less substantial: Hemingway, Juan Gris, Francis Picabia, Francis Rose, Thornton Wilder. She would go on in *Picasso* (1938) to round out her view of his artistry, but here, as he lamely reads his poetry, his effective participation in her imaginative life is over.

They meet again, in a gallery, as if in a fiction by Henry James, and their roles are reversed. *Let me see, she said. He let her see.* It is now Picasso who is apprehensive, uncertain, and Gertrude Stein who authoritatively defines him, whose maternal admonition becomes an aggressive embrace. Held by his lapels, shaken like a schoolboy, Picasso submissively yields like Molly Bloom.

> ah I said catching him by the lapels of his coat and shaking him, you are extraordinary within your limits but your limits are extraordinarily there and I said shaking him hard, you know it, you know it as well as I do, it is all right you are doing this to get rid of everything that has been too much for you all right all right go on doing it but don't go on trying to make me tell you it is poetry and I shook him again, well he said supposing I do know it, what will I do, what will you do said I and I kissed him, you will go on until you are more cheerful or less dismal and then

you will, yes he said, and then you will paint a very
beautiful picture and then more of them, and I kissed him
again, yes said he (*EA, p. 37*).

3

A Bitch is A Bitch is A Bitch is A Bitch. As we have seen, Hemingway did not find *The Autobiography of Alice B. Toklas* amusing.
Leo Stein would contemptuously marvel at his sister's arrogance in
the book. "There is not a statement of any importance regarding her
life before the war," he wrote to Mabel Weeks in 1933, "which is
not the product of an illusion of grandeur."[6] Matisse, Braque,
Salmon, Tzara, the nettled artists writing in *Transition,* saw accurately enough the fundamental act of transgression in the *Autobiography,* the muse/model step from her proper place in Cubism to
declare her own artistry. The *Autobiography* had this irate reader
in 1933-34, and for him the text was simply a piece of vindictive
treachery. The other reader, the one who made the *Autobiography*
a bestseller, happily confused Alice and Gertrude, relished the
gossip, and took the narrative straight as a funny memoir. Neither
reading did justice to the complicated texture of the book. The
brickbats did not harm Gertrude Stein. Because thrown so low
(prostitute, ignorant woman, mad queen), the insults of the *Transition* critics justified her attack. The dubious admiration of her
newfound public was another matter. If the first self-protective
reader could find no humor in her irony, the second disinterested
reader saw no irony in her humor. When Gertrude Stein came to the
United States in 1934, her name went up in lights on Times Square.
She was greeted with acclaim, but not as a literary genius.

Lecturing in America, the toast of several towns—New York,
Boston, Chicago, Hollywood—Gertrude Stein effectively found
herself in James Russell Lowell's quandary, trapped in the role of a
'humorist,' admired for 'humorous' work that did not represent her
'literary' style, and forced to point out the difference. "Is Gertrude
Stein serious?" James Branch Cabell would ask Alice B. Toklas.
"Desperately," she replied. "That puts a different light on it" (*WIR,*
p. 150), Cabell then remarked. The two terms Genius and Humor,
at least in Cabell's mind, were not compatible. From the start, it
would seem, the success of the *Autobiography* depended on a certain

misreading of it. Ellery Sedgwick, for example, had regularly rejected Gertrude Stein's submissions to the *Atlantic Monthly,* but in 1933 he was delighted to serialize four installments of the *Autobiography.* "During our long correspondence," he wrote apologetically to her, "I think you felt my constant hope that the time would come when the real Miss Stein would pierce the smoke-screen with which she has always so mischievously surrounded herself. . . . Hail Gertrude Stein about to arrive!"[7] The visible Gertrude Stein who at last appears in this prestigious journal, no longer hiding in the obscure double-talk that had tried Sedgwick's patience, is Alice's Gertrude, not the real Miss Stein. Sedgwick simply overlooked the signal: *I am not here.* For her part, present or absent, much like Mark Twain in 1875, Gertrude Stein was eager to appear in the *Atlantic,* to be certified as respectable, and if its readers chose to read the *Autobiography* as a humorous tale, "Old Times" in Paris, she would endure it. Yet the irony of Sedgwick's misreading followed Gertrude Stein in her sudden celebrity. She had protested her exclusion as an artist and now found her acceptance conditional, that she amuse.

On tour, Gertrude Stein would speak in all her lectures presumptively *as* a genius, boldly taking up, as would a genius, large questions about language and literature. Striking in her mannish figure, reading in her mellow voice, she confronted, in her own terms, the misreading of the *Autobiography,* the condescension of the Sedgwicks and the Cabells. This indeed was the real Miss Stein. "What is English Literature?" she asked in one lecture, and in another, "What are Master-pieces?" Her delivery was at once serious and humorous. To follow her in lecture across her ellipses ("And then came the wars of Napoleon and England then owned everything" [*WL,* p. 46]), across those truisms she had tuned into taut aphorisms ("And toward the end of the nineteenth century there was bound to be a change because after all nothing goes on longer than it can" [*WL,* p. 52]), auditors had to take a conceptual turn in their attention. *Nothing goes on longer than it can.* There is a trace of Josh Billings in that line. The lecture was not, however, a performance in which the auditors could relax and be joshed, nor was it a strenuous piece of argument, a lecturely lecture that took them step by step to a necessary conclusion. She meditated. Her thought passed through different resolutions, branched, broke off, began again. It was, as her writing always is, bare, self-centered in its "present thinking," so up front, here in the passage of utterance, in the speech rhythm, that its delivery was positively confidential. The auditor was not rhetorically addressed, not actively persuaded of anything, but rather let in on the activity of her thought. She took, in brief, the stance of a demonstrative genius whose mind is self-sufficient. "Do you feel the nineteenth-century writing as it is," she would ask in the lecture "What Is English Literature." "I hope so. I do" (*WL*, p. 52).

The lectures were therefore object lessons in the complexity of Gertrude Stein's humorous intelligence. She spoke simply; she went directly to the fundamental question—"What is poetry and if you know what poetry is what is prose"—and there humorously turned the question over. "There is no use in telling more than you know, no not even if you do not know it. But do you do you know what prose is and do you know what poetry is" (*WL*, p. 125). So Gertrude Stein begins the lecture, "Poetry and Grammar," sidelong, at an angle. She will explain that a noun is a name, and what that means. "Call anybody Paul and they get to be a Paul call anybody Alice and they get to be an Alice perhaps yes perhaps no, there is something in that, but generally speaking, things once they are named the name does not go on doing anything to them and so why write in nouns" (*WL*, p. 125). Is that funny? perhaps yes perhaps no. The Name in question is surely the Patronymic, the Categorical Name, the Subject of the Right Sentence that this deft, disarming speaker wrongs. The thinker who speaks in the passage simply rephrases the question of the Nominalists in the Middle Ages, raises an old question, but the thought is politicized by the style, displaced into another discourse, the plainest of plain speech, and therein changed, renewed. We come in *at* the question (the independent existence of the prior notion) from a different place in discourse, not *at* the Patronymic *through* the Patronymic, at Aristotle through Aristotle, but sidelong, at an angle, in an undulating sentence, from a nameless site, Gertrude Stein's shifty *I. call anybody Alice and they get to be an Alice.* The speaker had herself suffered some adverse nomination, some trouble with the name Alice. Shakespeare writes "A rose by any other name would smell as sweet." Gertrude Stein, who also knew about roses, rethinks the position: *call anybody Alice and they get to be an Alice.* And there in the hall sat Alice B. Toklas.

Because no 'humorist' manipulated the course of this style, stood apart from its effect, the nervous question of course arose: Is Gertrude Stein serious? She made large claims, larger even than those made by 'Alice' in the *Autobiography*. Lecturing in New England, Gertrude Stein compared herself to Shakespeare: "I don't care to say whether I'm greater than Shakespeare, and he's dead and can't say whether he's greater than I am."[8] From afar, reading the newspaper clippings in Italy, Leo Stein followed the progress of his sister's tour with disbelief. "She takes herself seriously," he wrote to Mabel Weeks, "and turns down several engagements because of the crowd. Apparently if she wanted to do the clown act on her own, she could make a lot of money, etc. The real clowns are not Gertrude, but the university people who ask Gertrude to lecture" (*JIS*, p. 153). At the University of Chicago, Aristotle's shrine in America, she again took on the Father and said "violent things" to Mortimer Adler about the History of Ideas.

> What are the ideas that are important I asked him. Here said he is the list of them I took the list and looked it over. Ah I said I notice that none of the books read at any time by them was originally written in English, was that intentional I asked him. No he said but in English there have really been no ideas expressed. Then I gather that to you there are no ideas which are not sociological or government ideas. Well are they he said, well yes I said (*EA*, p. 206).

Gertrude Stein recognized the "intentional" authority behind that repression. There was nothing wrong with a 'History of Ideas.' The problem was with the list. "Every week they took a new idea and the man who had written it and the class read it and then they had a conversation about it" (*EA*, p. 206). She told Adler that he was "singularly unsusceptible" to ideas that were outside "regulation," not on his list, and to Robert Hutchins, whose students she stirred into passionate discussion, she explained "and then I said you see why they talk to me is that I am like them I do not know the answer, you say you do not know but you do if you did not know the answer you could not spend your life in teaching but I I really do not know, I really do not, I do not even know whether there is a question let alone having an answer for the question" (*EA*, p. 213). Fathers have questions. Fathers have answers. In the *agon* of the Writing Lesson, in this seminar where Adler and Hutchins hurl the

Great Books, those heavy tomes, Gertrude Stein takes Huck's position, which is skeptical. *I am like them I do not know the answer.*

Throughout the late thirties, writing now as a popular literary figure, if not as an acknowledged genius, Gertrude Stein would effectively interpret her discourse, explain her style, in several different modes. The lectures are exemplary, at once abstruse and anecdotal; the presentation of Gertrude Stein, an elaboration of her text. Yet the celebrity, 'Gertrude Stein,' the 'Gertrude Stein' Alice created in the *Autobiography,* is a problem in this writing, the trap of an identity not unlike the one she had struggled from in *Tender Buttons.* There are few masterpeices, she would argue in the lecture "What Are Master-pieces," "because mostly people live in identity and memory that is when they think. They know they are they because their little dog knows them, and so they are not an entity but an identity" (*WL,* p. 153). She returns to her dog (Basket, her poodle; Ellery Sedgwick greeting the "real Miss Stein"; the dumb reader) in the *Geographical History,* establishing a refrain in which she insistently distinguishes psychology and ontology, separates human nature from the human mind, and draws a line between 'Gertrude Stein' and Gertrude Stein's writing.

> I am I because my little dog knows me, even if the little dog is a big one, and yet the little dog knowing me does not really make me be I no not really because after all being I I am I has really nothing to do with the little dog knowing me, he is my audience, but an audience never does prove to you that you are you (*GHA,* p. 113).

Everybody's Autobiography is so perversely dependent on the context of the Toklas narrative that it is, properly speaking, an epilogue (or response) to the first book. An introduction hinges the two narratives: "Alice B. Toklas did hers and now everybody will do theirs" (*EA,* p. 3). Gertrude Stein then reports a series of conversations with David Edstrom, Dashiell Hammett, and Mary Pickford. In her talk with Hammett she complains that women writers in the nineteenth century "never could invent women they always made the women be themselves seen splendidly or sadly or heroically or beautifully or despairingly or gently, and they never could make any other kind of woman" (*EA,* p. 5). She is in Hollywood. Mary Pickford, who played these glamorous roles on the screen, regards Gertrude Stein suspiciously as a rival star and decides to keep her distance.

Hammett patiently explains the narcissism of male writers. "It is nice being a celebrity," Gertrude Stein observes, "a real celebrity who can decide who they want to meet and say so and they come or do not come as you want them" (*EA,* pp. 3-4). People approach her on the street. Her books are in the shop windows. Her photograph appears regularly in the newspapers and magazines. Mary Pickford might well look upon her with jaundice. But what other kind of woman is Gertrude Stein? Having escaped the significance of Picasso's portrait in the *Autobiography* (and challenged Aristotle in Chicago), she had set another image, that of the esoteric celebrity, in its place, and the problem in this new autobiography is once again to assert her difference, her human mind against her human nature, and disappear like Whitman at the end of "Song of Myself," like Huckleberry Finn. But the success of the first autobiography, the pleasure of being a celebrity, mesmerizes her. Suddenly she is rich, everybody knows her, she has a public. It leaves her speechless, so she writes in *Everybody's Autobiography,* unable to write. This crisis, her sudden confusion of the external and the internal, plays throughout the text. "It is all a question of the outside being outside," she asserts, "and the inside being inside. As long as the outside does not put a value on you it remains outside but when it does put a value on you then it gets inside or rather if the outside puts a value on you then all your inside gets to be outside" (*EA,* p. 47). The destruction of her Crusoe life, her changed position as a writer, had radically altered her stance as an autobiographer.

To return to the form, then, Gertrude Stein had first to justify doing it. She could say legitimately, and did, that it was now her turn, Alice having told her story, but what then was she to write about, and from which point of view? She could write about her American tour, life in Bilignin, her work, her past, visiting notables, but in so doing she inescapably wrote the referential discourse her first autobiography had so wickedly emptied of relevance. That revenge (*I am not here*) falls at last upon the writer of *Everybody's Autobiography.* "Anything is an autobiography," she declares in the introduction, prefacing her talk with Hammett, "but this was a conversation" (*EA,* p. 5). Given her own sportive approach to literary form, this sanction is sufficient, but in fact the magisterial *I* that finally seizes Alice's story, that plays whimsically with philosophical discourse in the *Geographical History,* is troubled and uncertain in this wavering narrative.

What are the resources of her inside now that so much of it is outside? The astonishment of her American tour and the impending strife in Europe (war in Spain, unrest in France) are compressive forces that obviously confuse her perspective, but as well it is the telling of her own past, her writing *about* herself, that also vexes the sureness of her solitude. How did she come to be called Gertrude Stein? The question emerges when someone asks what skin the peau de chagrin was made of. The word is looked up. Peau de chagrin "was made of anything mule calf or horse and I said how did it happen to be called peau de chagrin and Madame Giraud said and how did you happen to be called Gertrude Stein." The arbitrariness of the sign is once again affirmed, names are nouns that tell us nothing, but then she fixes on this haphazard name, Stein, her name, and at once stoically accepts and defiantly refuses it.

> Steins were called Steins in the time of Napoleon before that any name was a name but in the time of Napoleon in any country he went through the name of any one had to be written and so they took the name they gave them and Stein was an easy one. Then when any of us were named we were named after some one who is already dead, after all if they are living the name belongs to them so any one can be named after a dead one, so there was a grandmother she was dead and her name not an easy one began with G so my mother preferred it should be an easy one so they named me Gertrude Stein. All right that is my name (*EA,* p. 115).

The passage occurs in the midst of a meditation on death. Gertrude Stein takes up ambivalently the burden of her name, Gertrude Stein, this peau de chagrin. "Identity always worries me," she concludes, "and memory and eternity" (*EA,* p. 115). It is as though she suddenly perceives the thesis of classical autobiography: that it is a summation, the presentation of a self about to die, a prelude to biography. The noun names. It identifies. It is the skin of a dead thing that has nothing to do with what the dead thing was. Names are taken from those already dead. We wear our names as we wear the skins of dead animals. In *Everybody's Autobiography* Gertrude

Stein's long attack on the coherence and stability of the noun takes a desperate turn. Here she is, then, wearing her dead grandmother's *G*: Gertrude Stein.

When Gertrude Stein now contemplates the hierarchical domain of the patriarchy, and all its intimidation, her view is not that of an escaped slave, malicious, alert, deceptive, but rather the resigned view of the historian and autobiographer who wears in her name the dead grandmother's *G*. It was Napoleon, after all, who made the Steins become Steins. "Everybody nowadays is a father," she writes, "there is father Mussolini and father Hitler and father Roosevelt and father Stalin and father Lewis and father Blum and father Franco is just commencing now and there are ever so many more ready to be one" (*EA*, p. 133). Those periods of history where fathers loom and fill up everything, she observes, are always the "most dismal ones." The oppressive presence of her own father is recalled, and the importance of her brothers, especially Michael and Leo, and these familial politics are then framed by the larger issue of the patriarchy itself, the world ruled by fathers. "Sometimes barons and dukes are fathers and then kings come to be fathers and churchmen come to be fathers and then comes a period like the eighteenth century a nice period when everybody has had enough of anybody being a father to them . . . just now everybody has a father, perhaps the twenty-first century like the eighteenth century will be a nice time when everybody forgets to be a father or to have been one" (*EA*, p. 142). Gertrude Stein's struggle in *The Autobiography of Alice B. Toklas* to escape her identity as the lady in Picasso's portrait, to break into the Palace of Modern Art, and upset a few pedestals, becomes a dream in *Everybody's Autobiography,* the dream of parricide, king killing, the "nice period" of revolt when the very principle of identification (Napoleon's command, the father's business) is shattered.

Out of all this grim study, this fingering of the peau de chagrin, comes *Ida, A Novel,* in 1941. It is Gertrude Stein's humorous farewell to the problem of her wrongness, the question of identity, and it ends, serenely, with "Yes."

4

There are two fictions entitled *Ida*. The first *Ida* appears as a little *Nachtmusik* in Page Cooper's *A Boudoir Companion* (1938). It begins: "Ida is her name," and then promptly confides "You might as well just as well call her Bessie as call her Ida and if nobody likes that you might call her Emily. Perhaps Henrietta might be better because you can say Henrietta won't let her. But now let's be serious as ever is and her name is Ida, dear Ida."[9] There are seven tiny chapters in this briefest of novelettes, which is really a bedtime story told in a comforting parental tone for very large children, those who know, having read *War and Peace* and *Bleak House,* "There is always that, he says she says, there is always that" (*HWW*, p. 46). Indeed this first *Ida*, which skips merrily past Plot and Character, belongs to a sequence of tales Gertrude Stein wrote between 1936 and 1940 for children, strange tales: *The Autobiography of Rose, The World Is Round,* and *To Do: A Book of Alphabets and Birthdays.* The *Autobiography of Rose* begins: "How does she know her name is Rose" (*HWW*, p. 39), and it is a tough question for the little Rose to whom the fiction is dedicated, Rose Lucy Renee Anne d'Aiguy, the daughter of friends in Bilignin. In *The World Is Round,* another Rose, perplexed by the circularity of introspection "*who are you who are you,*" will finally carve on a tree trunk "*Rose is a Rose is a Rose is a Rose.*"[10] As for the Ida in *The Boudoir Companion:* "Ida used to sit and as she sat she said am I one or am I two" (*HWW*, p. 45). At this far remove in Gertrude Stein's writing, in a fictive space somewhere between Lewis Carroll's Wonderland and L. Frank Baum's Oz, we are curiously back before the blind glass that is the text of *Tender Buttons,* in double-talk.

Written in the aftermath of Gertrude Stein's autobiographical narration, her own adventure in self-description, these tales for children begin by questioning the self reflected in the name and discover therein a prosy field of discursive play where contradiction, absurdity, nonsense, are the postulates of experience. "She knew, she knew that five is more than ten she knew that six is more than eight, she knew the weight, the real weight of the slate it was a large slate upon which she wrote, she did not really write but on the slate there it was, it was Ida" (*HWW*, p. 46). It is the question of the name that makes the play possible. Action is not important in these tales, but thinking is. These are, after all, little girls, little Rose and little Ida, who are asked to discover their identity in a scholastic discourse that has already defined them. The urgent question of the little girl who is alienated by her identification (her name, her role, her place in the world), *why,* typically receives a formulary response: *because the world is round.* Little Rose endures a Writing Lesson in *The World Is Round,* learns the natural law of the universe, the clocklike articulation of its movement, and the prospect fills her with sorrow.

> The teachers taught her
> That the world was round
> That the sun was round
> That the moon was round
> That the stars were round
> And that they were all going around and around
> And not a sound
> It was so sad it almost made her cry (*TWR,* p. 21).

The world is round, the world is right, that is the weight of the slate on which is written: *Ida, Rose.* Little girls are depressed and irrational in this round and rational world, as Gertrude Stein tells the story, and their only weapon in the struggle (which is largely verbal) is contradiction. If you look down at the ground, Rose insists, "you see that the world is not round" (*TWR,* p. 39). It is, of course, a grown girl, the teller of the tale, who reports without correction that five is more than ten, who invests the right roundness of the world with such a feeling of wrongness.

Am I one or am I two? As we have seen, Gertrude Stein's humorous style originates in the double-talk of *Tender Buttons,* in that humor which freely traverses the primary symbolic orders in discourse: the realm of the Mother (household speech), the sphere of the Father (philosophical writing). The way this double-talk is written changes as Gertrude Stein's understanding of her own duality changes. In *Tender Buttons* it is charged with sexual reference ("The sister was not a mister."), with the politics of the new "arrangement." In *Lifting Belly* double-talk simply becomes duet. Double-talk in the *Autobiography of Alice B. Toklas* is literally the talk of the double, Alice's speech 'innocently' transcribed, ironically circumscribed, and in the *Geographical History* the style reappears in the echoing play of "I am I I." That is, the style varies, but its motive remains the same, to keep Gertrude Stein, as a writer, out of the fixation of a particular identity, *he said she said,* out of the power of the Name, in the present motion of her thinking. How, then, does twice-born Ida fit into this characterization of Gertrude Stein's humorous writing? Doubles abound in *Ida, A Novel,* which begins: "There was a baby born named Ida. Its mother held it with her hands to keep Ida from being born but when the time came Ida came. And as Ida came, with her came her twin, so there she was Ida-Ida."[11] As a lonely young girl, whose only confidante is her blind dog, Love, Ida will write letters to herself, to the other Ida whom she calls Winnie. Winsome Winnie is a "suicide blonde," the winner of a beauty prize, a veritable Miss America. She is obviously a young girl's fantasy of herself as adorable, unapproachable in her unreal beauty, a *femme fatale* pursued by men, and yet, after all, she has nothing to do with the reality of shy Ida, whose sexual confusion is profound. In *Ida,* it would seem, Gertrude Stein returns through the analytic framework of the *bildungsroman* to the psychological and social origin of her style, to the poignant double-talk of the adolescent girl, as if to describe there a schizophrenic speech barely escaped. Ida will have to kill this winsome twin, the beauty queen, and she does.

Gertrude Stein's approach in *Ida* is therefore complex, though the style is rigorously simple. In 1937, as she began to work on the novel, she intended "to write about the effect on people of the Hollywood cinema kind of publicity that takes away all identity."[12] That is, she is still close to the problem of her public recognition, the ambiguity of her fame, still struggling with the 'Gertrude Stein' her misreaders had misunderstood in the *Autobiography of Alice B. Toklas.* It is in this period that she writes fables for little girls, recalling the problem of identity for the child. How hard it is for a little girl, for a grown woman, struggling in the round world without the sanction of a masculine ego, to be one, singular, single, and not two persons. In 1937 another example of the problem is vividly before her, a scandal that strangely mirrored her own struggle. As she first drew her picture of Ida, Gertrude Stein had in mind, so she told Carl Van Vechten, the character of Mrs. Simpson, formerly Wallis Warfield, truly a *femme fatale,* soon to be the Duchess of Windsor. When the young Gertrude Stein had lived with Leo in Baltimore at 215 East Biddle Street, a young Wallis Warfield had lived directly opposite at 212 East Biddle. In England during the spring of 1937 for the London opening of her ballet, *A Wedding Bouquet,* Gertrude Stein found that all the talk was of the infamous

Mrs. Simpson and the King. The coincidence was apt, and she considered it.

Here, after all, are these two famous American women in the twentieth century who struck out along such radically different paths for *gloire,* for splendor, to shine, from East Biddle Street, Baltimore. The similarity of ambition and the contrast of method make their story an exemplary tale. For the one works her way to power, as of old, through marriages, through the manipulation of male vanity, whereas the other stands resolutely in her own unattractive genius, refusing to court favor, refusing to please. It is a tale to be considered. There is indeed a murky coalescence of Gertrude Stein and Wallis Warfield in the double figure of Ida-Ida and Ida-Winnie. Although Gertrude Stein rewrote *Ida* several times, significantly changing her conception of the novel, some of her earlier satiric intent is still present in the text. She leaves intact, for example, the funny contradiction of Ida's marital status. Ida marries casually, the marriages end casually, she forgets she was married, she asserts she is unmarried, the narrator doesn't seem to know, we certainly do not know, until at length Ida settles down with a compliant Andrew. And what does Ida do? She eats, she rests, she talks, she travels, she sits down, she gets up, she goes out, she comes in, she is continually involved with men. Poor Wallis Warfield, poor Ida. When *Ida* appeared in 1940, Gertrude Stein made sure that the Duchess of Windsor received a copy. The Duchess read the book, and wrote "I hope to emerge from this literary labyrinth with some idea of Ida's thoughts and ways" (*GIP,* p. 306). Gertrude Stein had changed her direction in the final *Ida,* but inside the text, behind Ida-Ida, is the elusive figure of a much-married, essentially forlorn, restlessly idle socialite who lives in the glass of fashion, talked about, discussed. For all her marriages, the different identities she takes on as Mrs. and Mrs. and Mrs., she remains singly Ida. And this is the turn. Ida has no last name to bind her to the legality of the patriarchy, and so, unlike Wallis Warfield, she never becomes its victim.

This socio-political aspect of *Ida,* partially effaced, can easily be read as the novel. For Donald Sutherland, "*Ida* is strictly speaking no novel at all but belongs to the tradition of the philosophical farce or romance which is probably at its purest in Voltaire's *Candide*" (*GSBW,* p. 154). Yet much of *Ida* is ultimately drawn from Gertrude Stein's life, and the feeling of the prose, though often droll, is not farcical. There are surprising interpolations: a haunting essay on the nature of the sign as superstition, several doggy dramas, and the menu of a dinner. Anecdotes and passages from other work in the period are woven into the narrative, and of course the second Ida is before the question that confronts the first Ida in the novelette. Am I one or am I two? "More than any other single composition," Richard Bridgman observes, "*Ida* incorporates a variety of material from Gertrude Stein's other pieces" (*GIP*, p. 307). The borrowing is eclectic and far-ranging. In telling the story of Ida's "funny" sexual experience in church, Gertrude Stein would reach back to a composition, "The Temptation," written in 1895 at Radcliffe. To this extent, *Ida* is an assemblage of topics, a pastiche of fiction, fantasy, fable, hung on the skeletal structure of the *bildungsroman*. In *Ida, A Novel*, the sequence of Childhood, Youth, and Maturity obtains, even though the transitions are remarkably obscure. Whatever might be said of its construction or its form, this much is true: what holds *Ida* together is the command of Gertrude Stein's measured style, what carries it along is the sweet serenity of the narration. "So Ida was born and a very little while after her parents went off on a trip and never came back. That was the first funny thing that happened to Ida" (*Ida*, p. 8). It is the humor, the mood, the feeling of this simple style, so like Huckspeech, that governs any reading of *Ida*.

How is *Ida* a humorous text? "There was nothing funny about Ida," Gertrude Stein tells us, "but funny things did happen to her" (*Ida*, p. 12). Disaster befalls Ida, and all the agonies of change. First she must undergo the trauma of a hard birth, then she suffers the early and inexplicable loss of her parents, after which, frightened, lonely, confused, she is moved from great-aunt to grandfather. Ida begins, in effect, the dislocated life of an orphan, a fact which increasingly alienates her in herself. She speaks of her feelings to her dog (Love, who is blind, and later a second dog, Iris) and she communes with her imagined twin, the suicide blonde. To others, as Ida, she is a steadfast enigma. Ida's rough beginning is in fact an enhanced outline of Gertrude Stein's own childhood. Amelia Stein dies when Gertrude is fourteen, and Daniel Stein, a disappointed and indifferent father, dies three years later, to the considerable relief of his children. Like Gertrude and Leo, who come (guiltily) after the death of two infant siblings as replacement, as substitution, Ida-Ida is born into the family after the death of little twins shamefully born, "oh many years ago," to the great-aunt, and buried "under a pear tree and nobody knew" (*Ida,* p. 7). The unknown soldier who did this to the great-aunt will reappear in *Ida* as a lurking figure behind some trees, as the brisk young officer so peremptory in his flirtation with Winnie, always threatening, always pressing. The twin, Winnie, is constructed, almost as a sacrifice, for this male figure. Men follow Winnie home only to find Ida.

> He followed Winnie.
> He did it very well.
> The next day he went and rang the bell.
> He asked for Winnie.
> Of course there was no Winnie.
> That was not surprising and did not surprise him.
> He could not ask for Ida because he did not know Ida.
> He almost asked for Ida. Well in a way he did ask for Ida.
> Ida came.
> Ida was not the same as Winnie. Not at all (*Ida,* p. 26).

These are the "funny things" that happen to Ida in her pitiable struggle to establish a secure relation with reality through the dialectic of Ida-Ida, Ida-Winnie. She is everywhere confronted by the inadequacy of her defense, made painfully aware of her difference, and so, at last, winning Winnie is a failure. Clearly enough, Ida's *I* is formed through the agency of a double-talk at once defensive and desperate. This heavy piece of business, the location of the self in the *imago,* lies in fragmented Ida's projection of the alluring Winnie, in her question, *am I one or am I two.* To break out of the circle of the *Innenwelt* into the *Umwelt,* this quest informs the reflective *bildungsroman* with its purpose.

Such novels give us the fiction of that break, of sudden revelation, render, through the self-realization of the hero, at once the myth and value of identity. Such a climax does not occur in *Ida.* She can only discover who she is not, discover the negativity of her *I.* Ida is Ida is Ida is Ida. So Gertrude Stein removes her from a system of nomination (her patronymical name is never given), withdraws her from that system of functions which produces the name of the hero, and sets her picture of Ida's life at odds with the portraiture of the form. We do not know Ida's last name; we learn nothing of her physical features, the color of her eyes, her stature. She is effectively disembodied. In the mirror of the *bildungsroman,* we see, at best, a barely described behavior: a subject, Ida, and the simplest of predicates. Ida moves, moreover, across the threshold of her adolescence not into the activity of a destiny, but rather into the passivity of a fate. If language is the mirror in which the subject seeks it verification, this language, the expression of the *bildungsroman,* the very mythology of the self, can only misname, misspell, who Ida is. To be a winning woman, Ida must engage in double-talk, create an alter ego, and this double-talk, this alter ego, is delicately poised between submission and freedom. Winnie at least enables Ida to say: *I am not here.* It is a psychological maneuver that bears some resemblance to the stylistic complexity of Gertrude Stein's impersonation in the *Autobiography of Alice B. Toklas.*

> What is it that you like better than anything else, he asked and she said. I like being where I am. Oh said he excitedly, and where are you. I am not here, she said, I am very careful about that. No I am not here, she said, it is very pleasant, she added and she turned slightly away, very pleasant indeed not to be here.
> The officer smiled. I know he said I know what you mean. Winnie is your name and that is what you mean by your not being here.
> She suddenly felt very faint. Her name was not Winnie, it was Ida, there was no Winnie (*Ida,* p. 29).

There is nothing funny about Ida, Gertrude Stein tells us, but funny things do happen to her. Here the vertigo, the nausea, of being confronted in her duplicity. "I am an officer," says the officer, "and I give orders. Would you, he said looking at Ida. Would you like to see me giving orders. Ida looked at him and did not answer" (*Ida,* p. 29). *Funny* is Gertrude Stein's humorous term in *Ida* for the hard brick of suffering thrown by Adversity, and the first funny thing that happens to Ida is the death of her parents. The mirror in which Ida speaks to herself, the mirror in which she first conceives Winnie, is the unseeing iris of her blind dog, Love. Love, says the bereft and unappealing child, is blind. Should be blind, but isn't. Love desires Winnie. Then this happens, the confusion of Ida's sexuality, the demolition of her ego's defenses. "Would you like to see me giving orders," the officer asks.

How is *Ida* a humorous text, a funny *bildungsroman*? Who takes down the high energy of the certain grief in Ida's life and discharges it funnily through the quirk of this simple style? The humorist, Gertrude Stein, who, in Part II of *Ida,* recites again her autobiography, this time in a man's voice. She tells us an anecdote about a cuckoo. I cite the passage in its entirety because of the excellence of its humorous ease. A man is speaking; he tells of a cuckoo, he tells of a woman writer. First the cuckoo sings:

> If you listen to me, if when you hear me, the first time in the spring time, hear me sing, and you have money a lot of money for you in your pocket when you hear me in the spring, you will be rich all year any year, but if you hear me and you have gone out with no money jingling in your pocket when you hear me singing then you will be poor poor all year, poor.
> But sometimes I can do even more.
> I knew a case like that, said the man.
> Did you said Andrew.
> She, well she, she had written a lovely book but nobody took the lovely book nobody paid her money for the lovely book they never gave her money, never never never and she was poor and they needed money oh yes they did she and her lover.
> And she sat and she wrote and she longed for money for she had a lover and all she needed was money to live and love, money money money.
> So she wrote and she hoped and she wrote and she sighed and she wanted money, money money, for herself and for love for love and for herself, money money money.
> And one day somebody was sorry for her and they gave her not much but a little money, he was a nice millionaire the one who gave her a little money, but it was very little money and it was spring and she wanted love and money and she had love and now she wanted money.
> She went out it was the spring and she sat upon the grass with a little money in her pocket and the cuckoo saw her sitting and knew she had a little money and it went up to her close up to her and sat on a tree and said cuckoo at her, cuckoo cuckoo, cuckoo, and she said, Oh, a cuckoo bird is singing on a cuckoo tree singing to me oh singing to me. And the cuckoo sang cuckoo cuckoo and she sang

> cuckoo cuckoo to it, and there they were singing cuckoo
> she to it and it to her.
> Then she knew that it was true and that she would be
> rich and love would not leave her and she would have all
> three money and love and a cuckoo in a tree, all three
> (*Ida*, pp. 124-125).

Cuckoo she to it and it to her, two experts in double-talk. Immediately after this important section on superstition, of which the cuckoo story is only a part, Ida and Andrew will fall in love. Where, after all, can a *bildungsroman* about a woman go, but into a romance? Gertrude Stein had read Henry James, knew *The Portrait of a Lady*, and had before her the example of Wallis Warfield.

Ida drifts through a series of desultory marriages in the middle section of the novel and then vaguely marries a Gerald Seaton. While married to Gerald Seaton, who is never anything more than the name Gerald Seaton, Ida falls in love with Andrew. She has been drifting all the while through an abstract landscape of different states and cities (Ohio, Virginia, Texas, Connecticut, Boston, Washington), on that aimless American road, moving through states of mind, qualities of mood. "It often was evening in Texas" (*Ida*, p. 59). None of these places place Ida, whose origin we never learn, whose last name is never given, whose destination is not discovered. So much for local color. Nor do we find here in 'Ohio' or 'Virginia,' these places, the furniture of the *bildungsroman*, those novelistic tricks of representation which position a character in his or her identity. "Nobody talked about the color of Ida's hair and they talked about her a lot, nor the color of her eyes" (*Ida*, p. 111). The nouns that define identity, the nouns that explain motive, are expunged from the narration. We have perfect access to Ida's mind, to her thoughts, her feelings, even to her letters, but we know nothing of her nature, her physical attributes, or the settings in which she lives, and so, as readers of the *bildungsroman*, of the romance, we must deal differently with her, this woman who exists apart from her body. When Andrew enters the novel, the disembodied *bildungsroman* becomes a disembodied romance. All that Gertrude Stein again records is the essential structure, and yet the nuances of Ida's relation to Andrew are minutely registered. Here, without the clutter of 'scenes,' without the delay of fine speeches, is the denouement of an affair.

Andrew never looked around when Ida called him but she really never called him. She did not see him but he was with him and she called Andrew just like that. That was what did impress him.

Ida liked it to be dark because if it was dark she could light a light. And if she lighted a light then she could see and if she saw she saw Andrew and she said to him. Here you are.

Andrew was there, and it was not very long, it was long but not very long before Ida often saw Andrew and Andrew saw her. He even came to see her. He came to see her whether she was there or whether she was not there.

Ida gradually was always there when he came and Andrew always came.

He came all the same.

Kindly consider that I am capable of deciding when and why I am coming. This is what Andrew said to Ida with some hesitation.

And now Ida was not only Ida she was Andrew's Ida and being Andrew's Ida Ida was more that Ida she was Ida herself.

For this there was a change, everybody changed, Ida even changed and even changed Andrew. Andrew had changed Ida to more Ida and Ida changed Andrew to be less Andrew and they were both always together (*Ida,* p. 90).

She calls out, he comes to see. It is the simplest of love stories, but not for an instant simplistic. For in the brevity of these spare strokes, Gertrude Stein precisely delineates the complexity of the political struggle in a love affair. Ida compels Andrew to yield his self-sufficiency, his 'freedom.' "Kindly consider that I am capable of deciding when and why I am coming. This is what Andrew said to Ida with some hesitation." The moment he must justify himself, he falters, expressing the bondage of his desire. Ida makes him see her Ida, admit Ida, and so (mirrored in his gaze) she becomes "Ida itself." More Ida, less Andrew. Their "almost marriage" remains problematical, a struggle, and near the end of the novel, feeling Andrew's dependence, Ida will briefly leave him. *Ida* ends with their reconciliation, but it is iffy.

> She dresses, well perhaps in black why not, and a hat, why
> not, and another hat, why not, and another dress, why
> not, so much why not.
>   She dresses in another hat and she dresses in another
> dress and Andrew is in, and they go in and that is where
> they are. They are there. Thank them.
>   Yes (*Ida*, p. 154).

So *Ida* ends, resigned, why not. Ida is in black; misfortune is female. First Gertrude Stein deprives the *bildungsroman* of its subject,
then she empties the romance of its subject. This life misfits its
fiction.

It is in the 'romantic' second half of the novel that Gertrude Stein
takes up the question of superstition, tells the story of the cuckoo,
and comes around metafictively to the whole question of her work,
her vision. What does humor know? It is the proper place to conclude this discussion of Gertrude Stein's writing, for here, in all the
sweetness of her Huckish innocence, Huckishly wondering about
superstition, she demonstrates the critical power of her humorous
intelligence. From the original double-talk of the dwarfs, female
male, who speak in perfect harmony, as *we*, Gertrude Stein will
derive a *credo* that constitutes her valedictory.

Ida and Andrew are at a social gathering where they hear a recital
of superstitions. Gertrude Stein has just previously speculated on the
nature of the sign, wondering Huckishly, "Why are sailors, farmers
and actors more given to reading and believing signs than other
people. It is natural enough for farmers and sailors who are always
there where signs are, alone with them but why actors" (*Ida*, p. 119),
so of course Ida and Andrew are interested in the nature of signs.
They encourage the storyteller with questions, urge him on, and are
gradually lost in the dispute of the superstitions, the contradiction
of the signs. Out of the fiction of *Ida*, we are abruptly in an older
narrative form, the medieval debate between allegorical animals, and
this form, as the sign-of-the-spider speaks, as the sign-of-the-cuckoo
speaks, as the sign-of-the-goldfish speaks, discloses an even older
narrative form, myth itself. Each sign proposes its myth, its structure
of meaning, *if/then*, its explanation of the world, and speaks absolutely for its priority.

> Listen to me I, I am a spider, you must not mistake me
> for the sky, the sky red at night is a sailor's delight, the sky
> red in the morning is a sailor's warning, you must not
> mistake me for the sky, I am I, I am a spider and in the
> morning any morning I bring sadness and mourning and
> at night if they see me at night I bring them delight, do not
> mistake me for the sky, not I, do not mistake me for a
> dog who howls at night and causes no delight (*Ida,* pp.
> 122-23).

So mythologies, religions, ideologies, discourses, strive for the distinction of their mastery, strive to be the sign of the truth, for their
existence depends on being first, in place, original — the first spider
seen at night, the first cuckoo heard in spring. And what sounds
through the cacophony of the fight, eerily, humorously, as the
storyteller renders it, singsong, is the Will-to-Power of the male ego
in His Story, in patriarchal history.

It is, after all, 1939-40 as Gertrude Stein finishes *Ida.* History
pours through her fable. These are heavy signs, full of strut, and fire.
The boots of the believers are everywhere. "Yes said a goldfish I
listen I listen but listen to me I am stronger than a cuckoo stronger
and meaner because I never do bring good luck I bring nothing but
misery and trouble" (*Ida,* p. 125). To which the cuckoo responds:
"Oh you poor fish, you do not believe in me, you poor fish, and I
do not believe in you fish nothing but a fish a goldfish only fish"
(*Ida,* p. 127). The spider, too, has his say: "You do not believe in
me, everybody believes in me, you do not believe in spiders you do
not believe in me bah" (*Ida,* p. 127). Each sign treats the other
ironically, seeks to supplant it, even though each sign is forced to
admit a flaw in its own authority, that it is itself superstitious,
and dependent. The surly goldfish fears and adores the shoe on the
table; the spider worships the portent of putting one's clothes on
wrongly in the morning. For all their bravado, their demand, the
signs are weak things. A single pressing voice speaks through all the
tales: "ooh ooh, it is I, no matter what they try it is I I. I" (*Ida,*
p. 128). It is, seemingly, the voice of Thanatos, of Discord, of Bad
Luck, who delivers the contradiction of the signs. What, then,
are we to believe in? How, then, are we to read History? Happily,
there is another voice in the text, another myth, and it is humorous.

The dwarfs said, And of whom are you talking all of you, we dwarfs, we are in the beginning we have commenced everything and we believe in everything yes we do, we believe in the language of flowers and we believe in lucky stones, we believe in peacocks' feathers and we believe in stars too, we believe in leaves of tea, we believe in a white horse and a redheaded girl, we believe in the moon, we believe in red in the sky, we believe in the barking of a dog, we believe in everything that is mortal and immortal, we even believe in spiders, in goldfish and in the cuckoo, we the dwarfs we believe in it all, all and all, and all and every one are alike, we are, all the world is like us the dwarfs, all the world believes in everything and we do too and all the world believes in us and in you (*Ida*, p. 128).

The voice that speaks in this myth, as *we*, as Adam and Eve telling us the creation myth in double-talk, is not ironic, aggressively asserting its singularity: *I am stronger, I am meaner.* The voice is dwarfish, the small voice of humor, embracing the loony plenitude of meaning in the world.

Notes

1. Cited in Janet Hobhouse, *Everybody Who Was Anybody, A Biography of Gertrude Stein* (London, 1975), p. 167.

2. "Testimony Against Gertrude Stein," *Transition* Pamphlet No. 1, Supplement to *Transition* (1934-35), nr. 23, ed. Eugene Jolas (The Hague: Servire Press, February, 1935), p. 14. All subsequent reference will be indicated *TAGS.*

3. Mark Twain, *Life on the Mississippi* (New York, 1968), p. 16.

4. Alice B. Toklas, *What Is Remembered* (New York, 1963), p. 23. All subsequent reference will be indicated *WIR.*

5. Gertrude Stein, *Everybody's Autobiography* (New York, 1973), p. 15. All subsequent reference will be indicated *EA.*

6. Leo Stein, *Journey Into The Self,* ed. Edmund Fuller (New York, 1950), p. 134. All subsequent reference will be indicated *JIS.*

7. Cited in Hobhouse, *Everybody Who Was Anybody,* p. 162.

8. *Ibid.,* pp. 189-190.

9. Gertrude Stein, *How Writing Is Written,* ed. Robert Hass (Los Angeles, 1974), p. 43. All subsequent reference will be indicated *HWW.*

10. ————, *The World is Round* (New York, 1939), p. 77. All subsequent reference will be indicated *TWR*.

11. ————, *Ida, A Novel* (New York, 1978), p. 7.

12. Cited in Bridgman, *Gertrude Stein in Pieces*, p. 306.

VIII

Epilogue: In the Snare of Mother-Wit

1

Aperson on horseback follows at a distance the cortege in *The Dead Father,* and as we near the site of interment, as we approach the end of the novel, this marginal person suddenly gallops up. It is Mother, responding to an unvoiced need. She sits there in the saddle, ignoring the undead Dead Father, who, for his part, is silently trying to remember her name. She awaits a request from her anxious daughter, her depressed son.

> Mother, Thomas said, we need some things from the store.
> Yes, Mother said.
> A ten-pound bag of flour. The unbleached.
> Mother produced a pencil and an envelope.
> Ten-pound bag of the unbleached, she said.
> We need garlic, bacon, tonic water, horseradish, cloves, chives, and chicory.
> Garlic, bacon, tonic water, horseradish, cloves, chives, chicory.

And so forth: eggs, butter, peanut oil, vermouth, beef bouillon, barbecue sauce. Mother repeats everything, writes it down, and then departs.

> Mother reined her horse about and rode away.
> I don't remember her very well, said the Dead Father. What was her name?
> Her name was Mother, Thomas said, let me have your keys, please (*DF,* pp. 169-170).

As Barthelme moves through this episode, introducing Mother, excluding Mother, he incisively describes the paradox of humorous writing in the postmodernist period. That is, he is humorously ironic, ironically humorous, somewhere betwixt the modes, measuring the son as he measures the father. Mother's appearance momentarily ruins Thomas's case, throws the suasion of his irony into doubt, and makes us look again at the project of Thomas's deconstruction, his

241

exposure of the father's vanity, the father's trickery. Mother-wit, Simon Suggs told us, kin beat book-larnin' at any game. Like Joyce in *Finnegans Wake,* the 'humorous' post-modernist gazes upon Willingdone's "big white harse," tries on the Lipoleumhat, which is too large and falls down over his ears—this mockery is easily shown—but how he represents that contraposed mother-wit, in which style, in which voice, that is another question, that is a problem. Here, then, is Mother. Barthelme allows us briefly to wonder: where has she been all along in this text, and why, until now, have we not really considered her, questioned her absence? How skeptical indeed is this doubting Thomas?

Her name was Mother. Doubting Thomas, the ironic son, keeps Dad firmly fixed in the past tense. It is his labor, to bury the Dead Father, to keep the pastness of the Father out of his present, to take the actual keys and refuse the symbolical ones. Yet Thomas is uncertain in this labor. He is stalked by the haunt that his *mythos* depends on the size of the Father, the situation of the Father. He does not greet Mother. He simply knows what she is for. This is precisely Mother's place in His Story, *The Dead Father.* She is peripheral, she has next to nothing to say, and this says everything. Her daughters (Julie, Emma) speak variously for her: chatter, deliver slinky asides, are capricious, resentful, devious. Mother's absence, Mother's silence, is therefore large—larger, it might be said, than the presence of this largest Father. As Thomas sees it, however, her story is properly a list of his needs, an endless tale written in pencil on an envelope. He does not inquire into the matter of Mother's absence. He, too, like a father, dictates to her—not *principia,* but needs. In the slide of this sentence, Thomas slips. He blames the Dead Father for having forgotten her—*Her name was Mother*—and then abruptly forgets her himself, turns briskly back into the business of the son-father story: *give me your keys.*

Thomas's contempt for the stupidity of the longwinded Father, who drones, who is destructive, does not free him from the assumption of paternal discourse. It merely places him in an ironic relation to that discourse, makes him the exhibitor of paternal folly, binds him closely to the object of the obsequies, the Dead Father. In his contempt for the father, the son does not find release from self-doubt, from self-hatred. The august lesson in *The Dead Father,* stonily observed, is the truth of repetition. "Your true task, as a son, is to reproduce every one of the enormities touched upon in this manual [*A Manual for Sons*], but in attenuated form. You must become your father, but a paler, weaker version of him" (*DF*, p. 145). So the novel reaches its dead-end, a hole in the gound, the terminal period. Into it goes the Father, summoning up at last his own rumbling fatherly version of James Joyce doing Anna Livia Plurabelle in *Finnegans Wake*, and with him goes his fiction, this fiction. He leaves behind allusion, reference, debris. After the Joycean coda, when artifice has become artifact, what is left to write? The writer can do grace notes. He can write and rewrite the Father's epitaph, do and redo that story, His story, *Grandfather said*. Such is the foreknowledge of the forefather, the fatherly irony that brackets the son's irony. *You will repeat me. My story is your story.* As we have seen, Thomas's brave doubt is dubious. What, then, is the nature of the skepticism that regards this paternal/filial exchange, the toil of the dragging, the trouble with transference, this dispute and that dispute, the will, the keys, the *droit du seigneur*? Who is outside the exchange, outside the father's will, watchful, looking in on the definition of the scene?

There is, as it were, a companion text to *The Dead Father*: Gertrude Stein's opera, *The Mother of Us All* (1946). She, too, addresses the authoritative speech of the forefather, a particular speech that is brilliantly chosen and re-presented. Susan B. Anthony plays with its sonority, subverts its appeal, questions its purpose. This speech is Daniel Webster's "Reply to Hayne" (1830), which is still generally considered the highest expression of American eloquence in the Jacksonian period. Knowledgeable men in the nineteenth century loved the speech, adored its ostensible power, relished its nuances. Senator Robert Hayne of South Carolina had launched a vituperative attack on the geopolitical strategy of the commercial North so effectively scathing that Northern politicians found themselves in a rhetorical showdown. It fell to Webster to define the Northern position, to demonstrate a significant difference in oratorical style, and this he coolly did with crushing argumentative blows. Given its context, the urgency of a constitutional crisis, and the dramatic setting—Webster on the Senate floor, the galleries packed with spectators—the speech is verily a thriller. In 1897 Henry Cabot Lodge would restage the drama: "At last his time had come; and as he rose and stood forth, drawing himself up to his full height, his personal grandeur and his majestic calm thrilled all who looked upon him.''[1] Webster's speech is displaced in *The Mother of Us All*, taken out of that context, seen through, witlessly delivered past Susan B. Anthony, who is not thrilled.

Daniel Webster.	When the mariner has been tossed for many days, in thick weather, and on an unknown sea, he naturally avails himself of the first pause in the storm.
Susan B. Anthony.	For instance. They should always fight. They should be martyrs. Some should be martyrs. Will they. They will.
Daniel Webster.	We have thus heard sir what a resolution is.
Susan B. Anthony.	I am resolved.
Daniel Webster.	When this debate sir was to be resumed on Thursday it so happened that it would have been convenient for me to be elsewhere.
Susan B.	I am here, ready to be here. Ready to be where. Ready to be here. It is my habit.
Daniel Webster.	The honorable member complained that I had slept on his speech.
Susan B.	The right to sleep is given to no woman.
Daniel Webster.	I did sleep on the gentleman's speech; and slept soundly.
Susan B.	I too have slept soundly when I have slept, yes when I have slept I too have slept soundly.
Daniel Webster.	Matches and over matches.
Susan B.	I understand you undertake to overthrow my undertaking.[2]

Daniel Webster, Daniel Stein—Gertrude Stein has earlier in the text given all that away. These are 2 of our 4 fathers. Susan B. Anthony shows us her motherly wit as she remarks along the course of Webster's speech, a motherly wit that is turned against the book learning of Webster's rhetoric. She has, in fact, her own speech, a 'true speech,' the direct utterance of her thought, which is set in contrast to Webster's 'false speech,' this contrived, rehearsed composition, "Reply to Hayne." Susan B. Anthony's "Reply to Webster" is delivered at home while she is "busy with her housework," and her audience is a timorous woman, Anne. She says: "They fear women, they fear each other, they fear their neighbor, they fear other countries and then they hearten themselves in their fear by crowding together and following each other . . . like animals who stampede, and so they have written in the name male into the United States constitution, because they are afraid of black men because they are afraid of women, because they are afraid afraid. Men are afraid" (*MUA*, p. 192). Indeed Webster is a pitiable figure in *The Mother of Us All*. He can't stammer, he is forced to admit, can't stutter, his speech is never within the exigencies of speech, and therefore he is doomed to speak perfectly all these ringing phrases. He is trapped in the rectitude of the "Reply to Hayne," in the rationality of a letter-perfect writing, and effectively deprived of the humanity of error, the humor of being wrong.

The skeptical intelligence that governs the play in *The Mother of Us All* is ironic in its representation of the forefathers (Webster, John Adams, Ulysses S. Grant, Thaddeus Stevens), but only to an extent. Susan B. Anthony wants to be written into the constitution, but she has no desire *per se* to be Hayne, to engage Webster in the terms of his discourse. The opera, for all its ironic effects, is finally humorous. In order to deliver itself, the text *must* be humorous, must show us Susan B. Anthony in the magnificence of her tolerance, because that is her meaning, her triumph. In all her struggle with the Father, fighting him on his ground, petitioning, politicking, she did not become the deadly Father. Barthelme affiliates with Gertrude Stein's perspective in *The Dead Father*, humorously fractures the intoning discourse of paternal authority, but only to an extent. What, after all, is the humorous resolution of *The Dead Father*? Groping for Julie's fleece, grumbling, the Father reluctantly gets down into his hole. We are left to imagine what Mother might think of all this as she pushes her cart through the supermarket, selecting the right bacon, the fresh garlic, the wrong brand of vermouth. The last, wonderfully apt word in *The Dead Father* is "Bulldozers." Barthelme draws in Thomas's shaky position the ironic stance of the postmodern humorist, and declares the resolution of his humor: "*Fatherhood can be, if not conquered, at least 'turned down' in this generation*" (*DF*, p. 145). It is the best Thomas might do, as a humorous doubter. Then the position is bulldozed, ironically.

As Barthelme demonstrates, this humorous modesty is a pose as well as a stance; there is some bad faith, some bullshit, in its profession, and yet, for all that, it is exactly in this resolve that the male humorous writer describes his *agon* in the sixties and seventies. He writes ruefully as a paler, weaker father, as a failed man. He presents himself as a writer who has turned down, formally and stylistically, the volume in patriarchal discourse. He identifies with the exemplary 'humor' of Gertrude Stein's position in *The Mother of Us All*; he will admit that men are afraid, and yet the question, the curiosity of his work, lies in his representation of mother-wit. There is, for example, Mother in Kurt Vonnegut's *Slaughterhouse-Five* (1969), Mother in Richard Brautigan's *In Watermelon Sugar* (1968), and Mother in Philip Roth's *Portnoy's Complaint* (1969). The status of mother-wit in these novels (which generally depict men as crazed) establishes the measure of their irony. Mother becomes, in any case, the question of humor.

2

Kurt Vonnegut begins *Slaughterhouse-Five* by elaborately explaining to an irate mother the kind of war novel he is going to write. She is the wife of an old comrade whom Vonnegut visits, to pick through shared memories of World War II, and she greets him with icy dislike. She thinks he will write in the mode of Norman Mailer and James Jones. "You'll pretend you were men instead of babies," she angrily declares, "and you'll be played in the movies by Frank Sinatra and John Wayne or some of those other glamorous, war-loving, dirty old men. And war will look just wonderful, so we'll have a lot more of them." It is, of course, a mistake. Vonnegut is going to write a novel that will depict the lunacy of World War II, give us heroic Roland as Roland Weary, that will show us one of *our* war crimes, the firebombing of Dresden.

> So I held up my right hand and I made her a promise:
> 'Mary,' I said, 'I don't think this book of mine is ever going to be finished. I must have written five thousand pages by now, and thrown them all away. If I ever do finish it, though, I give you my word of honor: there won't be a part for Frank Sinatra or John Wayne.

'I tell you what,' I said, 'I'll call it "The Children's Crusade." '
She was my friend after that.[3]

Here, then, is the humorist, affable, low key, the volume turned down. He will weave two narratives through *Slaughterhouse-Five*: the ironic tale of Billy Pilgrim, a Candide who inexorably bumbles his way from Ilium, New York, to Dresden and is present at the fiery event; and a loony story, the one we must look through a "time window" to read, the humorous tale of Tralfamadore. In the relation of these two narratives, Vonnegut raises a familiar question. Here is the contingent world ruled by Necessity, His story, which is written in the 'serious' mode of Voltairean satire, and there is the 'free' other-world of the imagination, composed in the form of humorous fantasy. In historical time, Billy Pilgrim is determined, merely reactive, a pawn moved about by incomprehensible forces; in the poetic time of the eternal present, out the window, through the looking-glass, he is 'free,' a space traveler. To get out of His story, where fiery bricks rain down from the sky on Dresden, Billy Pilgrim withdraws his belief in its reality, its truth, and leaps into fantasy. This jump constitutes the humorous resolution in *Slaughterhouse-Five*, its transformation of suffering. Yet the Tralfamadorian fantasy, even as Billy Pilgrim imagines it, does not set him free. It is simply a narcissistic trance, a pipedream that keeps him safe, that gives him pleasure. We are effectively back before the whitewashed fence regarding its suspicious gleam. Vonnegut ironically renders this resolution as the necessary lie of humor. To get out of His story, Billy Pilgrim must enter the discourse it excludes, move from the rational to the irrational, from His story to her story, and this movement, for all its lyrical whimsy, is plainly regressive.

It is the ideal mother in *Slaughterhouse-Five*, not the actual one, who is significant. Mrs. Pilgrim, a "perfectly nice, standard-issue, brown-haired, white woman with a high-school education," has nothing to say to her son. "She made him feel embarrassed and ungrateful and weak because she had gone to so much trouble to give him life, and to keep that life going, and Billy didn't really like life at all" (*SH5*, p. 88). On Tralfamadore Billy Pilgrim lives inside a sealed bubble and enjoys the comfort of an artificially created environment. He is absolutely dependent on the Tralfamadorians. He is in their zoo. They give him Montana Wildhack, a voluptuous movie actress, for a mate, and she quickly becomes a mother. Here Billy Pilgrim, who "didn't really like life at all," lives in delight. He is the child-father, she the mother-wife. There is no history in the bubble, just stasis. Tralfamadorian knowledge, which considers death a "bad condition in that particular moment" (*SH5*, p. 23), has nothing to do with history, could only say of World War II, of destroyed Dresden, that it was a "bad condition in that particular moment." It is the trite knowledge we regain when we regress to an infantile state, when we slip into the poetry of psychosis, return to our innocence. The knowing humorist, writing ironically, represents the lore of mother-wit as a lure. Montana Wildhack has the body of Dewey Eula Lena Dell and the mind of Miss Lonelyheart's girlfriend, Betty. She is the centerpiece of the fantasy, humor's cherished object, the restorative that guarantees our sense of humor. Vonnegut draws a cartoon of her bosom. A junk-store locket dangles between her breasts. Humor's eternal verity is written on the talismanic heart:

> God grant me the serenity to accept the things I cannot change, courage to change the things I can, and wisdom always to tell the difference (*SH5*, p. 181).

Slaughterhouse-Five at length places its intelligence as a humorous text beside titty. Here I am, says Humor, I *am* titty. The humorist who writes such pap, produces the warm milk in this cliché, suffers a death as a writer, follows Billy Pilgrim into the bubble, and Vonnegut everywhere makes his ironic disclaimers. Inside this very locket, for example, is a photograph of Montana Wildhack's "alcoholic mother," but it is a "grainy thing, soot and chalk." Like Mark Twain in *Tom Sawyer*, this 'humorist' exposes his mode, reveals the operation of the humorous lie. Billy Pilgrim's escape into a private world of fantasy is just a simpler, funny version of the ironic distance Vonnegut establishes in his text. How, then, do we respond to Dresden on the morning after, when we look over the melted landscape and see picture after picture of horror? Humor has its place, Freud tells us, among the great series of methods which the human mind has constructed in order to evade the compulsion to suffer. It occurs in the series that begins with neurosis and culminates in madness. That is exactly how Vonnegut represents humorous thought in

Epilogue: In the Snare of Mother-Wit

Slaughterhouse-Five. It appears somewhere between ironic alienation and madness. The humorous impulse is always manifest as a desire in Vonnegut's style, but the ironist who directs the style, who smuggles a photograph of an "alcoholic mother" into the funny locket, does not really take humor seriously. Humor does not propose questions in *Slaughterhouse-Five*; it creates Tralfamadore.

Out of history, out of irony, where is the humorist? We find him again in the dubious paradise of Richard Brautigan's *In Watermelon Sugar,* and he is again writing sweet stuff in the sweet style. He lives under the rule of mother-wit in a matriarchy. The unspoken communal law in iDEATH is the denial of the *i*. We are in a postcapitalist, postpatriarchal world, in the pastoral language of watermelon sugar. Pauline's power to determine the muted discourse in iDEATH resembles the power Miss Lonelyhearts discerns in Betty, that feminine power to limit experience arbitrarily. This is, in part, how Brautigan defines mother-wit in the novel. No more fighting, Pauline insists, no more despair. The denial of the *i*, of aggressive masculine individuality, opens up the possibility of all sorts of simple pleasures, all kinds of enjoyable agrarian pursuits. Dinner, for example, is pleasant, and handcraft flourishes. Yet the loss of the *I,* so it would seem, results in a loss of vision, of what can be seen, and spoken. Her story, humor, excludes his story, irony. There are "watermelon bricks made from black, soundless sugar" in iDEATH, and these "seal off the forgotten things forever."[4] Yet the writer of *In Watermelon Sugar* is a doubting Thomas who doubts his resistance to matriarchal rule, doubts his distrust of mother-wit. He places before us the spectacle of inBOIL, the displaced, furious, alcoholic patriarch who lives outside iDEATH near the Forgotten Works, the ruins of His story. inBOIL finally bursts into the trout hatchery where all the nullified sons have gathered, and here, in the hatchery, on sacred ground, he instructs the skeptical sons in the art of dying. He cuts himself up piecemeal, a thumb, a nose, an ear.

> Pauline suddenly started to leave the room. I went over to her, almost slipping on the blood and falling down.
> 'Are you all right?' I said, not knowing quite what to say. 'Can I help you?'
> 'No,' she said, on her way out. 'I'm going to go get a mop and clean this mess up.' When she said mess, she looked directly at inBOIL.

She left the hatchery and came back shortly with a mop. They were almost all dead now, except for inBOIL. He was still talking about iDEATH. 'See, we've done it,' he said.

Pauline started mopping up the blood and wringing it out into a bucket. When the bucket was almost full of blood, inBOIL died. 'I am iDEATH,' he said.

'You're an asshole,' Pauline said.

And the last thing that inBOIL ever saw was Pauline standing beside him, wringing his blood out of the mop into the bucket (*IWS,* p. 95).

inBOIL *is* an asshole. We see Pauline briefly as *Mutter Courage,* tough, unfazed, cleaning up the mess destructive men make. Still, inBOIL's ridiculous suicide has about it some element of exemplary sacrifice. He makes his benumbed sons confront the amputation of their *I.* He forces them to witness what is repressed in iDEATH. Life in iDEATH, after all, is rather like life in the Tralfamadorian bubble. The tranquility of this space requires constant insulation, a certain temperature, good nourishment, and the prompt flushing away of discordance, difference, of anything that questions the perfection of the tranquility. No one writes books in a matriarchy. The narrator of *In Watermelon Sugar,* however, is struggling to write a book, and he is stricken with anxiety as he feels the alienation of the task, as he realizes the insistent treason of his adamant *i.* He is withal a lonely heart who can't quite bring himself to admit that Pauline does not satisfy him. His fellow communards amiably offer him topics for his book: 'Pine Needles,' 'Clouds' — tiny topics, drifty topics. They have themselves, in momentary fits of creativity, sculpted great replicas of zucchini and snapbean. The narrator politely evades questions about his book, and we know why. The subject is *i.*

Like the doubting Thomas in Barthelme's novel, Brautigan's narrator rejects the inboiling father. He has turned down the volume of the authorial *I* to an anonymous *i,* and he writes using pap, the ichor of watermelon. He has gone figuratively on a pilgrimage to search out that other style, a writing shorn of aggressive wit, empty of prepossessing knowledge, and he finds himself in iDEATH, in Mother's world, in maternal discourse, where he seethes in secret complicity with the rejected father. It is a dilemma that Brautigan describes in the geography of his fiction. Here is iDEATH where the talk is simple and sweet, where Pauline assures everyone the harmony of good humor, and there is the zone of the Forgotten Works where Choler (inBOIL) resides, where discourse is harsh and inquisitive. The writer hovers in his speculation, striving to write earnestly a sincere prose as he struggles hypocritically with his subject. He wants to be humorous, to be in Pauline, with Pauline, to be free of the alienation of irony, but the only humor he can manage is melancholy.

The nineteenth-century humorist, as we have seen, projected a consciousness outside the realm of writing, a character, a voice, situated in "natur," that enabled him or her to break back into writing with a fractious question. For Vonnegut and Brautigan, exemplary humorists writing self-reflexively in the postmodern period, that consciousness outside writing, outside history, in "natur," is far from funny. *Slaughterhouse-Five* is dutifully dedicated to the Mother, the stern Mary O'Hare, who likes to think of men as big babies. That indeed is how Vonnegut represents them in the novel: the men who pass through his muster are, for the most part, crazed big babies, and the biggest baby of them all is Billy Pilgrim. *In Watermelon Sugar* gives us Pauline's incontrovertible judgment of the self-mutilated inBOIL—"Asshole"—and a wide assortment of childlike communards. Yet the adoption of the maternal perspective, this scathing mother-wit, produces a certain anxiety in the wryly soft-spoken humorist, if only because it is so contemptuous, so unforgiving. If the phallocentric universe of patriarchal discourse, with its brawling treatises and combat fiction, its sharp-pointed stylus, is to be turned down, what are the resources of the opposing discourse? We contemplate in each fiction the milky mind of a feminized man. Mother-wit, speaking for nurture from "natur," deals out the clichés of optimism, draws the writer into the confinement of her sugary language where, as a writer, as a man, he perishes. Pauline, who has no interest in the Forgotten Works, likes to see her mealymouthed men in their proper place.

> Pauline was just getting ready to serve dinner. Everybody was sitting down. She was happy to see me. 'Hi, stranger,' she said.
> 'What's for dinner?' I said.
> 'Stew,' she said. 'The way you like it.'
> 'Great,' I said.

Epilogue: In the Snare of Mother-Wit

> She gave me a nice smile and I sat down. Pauline was wearing a new dress and I could see the pleasant outlines of her body.
>
> The dress had a low front and I could see the delicate curve of her breasts. I was quite pleased by everything. The dress smelled sweet because it was made from watermelon sugar (*IWS*, p. 17).

Like Faulkner, like West, the postmodern humorist ironically encircles the figure of humor, those "mammalian ludicrosities," and to this extent his writing simply reiterates the plight of his melancholy. The result is awful. Roth will take the theme of substitution, breast for phallus, to its absurd extreme. On February 18, 1971, somewhere between midnight and four A.M., a bookish man of great learning, David Alan Kepesh, becomes a breast. That is bad enough, but what is worse is that as a breast, a rosy-nippled titty, Kepesh still thinks and speaks as a man. Roth brings us up very close in *The Breast* (1972) to the humorous figure, and there it is, a "big brainless bag of tissue, desirable, dumb, passive, immobile, acted upon instead of acting, hanging, *there,* as a breast hangs and is *there.*"[5] Although he is one, Kepesh never achieves the hanging balance of such thereness. Throughout the tale of his transformation, he boils with self-consciousness, with fear and analysis. Kepesh becomes a breast, the humorist identifies with mother-wit, but neither Kepesh (as it turns out) nor the humorist can produce the milk of human kindness, be the real thing. This masculine breast can only complain, is only for beating.

"Men are afraid," Susan B. Anthony magisterially declares in *The Mother of Us All.* It is the brick Roth takes up in *Portnoy's Complaint,* this hard thrust of mother-wit, and the amplified report of its hit is what distinguishes the novel in postmodern American literature. Afraid of what? Afraid of women, of Gorgon and Medusa, the Weird Sisters, afraid of the breast. "*My Alex,*" Sophie Portnoy tells her friends, "*is suddenly such a bad eater I have to stand over him with a knife.*"[6] Various bricks fly in the novel. Portnoy will desperately throw book learning at mother-wit, hurl *The Grapes of Wrath* and *The Souls of Black Folk* at Mary Jane Reed, even though the oral tradition circumscribes the gesture with its fixed principle: mother-wit kin beat book-larnin' at any game. Roth returns to the site of the Writing Lesson in *Portnoy's Complaint,* that place where right and wrong, the clean and the unclean, are established, and effectively does the scene twice, shows us Portnoy first as pupil and then as teacher. Numerous comic traditions appear in the narrative: Gimpel the Fool and Lenny Bruce are discernible in Portnoy's monologue, and yet it is withal the project of humor that is before Portnoy in his complaint. He has lost his manhood, his limp phallus hangs like a "big brainless bag of tissue," and this is not funny. He has lost his manhood, and his sense of humor. To this summary text, we now turn.

3

> *dir willa polish the flor by bathrum*
> *pleze & dont furget the insies of win-*
> *dose mary jane r* (PC, p. 231).

The note Mary Jane Reed leaves for the maid, because it is rongly ritten, decides her fate in *Portnoy's Complaint*. When Portnoy finds it, he immediately recognizes it as a little piece of Huckspeech, the "work of an eight-year-old." He considers the extent of her misspelling, *clean* is usually spelled with a *k,* and then he focuses, epiphanically, on *dear,* which she variously spells as *dere, deir, dir.* "It nearly drove me crazy" (PC, p. 208), Portnoy humorlessly reports, spelling out each error for the benefit of his silent analyst, Dr. Spielvogel. The single sign, *dir,* brings into question the importance of culinary codes, sexual mores, and stylistic modes. It is the very emblem of that desire which does not recognize propriety, difference. "I would never eat *milchiks* off a *flaishedigeh* dish," Portnoy has earlier told us, "never, never, never" (PC, p. 13). He has already passed through the Writing Lesson, is in the rectitude of writing, whereas she is still in it, flunking the course, making error after error. She is not a clean dear, dumb *dir* reveals her trashiness, and therefore she could never become a proper wife. It is necessary for him to recall who he is, who she is, evidently Krazy, and what he is doing with her. Standing in their apartment, holding her note, Portnoy contemplates the misspelled sign of humor and soberly realizes the full measure of its wrongness.

He is, after all, an energetic careerist, the Assistant Commissioner for Human Opportunity in New York, an intellectual who knows the Mayor, who knows the Judge, who has a sense of style. Like Tom

Sawyer, Portnoy is well read, a plausible rhetorician, and the tireless producer of fantasies. Mary Jane Reed is at once a "pathetic screwy hillbilly cunt" (*PC*, p. 151) and the "fulfillment of all my lascivious adolescent dreams" (*PC*, p. 214). Roth stresses the analogy, makes us see *Portnoy's Complaint* as a rearrangement of *Huckleberry Finn*, a reopening of its question. He will compose a 'raft idyll,' reconstitute the argument between Huck and Jim, and give us, in fine, Tom's toil in Portnoy's betrayal of Mary Jane Reed. We have only to keep our 'characters' straight, to understand who is speaking and where the value of Huckspeech is in this discourse. Portnoy indeed shares Tom Sawyer's dilemma, and *dir* arouses him to the risk. How is Tom to get the feeling of Huck's uncivilized existence, live in the locus of *dir*, without also suffering Huck's vulnerability, enduring Huck's dirt? It is a problem, keeping Huck Huck, and yet safely delineated. For one thing, Huck is a reluctant player in Tom's fantasies, often obstinate, and he is dangerously capable of criminal acts, actual crimes in the real world. For another, and this is the hard part of it, Huck would like to emulate Tom. Portnoy is similarly confused in his regard of Mary Jane Reed. He takes delight in her sexual amorality, is drawn to her wildness, and at the same time he is repelled by it, threatened. So he plays her mentor, dutifully 'raises' her consciousness, makes her aware of her ignorance, and finds himself evading Mary Jane's insistence that they be married. She wants to settle down, to become a mother. When we last see her in *Portnoy's Complaint*, she is clinging to a hotel window in Athens, threatening suicide. She has been brought to this impasse by the manipulation of a literary fellow whose confused instruction, like Tom Sawyer's in *Huckleberry Finn*, has proved disastrous.

These several signifiers of Huckspeech, the hazy reference of the idyllic episode in Vermont, the stylistic murmur of *dir*, constitute the fissures in Portnoy's complaint, are the flaws in its otherwise bright, brassy, comic surface. Briefly rendered, fragmentary, they disclose the 'humor' that lies outside the glib scam of Portnoy's duplicitous irony, give us a glimmer of Roth's own fragile sense of humor. He, too, has a problem with Portnoy, and it is like Mary Jane Reed's: how to get around this expert complainer, get past his superlative defenses, in order to deliver the *swoosh* of humorous pleasure? For the complaint, as a form, is tightly organized to exclude pleasure. It will, on the other hand, admit our criticism, solicit our interpretation. To that end, Portnoy throws open the bathroom door on the Human Spirit, on Noble Reason, on Father and Son, shows them in the labor of creation, throws open the household door on Jewish paranoia, reveals its nuttiness, goes grimly from door to door. Nothing is to be repressed, or shut up, in this complaint.

That is, Portnoy is perfectly aware of how he wrongs women, and why he wrongs women. He has in hand the appropriate Freudian text, "The Most Prevalent Form of Degradation in Erotic Life." He has obviously read Erich Neumann's treatise on the Terrible Mother. Well versed in mother myth, he knows about Bata, the She-Bear, and Jocasta, about Ariadne and the life-saving thread that, after awhile, becomes sticky. A dedicated reader of the *Partisan Review,* he is also hip to the parlance of sexual politics, the terms of its ongoing debate. He can explain why he rejects Kay Campbell, 'The Pumpkin'; why he rejects Mary Jane Reed, 'The Monkey'; why he mauls Sarah Maulsby; why he collapses like a baby before Naomi, 'The Jewish Pumpkin'; and then take the listener directly to the source of his problem, the origin of his complaint, his Mother. Ah, this fatal amour, this first maternal mirror in which is foretold all the subsequent maidens, the forlorn demoiselles. Here Portnoy is eloquent. He remembers incestuous caresses, beef bleeding in the sink, the awful conflict in his feeling for Mother. In that knowledge, with that knowledge, he preempts our moral judgment of his action. He has already himself made that judgment, worked out the criticism, made all the connections, but what good does it do him or Mary Jane Reed, all this knowledge?

Knowledge and power. It is what the routine of the Writing Lesson always presents. A book is thrown, a brick is hurled, [knowledge is pain]. Humor receives it, this piece of learning, and questions it, misrepresents the mastery of the knower, and therein transforms the knowledge, changes its terms, make the brickish text supple, not injurious at all (knowledge is pleasure). In bed with Freud's essay "The Most Prevalent Form of Degradation in Erotic Life," Portnoy studies the one moment in his life when he briefly beheld the inside of rapture. He has just read Freud's description of "fully normal" love, that it is a union of tender and sensuous currents of feeling, and is reminded of an illicit weekend spent with Mary Jane Reed in the New England countryside. Currents, streams, confluence: it is withal life on the raft, this Freudian conception of love, and what Portnoy sees, Freud in one hand, phallus in the other, is a vision of that other Portnoy who, for a moment, an episode, seems capable of Huckish abandonment. "And *swoosh,* there was sensual feeling mingled with the purest, deepest streams of tenderness I've ever known! I'm telling you, the confluence of the two currents was terrific" (*PC,* p. 210). Yet in the pastoral landscape, nestled beside Mary Jane, bathed in postcoital bliss, Portnoy does not driftily recall the rapture of *Huckleberry Finn.* He thinks of the rape in Yeats's poem, *Leda and the Swan,* and delivers it from memory:

> Did she put on his knowledge with his power
> Before the indifferent beak could let her drop?

Knowledge and power. Portnoy's recitation spoils the mood, makes Mary Jane vaguely anxious. He realizes that he has "drawn attention to the chasm: I am smart and you are dumb" (*PC,* p. 217) and will look for a polite way out of the embarrassment. Who wrote that poem? she wants to know. The subsequent exchange rearranges, in modern terms, the classical form of the humorous act in American literature, and Portnoy, whose mind is always in the wrong text, is blind to it. Yeats, he replies. Who is Yeats? she inquires. An Irish poet, says Portnoy. Inescapably, the poem is discussed. He takes a fast trot through it, explains the myth, who Agamemnon is, and distances the poem as a literary fact, as historical reference. She will literally feel her way through the poem, draw his hand, at one point, between her own loosening thighs, and later, when Portnoy demands "Feel my feather," reach out and seize at once his nose and his phallus. " 'A *Jew*-swan!' she cried, and grabbed at my nose with the other hand. 'The indifferent beak! I just understood more poem' " (*PC,* p. 220)! As Mary Jane feels her way through the poem, loosening its joints, reversing its logic, she turns its hard 'truth,' the hard truth of Portnoy's ardent recitation, into humorous pleasure. There is another kind of knowledge, human knowledge, that is not based on force, and here it is. The finery of Portnoy's plumage, his show of learning, is parted, and we look in on him, the *Jew*-swan, this nervous fellow who will violate her, who will drop her. So this is metaphor, Mary Jane Reed declares, this for that, this indifferent beak for that indifferent beak. "Marvellous," Portnoy exclaims, quick with his approval. Metaphors lead one to another, and this particular sequence is for him perilous. "*Now* can I fuck you?" (*PC*, p. 220) he impatiently asks. The exchange ends. What comes next is Portnoy's discovery of her note, his appalled reading of *dir*.

The humorous question reappears in *Portnoy's Complaint*, but at a distance, and what we principally see of it, even as it libidinally flashes *dir* before us, is its rigorous exclusion. Roth's stylistic marking in the text draws large the place of Portnoy's confinement in discourse. When id says *dir*, throatily, the super-ego sends its messages through the headlines of the *Daily News*: "ASST HUMAN OPP'Y COMMISH FOUND HEADLESS IN GO-GO GIRL'S APT" (*PC*, p. 181)! Portnoy's delivery flinches between these dictations, *yes* and *no*, and is written, appropriately, in a between style, in a between mood. "Sure, I say *fuck* a lot," Portnoy tells us, "but I assure you, that's about the sum of my success with transgressing" (*PC*, p. 139). In *Portnoy's Complaint*, it might be said, Roth writes a reconnaissance of the humorous style. Like Portnoy, he stands before the misspelled sign, contemplates the scandal of his project— to go wrong, be wrong, write wrongly—and reveals the qualm. Unlike Portnoy, he sees what the Assistant Commissioner does not see, the blind spot in Portnoy's complaint, the hidden qualm. The humorous tolerance of *dir* is what happily lies at the end of therapy, whether before Dr. Spielvogel or in self analysis, and yet this is not the direction Portnoy's analysis takes. As he retells his tale, explains this, justifies that, the tale picks up momentum, shoots ever faster toward hysteria, and this is where the discourse ends, not in humor, but hysterically, with an outcry.

What drives Portnoy crazy, Roth humorously recognizes, is not the insistence of *dir*, but the ideological constraint of his knowing discourse, this analytical double-talk which poses mother-wit as the problem and the solution. The proper object of Portnoy's complaint is therefore the complaint itself, the one thing he does not question. It is formally installed for us at the beginning of the text as an abstract of the article Dr. Spielvogel has written for the *Internationale Zeitschrift für Psychoanalyse*, an article that promptly traces the symptoms of his malady back to the "mother-child relationship," puts the blame on Eve. That was the first complaint, after all, and the first representation of mother-wit. The history of the complaint, which begins properly in Genesis, is the history of that representation, an ambivalent figuring of the feminine. There is Eve, Lilith, and, farther back, the Venus of Willendorf, the uroboric circle, and it is in this series that Portnoy locates the meaning of his mother and Mary Jane Reed. His complaint is not the rarefied complaint, and yet, for all his racy diction, he classifies: Pumpkin, Monkey, et cetera. This history of masculine representation, whether sacred or profane, necessarily misrepresents the lower case humanity of Sophie Portnoy, of Mary Jane Reed, and drives them crazy, makes them hysterical. "And yet now that she is hollowed out," Portnoy admits, nervously regarding his mother after her hysterectomy, "I cannot even look her in the eye" (*PC,* pp. 75-76). The women who strike fear in Portnoy's breast are those whose reality escapes the hold of their trope—the mother whose womb is gone, the maiden who changes from whore into wife—those women whose demands are less than symbolic, merely human, who bring the entire history of complaint, of that representation, into question. These are the women who do not understand their place in writing, in what has been written, whose illiterate wrongness shines in *dir.*

The science of complaining, which is a patriarchal discipline, will tell Portnoy everything he wants to know, will unrepress repression, 'understand' his profanity, tell him where the problem is—Mother—conceptualize her significance, categorize her speech, give him the power of substitution, the trick of metaphor, enable him to play, godlike, the game of presence/absence, let him have it both ways, so long as he remains in its power, in the circularity of its double-talk. Nothing is without it, this complaint assures Portnoy, taking everything into it. Complaint is Portnoy's birthright. So the complainer takes on his plumage, gets into his swan-suit, proclaims his knowledge, and sings his swan-song. He will indeed draw the definitive picture of the self, spell Love "l-u-s-t," even as he insists, elsewhere, that *fuck* and *dir* must be somehow commingled in order for rapture to occur. It is a big heavy brick, this complaint, this Jovian knowledge, and Roth takes its measure. Here, of course, the humorous question begins.

⌒*Notes*

1. Henry Cabot Lodge, *Daniel Webster* (Boston and New York, 1897), p. 182.

2. *Selected Operas and Plays of Gertrude Stein,* ed. John Malcolm Brinnin (University of Pittsburgh Press: Pittsburgh, 1970), pp. 165-166. All subsequent reference will be indicated *MUA.*

3. Kurt Vonnegut, *Slaughterhouse-Five* (New York, 1969), p. 13. All subsequent reference will be indicated *SH5.*

4. Richard Brautigan, *In Watermelon Sugar* (New York, 1968), p. 126. All subsequent reference will be indicated *IWS.*

5. Philip Roth, *The Breast* (New York, 1972), p. 87. There are, of course, numerous representations of the breast in contemporary humorous literature. In the film, *Everything You Ever Wanted To Know About Sex,* a huge rampaging breast, remorselessly squirting jets of sticky milk, will pursue a flylike Woody Allen.

6. ————, *Portnoy's Complaint* (New York, 1969), p. 47. All subsequent reference will be indicated *PC.*

Index

Index

Index

Neil Schmitz is professor of English at the
State University of New York at Buffalo.
He has written numerous essays on American
literature and is a frequent contributor to
the *Partisan Review*.